Assessment Across Online Language Education

Advances in CALL Research and Practice
Series Editor: Greg Kessler, Ohio University

This series is published in cooperation with the Computer Assisted Language Instruction Consortium (CALICO). Each Spring just prior to the CALICO annual conference the series publishes one volume comprised of original studies on a specific topic.

Published:
Landmarks in CALL Research
Edited by Greg Kessler

Learner Autonomy and Web 2.0
Edited by Marco Cappellini, Tim Lewis, and Annick Rivens Mompean

Assessment Across Online Language Education

Edited by Stephanie Link and Jinrong Li

SHEFFIELD UK   BRISTOL CT

Published by Equinox Publishing Ltd.

UK: Office 415, The Workstation, 15 Paternoster Row, Sheffield, South Yorkshire
        S1 2BX
USA: ISD, 70 Enterprise Drive, Bristol, CT 06010

www.equinoxpub.com

First published 2018

British Library Cataloguing-in-Publication Data

A catalogue record for this book is available from the British Library.

ISBN-13   978 1 78179 701 3   (paperback)
ISBN-13   978 1 78179 702 0   (ePDF)

Library of Congress Cataloging-in-Publication Data

Names: Link, Stephanie, editor. | Li, Jinrong (Applied linguist), editor.
Title: Assessment across online language education / edited by Stephanie Link
    and Jinrong Li.
Description: Bristol, CT : Equinox Publishing Ltd, [2018] | Series: Advances
    in CALL research and practice | Includes bibliographical references and index.
Identifiers: LCCN 2017050400 (print) | LCCN 2017040446 (ebook) | ISBN
    9781781797013 (softcover) | ISBN 9781781797020 (epdf)
Subjects: LCSH: Language acquisition--Ability testing. | Language
    acquisition--Ability testing--Evaluation. | Language transfer--Ability
    testing--Evaluation. | Language and languages--Study and
    teaching--Computer-assisted learning. | Language
    acquisition--Computer-assisted learning. | Language and
    languages--Computer-assisted instruction. | Language and languages--Study
    and teaching--Computer network resources. | Second language
    acquisition--Computer-assisted instruction. | Intercultural
    communication--Study and teaching. | Education, Bilingual. | Educational
    technology.
Classification: LCC P118.7 .A774 2018 (ebook) | LCC P118.7 (print) | DDC
    428.0076--dc23
LC record available at https://lccn.loc.gov/2017050400

Typeset by S.J.I. Services, New Delhi
Printed and bound in Great Britain by Lightning Source UK Ltd., Milton Keynes and Lightning Source Inc., La Vergne, TN

Contents

PART THREE
ASSESSMENT TOOLS FOR ONLINE ENVIRONMENTS

PART FOUR
FUTURE DIRECTIONS FOR ONLINE LANGUAGE ASSESSMENT

Acknowledgments

We would like to take this opportunity to thank all the reviewers of the 2018 Advances in CALL Research and Practice book series. Without the effort and expertise that you contributed to reviewing, it would have been impossible to maintain the high standards of the edited volume.

Stacy Amling	Iowa State University
Adolfo Carrillo Cabello	University of Minnesota
Claudia Cornejo Happel	Georgia Southern University
Sarah Huffman	Iowa State University
Hee Sung (Grace) Jun	Seoul National University
Edna Lima	The Ohio University
Shannon McCrocklin	Southern Illinois University-Carbondale
Moonyoung Park	Chinese University of Hong Kong
Jim Ramali	Iowa State University
Julio C. Rodriguez	University of Hawaii-Manoa
Ruslan Suvorov	University of Hawaii-Manoa
Aysel Saricaoglu	TED University
Sinem Sonsaat	Iowa State University
Jing Xu	Cambridge Assessment

1 The Online Language Learning Imperative: Maximizing Assessment Practices to Ensure Student Success

Stephanie Link* and Jinrong Li**

Introduction

The development of research on language learning technologies since the introduction of Web 2.0 tools (O'Reilly, 2005) has been both rapid and transformative. On the one hand, the advancement of technology has continued to facilitate language learning by providing access to more authentic learning materials (e.g., Becker & Sturm, 2017), enabling the flexibility of learning regardless of time and location (e.g., O'Dowd & Lewis, 2016), and strengthening individualized and dynamic learning experiences (e.g., Cowan, Choo, & Lee, 2014; Hassani, Nahvi, & Ahmadi, 2016; Heift, 2010; Ziegler et al., 2017). On the other hand, innovative technologies aiming to facilitate communication, participation, and collaboration have also created many unprecedented language learning opportunities. This, together with the paradigm shift in research on second language acquisition from *cognitive* to *social* orientation (Firth & Wagner, 1997, 2007; Lafford, 2007), has contributed to the ever-growing body of research on technology-mediated language learning through collaboration (e.g., Nishioka, 2016; Thorns & Poole, 2017; Wang, 2014; Warner, 2017) or community-based practices (e.g., Andes & Claggett, 2011; Martin-Beltran, 2013; Sauro, 2017). More importantly, technology has become "pervasive" and "interwoven with human activity" and it is difficult to imagine language teaching without some form of technology (Chun, Kern, & Smith, 2016: 65).

The expansion of online language learning opportunities has provided language teachers and learners with an increasingly diverse range of tools aiming to facilitate language learning in various contexts. However, CALL

* Oklahoma State University, USA; steph.link@okstate.edu
** Georgia Southern University, USA; jli@georgiasouthern.edu

researchers and practitioners do not have adequate knowledge about how online language learning may affect the development of learners' language proficiency. Admittedly, there is a lack of empirical studies on online language teaching and learning that employ standardized, valid measures of proficiency outcomes to assess the effectiveness of online language learning (Tarone, 2015). But more importantly, the lack of knowledge about the impact of online language learning signals the urgent need to go beyond replicating the assessment practices used in face-to-face instructional settings and rethink how to make the best use of the available technologies to assess online language learning more effectively, as rightly suggested by Rubio (2015). Furthermore, we believe online language teaching is a crucial element that shapes the impact of online language learning, and thus there is a need to continue to address the controversies and challenges that exist in the ongoing efforts to better understand aspects of assessment in online language teaching, including how to assess language teacher performance prior to, during, and after teaching online. Finally, we believe the advancement of language learning technologies presents great opportunities both to enhance assessments of learners' progress and language development and to strengthen ties between assessment, teaching, and learning.

Therefore, the purpose of this edited volume is to engage language teachers, researchers, and practitioners in the conversation on opportunities and challenges regarding assessments in online language education, to further the discussion on how to re-conceptualize the need and use of assessments in the online environment, and finally, to contribute to a better understanding of how assessment tools can affect online language teaching and learning. We use "assessment" in its broader sense to refer to the process of collecting information that is both systematic and substantively grounded (Bachman, 2004; Bachman & Palmer, 2010). This approach allows us to explore various aspects of online language learning and their impact on the development of learners' language abilities. We facilitate this conversation by dividing the volume into four sections: (1) *Assessing Learner Progress and Development* containing a discussion of assessment in a telecollaborative environment, an online Spanish class, and a language MOOC (massive open online course) for clinical terminology; (2) *Assessing Online Teachers* examining issues and challenges in assessing online teachers' effectiveness and teacher tech readiness for online instruction and online material development; (3) *Assessment Tools for Online Environments* with contributions toward new assessment tools, methods, and evaluations of existing resources and (4) *Future Directions for Online Language Assessment* with perspectives toward alternative assessments and a framework for establishing valid assessment practices online.

Assessing Learner Progress and Development

A major issue concerning the effectiveness of online language learning is the lack of empirical studies that measure online language learning outcomes with standardized and validated proficiency assessments, such as the American Council of Teachers of Foreign Languages (ACTFL, 2012) proficiency assessments or equivalent assessments. This problem was noted and discussed in the *Modern Language Journal*'s Perspectives column in the summer issue of 2015. Contributors to this column considered existing approaches to and evidence for documenting language learning outcomes in different online learning environments and identified the following research gaps: (1) findings regarding the effectiveness of online language learning are largely inconsistent due to the wide variety of instructional environments and models; (2) the number of rigorous longitudinal studies investigating learners' attainment of advanced levels of proficiency is very limited; and (3) empirical studies in this area rely heavily on achievement tests and thus there is little generalizable information concerning learners' proficiency attainment beyond the achievement of specific course goals.

A survey of empirical studies on the impact of *online language learning* published in major CALL journals between 2015 and 2017 indicates that these issues continue to exist. Table 1.1 summarizes the empirical studies identified, their instructional environments and models, and the measure(s) used in the assessing language learning in online environments.

As the summaries indicate, an overwhelming majority of studies published after 2015 continue to rely on achievement measures or student perception surveys to assess the impact of language learning in online environments. Only a few studies used standardized and validated measures of language proficiency (e.g., the Versant test in Moneypenny & Aldrich, 2016) or proficiency measures developed locally (e.g., the communicative efficiency rating scale in Gao & Hanna, 2016).

One of the difficulties of adopting standardized proficiency measures is the costs and challenges of test administration, particularly considering the physical locations of the learners (Lin & Warschauer, 2015). A more important issue, however, is that proficiency tests may not always fully capture learners' online language learning and development. In a study investigating the impact of *Rosetta Stone* (RS) on Spanish learning, for example, Lord (2015) demonstrated that although the participants did not have significant differences in their scores on standardized proficiency tests at the end of the study, the differences in their abilities to use Spanish during the interviews with the researcher were evident. Specifically, this study was carried out among 12 true beginners of Spanish who were divided into three

Table 1.1. Instructional environment, model, and assessment measures in research on online language learning

Author (year)	Instructional environment	Instructional model	Number of participants	Assessment measure(s)
Dugartsyrenova & Sardegna (2016)	blended learning	facilitate learning through multi-modal asynchronous CMC	26	researcher's field notes, activity log, survey, and interviews
Furniss (2016)	stand-alone instructional modules online for students' individual learning	help students develop pragmatic competence through CALL applications	34	tests of comprehension and pro-duction of the targeted routine formulas
Gao and Hanna (2016)	individual computer-assisted pronunciation training	explicit instruction on pronuncia-tion and practices	60	communicative efficiency ratings of pronunciation features in students' reading and spontaneous speaking
Garrett-Rucks, Howles, & Lake (2015)	hypermedia texts	cognitive theory of multimedia learning	70	reading format preference survey and questionnaire
Hong et al. (2016)	online games in realistic, 3D, virtual English-speaking environment	game-based language learning	12	proficiency assessments based on ACTFL guidelines
Kusyk (2017)	online informal learning of English (OILE)	usage-based language learning; dynamic systems theory	3	semi-structured interviews and a 15-minute writing activity every 6 weeks; CAF measures of the written productions
Lee (2016)	task-based activities in an online Spanish course	task-based instruction	48	post-study survey and interviews
Levak & Son (2016)	Skype and Second Life	improve listening comprehen-sion through computer-mediated communication tasks	35	pre- and post-tests of listening comprehension; perceived effectiveness based on interviews

Li (2016)	self-access web-based instructional units	explicit instruction and pragmatic consciousness-raising	36	metapragmatic assessment tasks and reflective e-journals
Liakin, Cardoso, and Liakina (2015)	mobile-assisted learning environment	automatic speech recognition based pronunciation activities	42	rating of the accuracy of the pronunciation and perception of the target segmental feature
Lin, Warschauer, & Blake (2016)	language learning social network sites	mixed types of exercises	4,174	perceived progress through survey & accuracy and complexity of language use in writing exercises
Moneypenny & Aldrich (2016)	Online Spanish course	ACTFL 5C standards	90	the Versant exam for Spanish
Scholz (2017)	massively multiplayer online role-playing games	extramural digital game-based language learning	4	frequency analysis of participants' emergent linguistic construction
Scida and Jones (2016)	hybrid Spanish courses	communicative language teaching	39	local tests of listening comprehension and linguistic knowledge; student perceptions
Terantino (2016)	individual use of mobile-assisted language learning (MALL) programs (5 apps)	multimodal vocabulary learning applications on iPad	7	pre- and post-tests of vocabulary recall and listening comprehension
Trinder (2016)	face-to-face, blended, and other environments	mixed	175	perceived usefulness and ideal environment for language learning through questionnaire
Tsai (2015)	blended English research paper writing course	CMS-assisted writing strategy instruction	247	holistic scoring of participants' written reports; participants' perceptions
Yang & Hsieh (2015)	blended learning of reading comprehension	to improve reading comprehension through peer questioning and response	50	TOEIC test of reading proficiency

groups: a control group that followed the typical face-to-face classroom syllabus, a RS group that did not attend classes or participate in other pedagogical activities except for the RS learning units and online activities, and a RS+class group that received face-to-face instruction in addition to the use of RS. All the participants took two standardized proficiency tests at the end of the study and participated in monthly interviews with the researcher. According to the test results, there were no major differences in terms of the participants' proficiency attainment. However, the interview data showed major differences between a participant in the RS group and another in the control group: whereas the RS learner rarely made any attempts to ask for help in Spanish to cope with possible communication breakdowns, the learner in the control group showed more willingness and facility in doing so. This example illustrates a second problem associated with the use of standardized and validated proficiency tests: language development over a relatively short period of time (e.g., a semester or several weeks) may be captured by objective and valid measures of learners' performance but not by standardized language proficiency tests.

Language proficiency is a broad concept that comprises a set of complex relationships among various factors (e.g., phonology, syntax, semantics, pragmatics, lexis), and proficiency tests are generally based on theories of language ability (Bachman & Palmer, 2010) and are used as an overall gauge of learners' ability to use the language (Bachman, 1990). Therefore, language proficiency tests may not always be the most effective or appropriate way to assess language learning in various online environments; instead, it is important to explore additional objective measures that can highlight the impact of online technologies and learning activities on specific areas of development. In other words, in order to better understand the impact of online language learning, it is necessary to not only explore available methods and tools of assessment of learning online but also re-conceptualize the purpose and use of assessments in online learning environments.

Moreover, *online language learning* covers a wide variety of instructional contexts with various instructors, pedagogical approaches, and tools (Table 1.1). Therefore, to assess the impact of online language learning in these various contexts through comparisons with learning outcomes in the face-to-face setting may not be valid or meaningful (Rubio, 2015). A more productive way is to explore the opportunities and challenges brought by online language learning environments and to consider how technology can strengthen assessment and help incorporate assessment into online language teaching and learning. Thus, in this volume, we begin with a set of three chapters that incorporate a mixture of assessments in different learning environments. Contributors in Part One, Assessing Learner Progress and Development, share their approaches to assessment of language learning in different online environments, examine issues that emerged in their efforts to document learning progress and measure learning outcomes, and discuss possible opportunities to address the issues along with recommendations for future research in this area.

In Chapter 2, Assessing Language and Intercultural Learning during Telecollaboration, Senta Goertler, Theresa Schenker, Carly Lesoski, and Sonja Brunsmeier focus on the assessment of learning outcomes in telecollaboration. In their report of a telecollaboration project between a pre-service class on intercultural competence for teachers of English as a foreign or second language at a German University of Education and a US undergraduate course aiming to develop advanced language skills, the researchers examine the correlation between various classroom-based measures of students' achievements and research-based measures of students' performance, and discuss the challenges of assessing the development of language and intercultural competence through telecollaboration. With the finding that the scores for the participants' language proficiency and language production were below expectations even though their scores on class performance measures were all satisfactory, the researchers consider possible reasons for the lack of correlation between the performance measures and provide suggestions for further research on assessments of learning outcomes in telecollaboration projects.

Much of the concern about the lack of empirical evidence for the impact of online learning probably also comes from the fact that there are fewer opportunities for the instructors to communicate with the students directly online and thus, in comparison to face-to-face learning, the instructor may not be able to closely monitor students' learning and progress. Therefore, means of documenting learning progress and assessing learning outcomes are more scarce for an online language course. This issue is further explored by Victoria Russell in Chapter 3, Assessing the Effect of Pedagogical Interventions on Success Rates and on Students' Perceptions of Connectedness Online. After identifying the urgent need to effectively assess the impact of pedagogical interventions on language learning outcomes in an online Spanish course, the researcher provides a synthesis of previous research regarding three important factors in effective online language learning: feelings of connectedness, foreign language anxiety, and beliefs about language learning. She then reports findings from an empirical study on how two pedagogical interventions affect students' success rates as measured by course grades and the three relevant factors. This chapter demonstrates that online pedagogical intervention may affect language learning indirectly through its influence on other relevant factors, and therefore these factors and how they may influence language learning online should be taken into account in future research on assessments of online language learning.

In Chapter 4, Language MOOCs: Assessing Student Knowledge and Comprehension of Clinical Terminology, Carrie DEMMANS EPP, Rae Mancilla, and Valerie Swigart share the results of their study on the learning of specialized vocabulary through a language MOOC informed by situated learning and the framework of the Community of Practice. In their effort to assess the change in students' knowledge of clinical terminology and their use of the terms in real-world settings, the researchers rely on a combination of observational data, student self-reports, and assessments of vocabulary knowledge. The chapter shows that studying with the language MOOC has led to an increase in vocabulary knowledge scores, which is also confirmed by students' self-reports. Meanwhile, the researchers discuss the importance of documenting learners' participation/use of the course materials in their investigation of the connections between students' behavior in the language MOOC and their performance as measured by course grades.

Assessing Online Teachers

Despite the challenges in assessing learning outcomes, online language education has brought new opportunities to inform pedagogical theory, research, and practice. In the coming years, "native CALL theories" (Hubbard, 2008: 387) will likely continue to emerge, expanding on what we currently know about language learning and technology and informing pedagogical decision-making. At the forefront of that development will hopefully be new insights into online language assessment as we move from not just "consumers" of theory (Levy & Stockwell, 2006: 139) but also "applicants" and perhaps "developers" of CALL theory. That is, from what is known about general teaching preparedness, teachers may not fully understand how to apply theory and research to daily practices (Crandall, 2000; Johnson, 2006; Kiely & Askham, 2012; Peacock, 2009; Wright, 2010). The same applies to teaching in online environments (Dooly, 2009; Dooly & Sadler, 2013). It is thus our necessity as a field to maximize the opportunities for teachers to apply knowledge to practice and become drivers of new theoretical developments. This call, however, relies heavily on adequate CALL teacher training to build technology-specific literacies (Compton, 2009). The struggle to provide adequate training and experiences for online teaching preparation is partially impacted by our ability to successfully evaluate our teachers' needs, which consequentially impedes development of the knowledge teachers have about instilling pedagogically informative assessment practices, among other areas. Therefore, the question of whether our teachers are ready for online course instruction, development, and assessment still remains.

Part Two in this book examines how to strengthen teachers to enhance assessment and the quality of online courses. Barbara Lafford, Carmen King de Ramirez, and James Wermers begin our discussion in Chapter 5, Issues and Challenges in the Assessment of Online Language Teacher Performance, with an overview of four key issues involved in the assessment of online language teaching (uneven training/uneven institutional expectations, faculty resistance to online teaching and to their assessment as online instructors, diverse backgrounds among online instructors, and varying instruments used to assess the performance of online faculty), the challenges these factors present for carrying out such assessments, and possible solutions for meeting each of those challenges. This chapter also includes brief findings from a pilot study that provided a rationale for the focus on these four issues associated with online instructor assessment.

Without much speculation, research has suggested that language teachers need a working knowledge of information and communications technology (Gilbert, 2013; Stickler & Emke, 2015). This technological competence has been well documented in literature; however, less emphasis has been placed on what teachers can do with that knowledge. In Chapter 6, Evaluating Teacher Tech Literacies Using an Argument-Based Approach, Jesse Gleason and Elena Schmitt evaluate whether teachers in a MS Bilingual Education & TESOL program are able to transpose their traditional face-to-face pedagogical knowledge to synchronous videoconferencing environments and have similar content learning opportunities as their on-ground peers. The authors contribute descriptive accounts of real-time challenges that teachers faced when training for online instruction. They also provide implications for assessing the development of teacher tech literacies in a situated context.

In the final chapter of the section, David Donnarumma and Sarah Hamilton explore how face-to-face teachers make the move to teaching online. Their chapter, titled Face-to-Face Teacher to Online Course Developer, is a small-scale study showing that readiness for online teaching is as much about the values and beliefs of the teachers as it is about their technological competence. Their findings demonstrate that communication and collaboration with colleagues, knowing your audience, and time management are factors that greatly influence teachers' perceived readiness for online course development.

Assessment Tools for Online Environments

With the interdisciplinary knowledge that exists between CALL research-ers and practitioners, there is a depth of experience that can be culti-vated to advance current assessment tools as well as build new innovative computer-based assessments. In fact, technology offers unique features for integrating tools for assessment and those for language learning in online instructional environments, potentially strengthening both assessment and instruction in this context. In the field of language testing, for example, such developments are pervasive. Researchers have explored means of using tech-nology for assessing writing through automated writing evaluation systems (Chodorow, Gamon, & Tetreault, 2010; Chapelle, Cotos, & Lee, 2015; Hoang & Kunnan, 2016), grammar through computer-delivered testing (Chapelle et al., 2010), speaking using videoconferencing technology (Nakatsuhara et al., 2017) and speech recognition software (Franco et al., 2010), listening using video-based listening tests (Ockey, 2007; Suvorov, 2015), and also reading with computer-adaptive functionalities (He & Min, 2017). While new assess-ments are being developed, few efforts have been made to bring those tech-nologies to the CALL community. Furthermore, the CALL community has limited access to these assessments, requiring partnering with language tes-ters, developing new valid assessments, or exploring the potential of existing technologies to supplement assessment efforts.

The articles in the third section of this volume focus on broadening our knowledge about how technology can be developed, improved upon, and even enhanced to fit online needs. In Chapter 8, Innovative Implementation of a Web-Based Rating System for Individualizing Online English Speaking Instruction, Hyejin Yang and Elena Cotos focus on validating the diagnostic uses of a web-based rating platform called R-PLAT, which captures mul-tiple aspects of language performance that can serve as the diagnostic evi-dence needed to inform transitioning from a face-to-face speaking course to an online course that is tailored to individual learners' abilities. Empirical evidence obtained from quantitative and qualitative data supports the judg-mental assumption that the diagnostic descriptors recorded via R-PLAT are indicative of target speaking ability levels used for placement into proficiency-based levels of the course. Overall, this work presents an exam-ple of how theoretically-grounded evaluation frameworks can serve to over-arch the validation of the uses of computer-based assessment tools for the purpose of shaping a strong learner-fit quality for online language teaching.

While emerging technologies can support a reformulation of assess-ments in online language education, existing technologies can also contrib-ute to this shift. In Chapter 9, A Systematic Approach to Vetting Reading

Comprehension Items for Inclusion in Cloud-Based Assessments, Fabiana MacMillan reports on the trial of a process for vetting reading comprehension items for inclusion in online placement and achievement assessments within Rosetta Stone. The results of this study have implications for the interface of assessment and language instruction in online programs, including suggestions for providing ever more specific information about learners' reading comprehension needs for use in individualized instruction.

The final chapter of this section, The Lingo of Language Learning Startups: Congruency between Claims, Affordances, and SLA Theory, by Gabriel Guillén, Thor Sawin, and Sarah Springer, focuses on the congruency between the claims and affordances of language learning startups and their relationship to instructed SLA theory. The authors' evaluation of archetypical startups (Memrise, Verbling, Bliu Bliu, Duolingo, Elsa, and ChattingCat) suggests that commonly-held language fallacies (the minimal effort myth, a preference for native speakers, or a focus on simplistic conceptions of language as isolated easily-translatable words) are prolific, and while language learning startups may promote themselves as being successful for developing language and assessing language acquisition, the quality of the learning products is still questionable. This chapter demonstrates that an objective evaluation of the online language learning products based on instructed SLA theory could help researchers and practitioners better understand the potential value of these products for language learning and learners' learning outcomes.

Future Directions for Online Language Assessment

As our efforts towards maximizing assessment practices in an era of online language learning persist, it it is evident that more insights are needed to determine where we go from here. The road to this understanding should lead to a clearer picture of where we want to end up; we believe that would be a place where effective assessments are used for measuring whole learner experiences in order to determine how learner dynamics would influence individual developmental trajectories, to predict success in students' future real-world language use, and to better inform teaching practices. The chapters in Part Four seek to provide insights in this regard. In Chapter 11, Toward Technology-Enhanced Alternative Assessment for Online Language Education, Zhi Li and Stephanie Link promote technology-enhanced alternative assessments to help account for the dynamic, multifaceted experiences taking place in technology-rich environments. They discuss the current roles of technology in designing and developing alternative language assessments and considerations for implementing technology-enhanced alternative assessments, including theoretical recommendations and evidence-based model discovery. Their chapter contributes to a more comprehensive understanding of how online learning experiences have the potential to complement traditional approaches to assessment and aid in efforts to simultaneously integrate learning and assessment into online language education.

Finally, Erik Voss completes the volume with Chapter 12, Argument-Based Approach to Validation in Online Language Education, in which he argues that teachers who use effective educational assessments will become better teachers. He highlights the importance of validation of learner-oriented assessment practices and presents an argument-based framework to support the evaluation of assessments. Material from this chapter can provide effective assessment information for evaluation of language learning and pedagogical practices in online language environments while setting the stage for future efforts to improve assessment practices in the field of CALL.

Conclusion

Assessment is a key component of language teaching and learning, with face-to-face and online contexts employing it as a central part of language development. This means that assessment represents a collection of ways by which CALL researchers and practitioners can assist students towards a better awareness of their learning processes and development. We thus argue for a more inclusive approach to language assessment in online education where there is potential for CALL scholars to engage in more fruitful dialogue with other discipline specialists (e.g., language assessors, NLP professionals, and SLA researchers). However, we contend that this potential will go unrealized until we acknowledge the impact that effective assessment practices can have on our understanding of language learning and acquisition online. If we want the field of CALL to grow exponentially in understanding how language development should be assessed in this era of technological discovery, we need to reach out to inform and be informed by other disciplines. As language testers have sought out knowledge from educational measurement and SLA researchers from natural sciences, sociology, and psychology, among others, CALL researchers and practitioners can team together with these other specialists to build upon our assessment practices.

Three directions for future research are particularly relevant. First, with the development of technology, there will be more possibilities to strengthen assessments of online language learning. Therefore, more research is needed to understand how to make the best use of the emerging tools to document learners' language development and assess learning outcomes. A second direction is to investigate how technologies can help incorporate learning and assessment seamlessly to improve online language teaching and learning experiences where cognitive, social, and affective factors can have huge impact. A better understanding of how these factors may influence online language learning is therefore also an important topic for future research. Third, given the nature and characteristics of online environments, language learning online may also be assessed indirectly through evaluation of relevant factors such as learner autonomy, language learning strategies, etc. There is growing interest among CALL researchers in how technologies can help develop autonomous language learning (Alzahrani & Watson, 2016; Lee, 2016; Smith & Craig, 2013) and thus contribute to learners' language development.

With the development of technology, it is increasingly difficult to distinguish face-to-face and online language learning, because technologies are widely used in face-to-face classrooms, and the element of real-time video-based communication is also incorporated in online language learning courses. Against this background, a more meaningful question to ask is how online and face-to-face language learning can benefit each other, and how the development of technology is blurring the boundary between the two. In the following chapters, contributors discuss in detail the challenges and opportunities in assessments brought by online language teaching and learning, and explore different ways to assess online language learning and teaching, and how assessments can help strengthen online language teaching and learning. It is our hope that this discussion will help reevaluate the knowledge we have about assessment across online language education.

About the Authors

Stephanie Link is an Assistant Professor of TESL/Applied Linguistics and Director of International Composition at Oklahoma State University. She earned her PhD from Iowa State University and a dual Master's degree from Winona State University in Minnesota, USA and Tamkang University in Taiwan. She primarily teaches graduate-level courses in TESL, grammatical analysis, language and technology, and research methods. Her research interests include the study of emerging technologies for language learning and assessment, written genre analysis, and L2 pedagogy.

Jinrong Li is an Assistant Professor in the Department of Writing and Linguistics at Georgia Southern University. Before that, she taught English in Beijing and ESL in Boston University and Iowa State University. Her research interests include Computer-Assisted Language Learning (CALL), the instruction and assessment of Second Language (L2) writing, and information literacy and writing pedagogy.

References

ACTFL (2012). *ACTFL Proficiency Guidelines 2012.* Retrieved from https://www. actfl.org/sites/default/files/pdfs/public/ACTFLProficiencyGuidelines2012_FINAL.pdf

Alzahrani, S., & Watson, J. (2016). The impact of online training on Saudi medical students' attitudes, awareness, and use of language learning strategies in relation to their developing autonomy. *Studies in Self-Access Learning Journal*, 7(1), 4–15.

Andes, L., & Claggett, E. (2011). Wiki writers: Students and teachers making connections across communities. *Reading Teacher*, 64(5), 345–350. https://doi.org/10.1598/rt.64.5.5

Bachman, L. F. (1990). *Fundamental Considerations in Language Testing.* Oxford: Oxford University Press.

Bachman, L. F. (2004). *Statistical Analyses for Language Assessment.* Cambridge: Cambridge University Press.

Bachman, L. F., & Palmer, A. S. (2010). *Language Assessment in Practice.* Oxford: Oxford University Press.

Becker, S. R., & Sturm, J. L. (2017). Effects of audiovisual media on L2 listening comprehension: A preliminary study in French. *CALICO Journal*, 34(2), 147–177. https://doi.org/10.1558/cj.26754

Chapelle, C. A., Chung, Y.-R., Hegelheimer, V., Pendar, N., & Xu, J. (2010). Towards a computer-delivered test of productive grammatical ability. *Language Testing*, 27(4), 443–469. https://doi.org/10.1177/0265532210367633

Chapelle, C. A., Cotos, E., & Lee, J. (2015). Validity arguments for diagnostic assessment using automated writing evaluation. *Language Testing*, 32(3), 385–405. https://doi.org/10.1177/0265532214565386

Chodorow, M., Gamon, M., & Tetreault, J. (2010). The utility of article and preposition error correction systems for English language learners: Feedback and assessment. *Language Testing*, 27(3), 419–436. https://doi.org/10.1177/0265532210364391

Chun, D. M., Kern, R., & Smith, B. (2016). Technology in language use, language teaching, and language learning. *The Modern Language Journal*, 100(S1), 64–80. https://doi.org/10.1111/modl.12302

Compton, L. K. L. (2009). Preparing language teachers to teach language online: A look at skills, roles, and responsibilities. *Computer Assisted Language Learning*, 22(1), 73–99. https://doi.org/10.1080/09588220802613831

Cowan, R., Choo, J., & Lee, G. S. (2014). ICALL for improving Korean L2 writers' ability to edit grammatical errors. *Language Learning & Technology*, 18(3), 193–207.

Crandall, J. (2000). Language teacher education. *Annual Review of Applied Linguistics*, 20, 34–55. https://doi.org/10.1017/s0267190500200032

Dooly, M. (2009). New competencies in a new era? Examining the impact of a teacher training project. *ReCALL*, 21(3), 352–369. https://doi.org/10.1017/s0958344009990085

Dooly, M., & Sadler, R. (2013). Filling in the gaps: Linking theory and practice through telecollaboration in teacher education. *ReCALL*, 25(1), 4–29. https://doi.org/10.1017/s0958344012000237

Dugartsyrenova, V. A., & Sardegna, V. G. (2016). Developing oral proficiency with VoiceThread: Learners' strategic uses and views. *ReCALL*, 29(1), 59–79. https://doi.org/10.1017/S0958344016000161

Firth, A., & Wagner, J. (1997). On discourse, communication and (some) fundamental concepts in SLA research. *The Modern Language Journal*, 81(3), 285–300. https://doi.org/10.1111/j.1540-4781.2007.00667.x

Firth, A., & Wagner, J. (2007). Second/foreign language learning as a social accomplishment: Elaborations on a reconceptualized SLA. *The Modern Language Journal*, 91, 798–817. https://doi.org/10.1111/j.1540-4781.2007.00670.x

Franco, H., Bratt, H., Rossier, R., Gadde, V.R., Shriberg, E., Abrash, V., & Precoda, K. (2010). Eduspeak®: A speech recognition and pronunciation scoring toolkit for computer-aided language learning applications. *Language Testing*, 27(3), 401–418. https://doi.org/ 10.1177/0265532210364408

Furniss, E. A. (2016). Teaching the pragmatics of Russian conversation using a corpus-referred website. *Language Learning & Technology*, 20(2), 38–60. https://doi.org/10.1007/978-3-319-41733-2_7

Gao, Y., & Hanna, B. E. (2016). Exploring optimal pronunciation teaching: Integrating instructional software into intermediate-level EFL classes in China. *CALICO Journal*, 33(2), 201–230. https://doi.org/10.1558/cj.v33i2.26054

Garrett-Rucks, P., Howles, L., & Lake, W. M. (2015). Enhancing L2 Reading Comprehension with Hypermedia Texts: Student Perceptions. *CALICO Journal*, 32(1), 26–51. https://doi.org/10.1558/calico.v32i1.26131

Gilbert, J. (2013). English for Academic Purposes. In G. Motteram (ed.), *Innovations in Learning Technologies for English Language Teaching* (pp. 117–144). British Council.

Hassani, K., Nahvi, A., & Ahmadi, A. (2016). Design and implementation of an intelligent virtual environment for improving speaking and listening skills. *Interactive Learning Environments*, 24(1), 252–271. https://doi.org/10.1080/10494820.2013.846265

He, L., & Min, S. (2017). Development and validation of a computer adaptive EFL test. *Language Assessment Quarterly*, 14(2), 160–176. https://doi.org/10.108/15434303.2016.1162793

Heift, T. (2010). Developing an intelligent language tutor. *CALICO Journal*, 27(3), 443–459. https://doi.org/10.11139/cj.27.3.443-459

Hoang, G. T. L., & Kunnan, A. J., (2016). Automated essay evaluation for English language learners: A case study of MY access. *Language Assessment Quarterly*, 13(4), 359–376. https://doi.org/10.1080/15434303.2016.1230121

Hong, J. S., Han, D. H., Kim, Y. I., Bae, S. J., Kim, S. M., & Renshaw, P. (2016). English language education on-line game and brain connectivity. *ReCALL*, 29(1), 3–21. https://doi.org/10.1017/S0958344016000173

Hubbard, P. (2008). Twenty-five years of theory in the CALICO Journal. *CALICO Journal*, 25(3), 387–399. https://doi.org/10.1558/cj.v25i3.387-399

Johnson, K. E. (2006). The sociocultural turn and its challenges for second language teacher education. *TESOL Quarterly*, 40(1), 235–257. https://doi.org/10.2307/40264518

Kiely, R., & Askham, J. (2012). Furnished imagination: The impact of preservice teacher training on early career work in TESOL. *TESOL Quarterly*, 46(3), 496–518. https://doi.org/10.1002/tesq.39

Kusyk, M. (2017). The development of complexity, accuracy and fluency in L2 written production through informal participation in online activities. *CALICO Journal*, 34(1), 75–96. https://doi.org/10.1558/cj.29513

Lafford, B. A. (2007). Second language acquisition reconceptualized? The Impact of Firth and Wagner (1997). *The Modern Language Journal*, 91, 735–756. https://doi.org/10.1111/j.1540-4781.2007.00666.x

Lee, L. (2016). Autonomous learning through task-based instruction in fully online language courses. *Language Learning & Technology*, 20(2), 81–97.

Levak, N., & Son, J.-B. (2016). Facilitating second language learners' listening comprehension with Second Life and Skype. *ReCALL*, 29(2), 200–218. https://doi.org/10.1017/S0958344016000215

Levy, M., & Stockwell, G. (2006). *CALL Dimensions: Options and Issues in Computer Assisted Language Learning.* Mahwah, NJ: Lawrence Erlbaum.

Li, Y. (2016). Learning to express gratitude in Mandarin Chinese through web-based instruction. *Language Learning & Technology*, 20(1), 191–208. http://dx.doi.org/10125/44452

Liakin, D., Cardoso, W., & Liakina, N. (2015). Learning L2 pronunciation with a mobile speech recognizer: French /y/. *CALICO Journal*, 32(1), 1–25. https://doi.org/10.1558/cj.v32i1.25962

Lin, C.-H., & Warschauer, M. (2015). Online foreign language education: What are the proficiency outcomes?.*The Modern Language Journal*, 99(2), 394–397. https://doi.org/10.1111/modl.12234_1

Lin, C.-H., Warschauer, M., & Blake, R. (2016). Language learning through social networks: Perceptions and reality. *Language Learning & Technology*, 20(1), 124–147. http://dx.doi.org/10125/44449

Lord, G. (2015). "I don't know how to use words in Spanish": Rosetta Stone and learner proficiency outcomes. *The Modern Language Journal*, 99(2), 401–405. https://doi.org/10.1111/modl.12234_3

Martin-Beltran, M. (2013). "I don't feel as embarrassed because we're all learning": Discursive positioning among adolescents becoming multilingual.

International Journal of Educational Research, 62, 152–161. https://doi.org/10.1016/j.ijer.2013.08.005

Moneypenny, D. B., & Aldrich, R. S. (2016). Online and face-to-face language learning: A comparative analysis of oral proficiency in introductory Spanish. *The Journal of Educators Online*, 13(2), 105–133. https://doi.org/10.9743/jeo.2016.2.2

Nakatsuhara, F., Inoue, C., Berry, V., & Galaczi, E. (2017). Exploring the use of video-conferencing technology in the assessment of spoken language: A mixed-methods study. *Language Assessment Quarterly*, 14(1), 1–18. https://doi.org/10.1080/15434303.2016.1263637

Nishioka, H. (2016). Analysing language development in a collaborative digital storytelling project: Sociocultural perspectives. *System*, 62, 39–52. https://doi.org/10.1016/j.system.2016.07.001

Ockey, G. J. (2007). Construct implications of including still image or video in computer-based listening tests. *Language Testing*, 24(4), 517–537. https://doi.org/10.1177/0265532207080771

O'Dowd, R., & Lewis, T. (eds.). (2016). *Online Intercultural Exchange: Policy, Pedagogy, Practice*. New York and London: Routledge.

O'Reilly, T. (2005). What is web 2.0. Retrieved from http://www.oreilly.com/pub/a/web2/archive/what-is-web-20.html?page=1

Peacock, M. (2009). The evaluation of foreign language teacher education programmes. *Language Teaching Research*, 13, 259–278. https://doi.org/10.1177/1362168809104698

Rubio, F. (2015). Assessment of oral proficiency in online language courses: Beyond reinventing the wheel. *The Modern Language Journal*, 99(2), 405–408. https://doi.org/10.1111/modl.12234_4

Sauro, S. (2017). Online fan practices and CALL. *CALICO Journal*, 34(2), 131–146. https://doi.org/10.1558/cj.33077

Scholz, K. (2017). Encouraging free play: Extramural digital game-based language learning as a complex adaptive system. *CALICO Journal*, 34(1), 39–57. https://doi.org/10.1558/cj.29527

Scida, E. E., & Jones, J. N. (2016). New tools, new designs: A study of a redesigned hybrid Spanish program. *CALICO Journal*, 33(2), 174–200. https://doi.org/10.1558/cj.v33i2.26053

Smith, K., & Craig, H. (2013). Enhancing the autonomous use of CALL: A new curriculum model in EFL. *CALICO Journal*, 30(2), 252–278. https://doi.org/10.11139/cj.30.2.252-278

Stickler, U., & Emke, M. (2015). Part-time and freelance language teachers and their ICT training needs. In U. Stickler and R. Hampel (eds.), *Developing Online Language Teaching: Research Based Pedagogies and Reflective Practices* (pp. 28–44). New York, NY: Palgrave Macmillan.

Suvorov, R. (2015). The use of eye tracking in research on video-based second language (L2) listening assessment: A comparison of context videos and content videos. *Language Testing*, 32(4), 463–483. https://doi.org/10.1177/0265532214562099

Tarone, E. (2015). Online foreign language education: What are the proficiency outcomes? *Modern Language Journal*, 90(2), 392–393. https://doi.org/10.1111/modl.12220

Terantino, J. (2016). Examining the effects of independent MALL on vocabulary recall and listening comprehension: An exploratory case study of preschool children. *CALICO Journal*, 33(2), 260–277. https://doi.org/10.1558/cj.v33i2.26072

Thorns, J. J., & Poole, F. (2017). Investigating linguistic, literary, and social affordances of L2 collaborative reading. *Language Learning & Technology*, 21(2), 139–156.

Trinder, R. (2016). Blending technology and face-to-face: Advanced students' choices. *ReCALL*, 28(1), 83–102. https://doi.org/10.1017/S0958344015000166

Tsai, Y.-R. (2015). Applying the technology acceptance model (TAM) to explore the effects of a Course Management System (CMS)-assisted EFL writing instruction. *CALICO Journal*, 32(1), 153–171. https://doi.org/10.1558/calico.v32i1.25961

Wang, Y.-C. (2014). Using Wikis to facilitate interaction and collaboration among EFL learners: A social constructivist approach to language teaching. *System*, 42, 383–390. https://doi.org/10.1016/j.system.2014.01.007

Warner, C. (2017). Designing talk in social networks: What Facebook teaches about conversation. *Language Learning & Technology*, 21(2), 121–138.

Wright, T. (2010). Second language teacher education: A review of recent research on practice. *Language Teaching*, 43, 259–296. https://doi.org/10.1017/S0261444810000030

Yang, Y.-F., & Hsieh, P.-Y. (2015). Negotiation of meaning to comprehend hypertexts through peer questioning. *Language Learning & Technology*, 19(2), 69–84. http://dx.doi.org/10125/44418.

Ziegler, N., Meurers, D., Rebuschat, P., Ruiz, S., Moreno-Vega, J. L., Chinkina, M., …, & Grey, S. (2017). Interdisciplinary research at the intersection of CALL, NLP, and SLA: Methodological implications from an input enhancement project. *Language Learning*, 67, 209–231.

PART ONE

ASSESSING LEARNER PROGRESS AND DEVELOPMENT

2 Assessing Language and Intercultural Learning during Telecollaboration

Senta Goertler,[*] Theresa Schenker,[**] Carly Lesoski,[***] and Sonja Brunsmeier[****]

Introduction

Telecollaboration has been a cornerstone of CALL research for over two decades with its own dedicated annual conference since 2015. While this research includes many accounts of successes and challenges in implementation (Hauck, 2007; Helm, 2015), the focus has primarily been on the pedagogical aspects and primary learning outcomes, such as language proficiency and intercultural competence. Less attention has been given to defining these learning outcomes in multiple areas at the same time, rather than in isolation, and to learning outcomes outside of communication. Furthermore, the validity of instruments used to evaluate outcomes of telecollaboration has rarely been assessed or reported, and in most studies, data have been coded by a single rater. Additionally, the assessment mechanisms used for evaluating learning have focused on research goals rather than pedagogical classroom goals.

This telecollaborative project was designed to improve (a) language skills by increasing target language production and intercultural competence through interaction with native speakers, and (b) content knowledge as defined in the syllabi through analysis tasks. Given the focus of this volume, and inter-rater reliabilities being extremely low, the discussion of content knowledge development was eliminated from this essay. Here, we adopt

[*]   Michigan State University, USA; goertler@msu.edu
[**]   Yale University, USA; theresa.schenker@yale.edu
[***] Michigan State University, USA; lesoskic@msu.edu
[****] Independent Researcher; s.brunsmeier@gmail.com

the intercultural knowledge and competence definition from Bennett (2008: 97) as: "a set of cognitive, affective, and behavioral skills and characteristics that support effective and appropriate interaction in a variety of cultural contexts." The overarching goal was the development and use of intercultural communicative competence, defined as "a complex of abilities needed to perform *effectively* and *appropriately* when interacting with others who are linguistically and culturally different from oneself" (Fantini, 2006: 12, emphasis in original). In terms of second language acquisition, this study is situated in the Interactionist Framework, specifically the assumption that output is an integral component of language development (Gass & Mackey, 2007).

In this study, students' performance was assessed from both a research and a classroom perspective. Specific grading criteria were developed for the course to assess students' learning outcomes on the basis of their telecollaboration records, blogs, synthesis projects, as well as overall class performance. From a research standpoint, telecollaboration records were assessed using amount of target language production and the intercultural competence rubric from the Association of American Colleges and Universities (AACU) (2010). Additionally, survey results and answers from reflective tasks were utilized for triangulation. Instruments were considered valid if they had high inter-rater reliability and if scores on instruments that are intended to measure the same construct had good correlations. The goal was to achieve 90% agreement on the ratings. Hence, in this study we compare students' performance on measures used for research purposes with those used for classroom purposes and assess inter-rater reliability.

Telecollaboration

Previous Research

Telecollaborative projects have been used in educational contexts for decades and what began with simple e-mail exchanges has developed into a myriad of projects utilizing technology in innovative ways. Telecollaboration can be defined as "the practice of engaging classes of geographically dispersed learners in online intercultural exchange using internet communication tools for the development of language and/or intercultural competence" (Helm, 2015: 197). Telecollaborative projects can vary in format, partnership setup, languages used, and goals associated with the project.

Learning Outcomes and Challenges

Much research has shown that both students and teachers view telecollaboration as positive and beneficial for language and cultural learning and the development of intercultural competence (Helm, 2015; Lee & Markey, 2014; Mahfouz, 2010). Studies indicate that students can increase their intercultural awareness and competence through telecollaboration (Bohinski & Leventhal, 2015; Chun, 2011; Van der Kroon, Jauregi, & Jan, 2015). Telecollaboration can also be beneficial for students' language skills in a variety of areas: pragmatic competence (Rafieyan et al., 2014), vocabulary knowledge (Yanguas, 2012), reading skills (Taki & Ramazani, 2011), oral skills (Lee, 2007), multiliteracy skills (Guth & Helm, 2012), and accuracy in writing (Stockwell & Levy, 2001), to name a few. Further benefits of telecollaborative learning include more equal student participation (Kötter, 2002) and social interaction (Arnold & Ducate, 2006), the development of critical thinking skills (Wu, Marek, & Chen, 2013), and increase in collaboration skills (Makaramani, 2015).

Naturally, not all telecollaborative projects lead to the intended learning outcomes. Tensions arising from institutional or logistical constraints, or differences in expectations can lead to miscommunication (Ware, 2005). Low participation and motivation, negative evaluations of the target culture, and failed opportunities for cross-cultural exchange can be the result (O'Dowd & Ritter, 2006). Other challenges include overcoming time zones and working with different institutional schedules (Helm, 2015), delays in asynchronous communication (Kötter, 2002), mismatched language levels and keeping students motivated (Kern, 1996), technological difficulties or unpreparedness, and ineffective tasks or lack of funding (Helm, 2015). Many challenges for instructors are connected to the assessment of telecollaboration. Instructors may struggle with how to deal with errors and error correction, and students might have difficulties understanding each other if their L2 text production contains many errors (Beatty, 2010).

Assessment of Telecollaboration Outcomes

The assessment of student learning through telecollaboration is a challenge many instructors face. While the assessment of language skills and communicative competence has used more widely accepted measurements, lack of second-rated samples puts the reliability of the results into question. A review of previous research reveals that many instructors grade telecollaboration based on participation, completion, ability to foster discussion, or a combination thereof, likely because this reflects socio-constructivist approaches which suggest that dialogic exchange encourages language learning (O'Dowd, 2010). Assessment of actual language or intercultural learning remains primarily a task researchers undertake after the telecollaborative project has been completed to evaluate potential effects of telecollaboration on student learning in a variety of domains by analyzing the stored data from the exchange. To assess and grade students' learning, instructors rely on a combination of tools, such as students' learning logs, journals or e-portfolios, peer-assessment, self-assessment, or the products created during the exchange (Dooly et al., 2008; Felix, 2003; Kabata & Edasawa, 2011). In many telecollaborative projects, participation and effort are the only criteria used to assess students' performance (Yang, 2011). Many instructors base their grading on amount of participation by requiring a certain length or number of messages to be exchanged (Ware & Kramsch, 2005; Weasenforth, Biesenbach-Lucas, & Meloni, 2002). Affective aspects of students' participation, and the extent to which they are able to keep the discussion going and develop relationships with their exchange partners is also part of many assessment rubrics (Arnold & Ducate, 2006; Weasenforth et al., 2002).

In most telecollaboration studies, language learning is assessed primarily for research purposes, and it is unclear if and how its assessment impacts course grading or is explained to students or if classroom and research assessments are assessing the same constructs. Research has assessed the effects of language gains in telecollaboration in myriad ways, for example by analyzing the speech produced by the students during the exchange. Some studies focus on subjective assessment of language comprehensibility by using trained raters to assess speech samples (Akiyama & Saito, 2016). Most studies look at specific aspects of language learning such as pronunciation (Bueno-Alastuey, 2010), lexical appropriateness and vocabulary learning (Akiyama & Saito, 2016; Perez, 2003; Yanguas, 2012), or syntactic complexity (Sauro, 2012; Schenker, 2016; Sotillo, 2000). Several studies have assessed negotiation of meaning as an indicator of second language acquisition (Kitade, 2006; Schenker, 2015; Tudini, 2003; Wang, 2006).

Researchers rely on a variety of models and tools to assess different language skills, including discourse analysis (Peterson, 2009), content analysis (Lomicka & Lord, 2012), lexical density or grammatical accuracy measures (Jin, 2013; Shang, 2007), ethnography of communication (Abrams, 2013), focus-on-form and collaborative episodes (Lee, 2008), socialist realist investigations (Belz, 2002), recognition and production tasks for vocabulary knowledge (Yanguas, 2012) and other vocabulary tests (Polat, Mancilla, & Mahalingappa, 2013), speaking tests (Satar & Özdener, 2008), and many more. Several studies make general claims about the language learning benefits of telecollaboration without any clear explanation about how this was assessed (Cardoso & Matos, 2013; Castillo-Scott, 2015).

The assessment of intercultural competence (IC) in telecollaboration is more challenging, and nuanced categories are needed for effective evaluation of this skill (Bohinski & Leventhal, 2015). O'Dowd (2010) points out that many instructors do not assess intercultural learning at all when conducting telecollaboration because of the difficulties associated with the definition and evaluation of IC development. Assessing the development of IC in telecollaboration is especially difficult due to the ethical questions that assessing concepts such as *openness to others* may raise (Byram, 2008), because IC is an extremely complex phenomenon and few instruments have been shown to be both valid and reliable (Spencer-Oatey & Franklin, 2009), and because many of its attributes are not easily observable or even definable (Witte, 2014).

To investigate the development of IC, many studies analyze cultural discussions between students based on different criteria and models, most commonly Byram's (1997) model of intercultural communicative competence (Belz, 2007; Liaw, 2006; O'Dowd, 2006; Schenker, 2012; Vogt, 2006; Ware & Kessler, 2014). A variety of tools have been used for the analysis of IC. Most frequently, researchers use qualitative analyses of students' contributions (Kramsch & Thorne, 2002; O'Dowd, 2006; Thorne, 2003; Toyoda & Harrison, 2002; Ware & Kramsch, 2005). Studies have investigated culture-related episodes in transcriptions of students' spoken interactions (Zakir, Funo, & Telles, 2016) or used discourse analysis of interaction transcripts (Menard-Warwick, 2009). Often, researchers look at some form of student production (reflective diaries or language produced during the telecollaboration itself) and try to find evidence of IC therein (Liaw, 2006; Woodin, 2001) with varying degrees of scientific thoroughness. Another set of studies rely on students' self-assessment, surveys or interviews, to assess their IC development (Kötter, 2003; Stickler & Emke, 2011; Thomé-Williams, 2016; Tian & Wang, 2010). Few projects discussed in research articles include detailed assessment criteria provided to the students like the project described by Schuetze (2008).

Methods

Building on the research discussed in the previous section, this exploratory study investigates different measures of success in learning through telecollaboration. This study is part of a larger research project and the focus here is on assessment. The larger study is grounded in an interactionist perspective of second language acquisition (Gass & Mackey, 2007) and an intercultural competence framework drawing from Bennett's (2008) model of intercultural competence as cognitive, affective, and behavioral skills and Byram's (1997) model, which divides IC into skills, knowledge, and attitudes. The study is guided by the following research questions intended to evaluate assessment tools: (1) Did students reach the expected learning outcomes as defined in the course syllabus (i.e., language production and IC goals)? (2) Did different measures intended to measure the same construct produce similar results? (3) Did raters assign similar scores on the research measures?

Context and Participants

The telecollaborative partnership was set up as a tandem exchange project between an advanced German language course focused on applied linguistics in the United States (n = 20) and a course focused on the teaching of intercultural competence for pre-service teachers of English at a University of Education in Germany (n = 16). It should be noted that one US student was a non-native speaker of English and one German student was not only a non-native speaker of German, but had very low proficiency in this language.

The course goal in the US (which is the course in focus here) was to improve learners' language skills to Advanced Low on the ACTFL proficiency scale through learning about linguistics (the structure of the language, language variation, and language acquisition) and conducting language analyses. The course included both formal (research papers, course presentations) as well as informal (interviews, class discussions, blogs, telecollaboration) communicative tasks to increase interactive opportunities and thereby language learning. Language analysis tasks, which required students to pay attention to language variation and also the structure of different types of discourse, were intended to help students notice gaps between their own production and norms in the larger language community. The communicative and analysis tasks focused on developing the language skills typical for Advanced Low such as moving from sentence-level language production to paragraph-length discourse, increasing ability and accuracy in narrating and describing across major time frames, presenting and supporting an argument, and hypothesizing. The language proficiency of students and their experience living in a target language community varied greatly in both courses. The intended language proficiency goal in the US course was Advanced Low; however, program-wide ACTFL assessments have shown that students in this level in that year ranged from Intermediate Low to Advanced Mid, with most students testing at Intermediate Mid. Furthermore, a program-wide benchmarking study (Goertler, Kraemer, & Schenker, 2016) also found similar results with students ranging from Intermediate Low to Advanced High in this course level with clustering in Intermediate Mid/High.

All the students in Germany were female, while the US class was mixed (9 female/11 male). The students were comparable in age, in their late teens and early twenties. The focus here is only on the US students, who were majors in German (9), minors in German (5) or just taking German for fun (6). Their (other) majors ranged from other Humanities fields to Social Science to the STEM fields.

Due to the differing semester schedules, the project was conducted during the second half of the US semester, which represented the first half of the German semester. Groups of three or pairs were formed based on random assignment once class lists were available for both courses. As out-of-class work, the students were supposed to complete one discussion task together per week communicating evenly in the two languages – though how they distributed English and German time and what technologies they used to communicate were entirely up to them. After task completion, students submitted an oral (e.g., Skype recording) or written (e.g., copies of emails) record of their interaction to their respective teacher. All tasks were designed to correspond with the topics discussed in both classes that week and were primarily open-ended questions drawing on students' personal experience, course material, and a common survey or other analyses that the partners completed independently and then compared in the discussion.

In both courses, the telecollaborative project also formed the basis for other class assignments. The US students had to use information from the exchange on several occasions and analyze it to complete their weekly blogging task. Additionally, the US students were strongly encouraged to use their telecollaboration interactions as the language sample for one of their last two research projects.

Materials

During the seven-week telecollaboration project, learners were given seven tasks, one of which they were allowed to complete without their partner. The complete course handbook with tasks and grading criteria can be found online (Goertler & Lesoski, 2015). The topics ranged from discussions of personal and national identity to subject matter discussed in the two courses, concluding with a reflection task about language learning in general and thorugh the project specifically, and their identity as language users.

Instruments

To assess learning outcomes for the purpose of assigning a course grade and for research purposes, all outside-of-class assignments and several in-class assignments were collected from the students. The present study focuses on the telecollaboration records. Additionally the following data points were used for triangulation: (1) the last two research projects focusing on language learning; (2) the blog tasks during the telecollaboration project part of the semester which focused on reflecting on the course, the project, language learning, and learner identity; (3) end-of-semester class feedback activities; and (4) perception surveys. The focus here is on the US class and the reliability and validity of the assessment criteria and instruments used for research purposes.

To answer the research questions, the goals stated in the syllabus (Goertler & Lesoski, 2015) were used to create grading criteria for classroom purposes and to set target scores for external scoring rubrics. To assess the validity of the instruments and rubrics in regard to assessing the constructs set as learning goals, correlations were run between scores intended to measure the same construct. To assess the validity of each research rubric, inter-rater reliability was measured.

From a teaching standpoint, the telecollaboration was considered successful if students (1) engaged with the tasks (i.e., completed the required number of tasks); (2) received scores above 80% on the tasks for classroom evaluation purposes (see below for more detail); and (3) had positive perception of the tasks. From a research standpoint, the telecollaboration was considered successful if there was demonstrated evidence of language and IC competence. How these constructs were measured from a research perspective, is discussed below. One big difference between the teaching and the research perspective was that evaluation from a teaching perspective was done by the teacher during the semester (i.e., it was not anonymous and no second rating was done); evaluation from a research perspective was conducted after the semester (i.e., students were assigned pseudonyms and two ratings were done).

Since the main point of the telecollaboration project was to engage students in conversations with members from the target language community, grades were largely effort- rather than performance-based. In the US classroom, students were awarded up to 10 points for each task (Goertler & Lesoski, 2015): (1) up to 6 points for task completion; (2) up to 3 points for paying attention to the partner; (3) up to 1 point for going beyond the task. As is typical in classroom assessment, only the main teacher (author 1) scored the assignments. The goal was to investigate whether the effort-based scores correlate positively with learning outcomes.

Furthermore, the study aimed to find out whether stronger participation results in better learning outcomes. One way of measuring the success of the task is to look at the completion rate of assignments. Of the seven tasks given, the lowest scored task was dropped, i.e., only six tasks were required for the US students. In the US class, ten students completed all seven tasks, six students completed six tasks, two students completed five tasks, one student completed one task, and one student did not complete any task, which means that on average, students completed six tasks.

For research purposes, the telecollaboration records were analyzed. For language skills, total target language use and percentage of target language use per task were analyzed as measured in words for written and minutes for oral data. From a language acquisition standpoint, the main purpose of the telecollaboration was to increase target language output, and hence other measures such as complexity and accuracy are not considered here.

The IC rubric developed by AACU (2010) was used by two raters to assess each US learner's IC in each task. The rubric builds on the intercultural frameworks defined by Byram (1997; 2006), and especially Bennett (2008, as cited in AACU, 2010) and divides IC into three categories: (1) Knowledge (a. cultural self-awareness; b. knowledge of cultural worldview frameworks); (2) Skills (a. empathy; b. verbal and nonverbal communication); and (3) Attitudes (a. curiosity; b. openness).

In addition to evaluating learning as exhibited in the telecollaborative tasks, the relevant blog posts (n = 19), research papers (n = 20), and feedback/survey responses (n = 17) from students were analyzed and are triangulated with the main results of this study when appropriate. There were two open-ended feedback forms in the course: one to reflect on the course goals and course components in relation to their own learning, and a second one to explicitly state what students liked about the course and what they would change. Additionally, students were given an anonymous survey about their experience with the telecollaboration, which was not part of course assignments. These assignments and documents were coded for any mention of the telecollaboration impacting students' language skills and intercultural competence.

Results

The first subsection below describes the results from the study from a class performance standpoint, followed by subsections focusing on the two outcomes: language learning and intercultural competence. General class results will be presented, but data will be triangulated for individual cases, whenever appropriate. Each student was assigned a pseudonym.

Class Performance

A variety of measures made up the final score for students in the US course. All of these assessments were intended to evaluate language skills and content knowledge, and to a lesser extent intercultural competence. Since the instruments are intended to assess the same constructs, it was hoped that there would be a positive correlation between the course grade and the average score on the telecollaboration. Of the 20 students, one student never completed the telecollaboration tasks and two students completed the tasks in an alternative format, which is why they have been excluded in this particular analysis. For the remaining 17 students, the average telecollaboration task score was 8.3 out of 10 with an average total of 58 points out of 70 (adding all points per task together); 60 points was considered a 100% for the grade, as only six tasks were required, and the average grade of these 17 students was 90%. All assignment types – when scored from a teaching perspective – had grading criteria that focused on (1) task completion; (2) content knowledge; (3) language skills; and to a lesser extent (4) intercultural competence. Non-parametric tests showed no significant correlation between course grade and average telecollaboration score. This could mean that the overall course grade and the telecollaboration grade measured different constructs despite both intending to measure the three levels of competence (language skills, intercultural competence, and content knowledge) or it could mean that students were differently able to demonstrate their abilities in different types of assignments.

Given that the focus of the last two research projects and the last six blog posts in the course was related to the discussions and experiences in the telecollaboration, and that they were occurring at the same time, it was hoped that students' performances would correspond with the relevant subset of these two grading categories. Non-parametric tests showed neither significant correlations between the average telecollaboration score and the average research project score nor between the average telecollaboration score and the average blog score. Either of the two explanations mentioned above is possible again. Yet, student comments in the exit survey suggest that the different assignment types worked differently for individual students. Furthermore, students were differently able to demonstrate their skills and showcase their knowledge depending on the interactivity of the assignment type and the formality of the assignment type. There was no clear pattern across students.

When students engaged with and completed the assignments, they met and exceeded the course expectations resulting in high scores. All participants scored high or very high in the course and on the research assignments. However, three students scored low in both computer-mediated communication (CMC) categories (telecollaboration and blog). Eight students scored high (85% or higher) in both the telecollaboration and the blogs. This matches the students' course feedback. All students considered the telecollaboration most beneficial in their reflective course essays, even the student who never completed the task. Most students also marked the telecollaboration as their favorite (i.e., most enjoyable) course component in their end-of-semester reflections. These results suggest that those assignment types students enjoyed most are also those in which they performed best. Yet, it is unclear whether they saw them as beneficial because they did well, or whether they did well because they perceived them as beneficial.

Language Learning

Two ACTFL trained teachers, the main instructor (author 1) and course assistant (author 3), used the ACTFL can-do-statements (https://www.actfl. org/publications/guidelines-and-manuals/ncssfl-actfl-can-do-statements) to assess the students' language level at the end of the semester. The students completed a role-play similar to those used in an Oral Proficiency Interview (OPI) and recorded themselves. Then the teachers and students used the recording to complete an ACTFL can-do-statement assessment. Most students self-assessed higher than the teachers assessed their language ability. For 13 of the 17 students (77%) who completed the self-assessment, the teachers agreed with each other on the ACTFL rating ranging from Intermediate Low to Advanced High. In the four cases in which the raters did not agree, they differed by one sublevel. Taking the lower assigned level in cases of disagreement, the distribution is as follows: two Intermediate Low, five Intermediate Mid, six Intermediate High, one Advanced Low, and three Advanced High. Hence, only 24% of the students met the minimum level goal of Advanced Low. These results match results for this level in official ACTFL exams as well as in a program-wide study utilizing instruments recommended by the Common European Framework of Reference (Goertler et al., 2016). It was hoped that the CMC assignments and the language analyses would improve language outcomes in comparison to previous semesters, but they did not in this short time frame. In fourth-year language courses, high-proficiency students dominate the in-class discussion thereby further limiting the amount of language output opportunities for lower-proficiency students. It was hoped that by using CMC (a feature known to equalize participation), students would have more output opportunities and thereby improve more than in previous years. Furthermore, by explicitly tasking students to compare their own language production vis-a-vis that of others or their own in different conditions or time periods, students would notice the gap in their language production and thereby improve their language.

Based on an interactionist perspective of language learning (cf. Gass & Mackey, 2007), interaction was assumed to contribute to language learning. Hence, target language use was measured as an indicator of language learning potential. The hope was that students would talk one hour per task (i.e., 30 minutes per student) or produce 500 words per student per task with the assumption that half of that would be in English and half in German. Table 2.1 summarizes the course results.

Only two pairs completed their interactions orally, one almost met and the other did not meet our target language production goals. In analyzing the written words in students' language output across tasks, it is obvious that there was a wide range of participation and target language production. Over the seven tasks, total written target language production ranged from 184 to 2,931 words per US student, averaging 922 words over the course of the project. Ignoring the outliers, most students produced between 800 and 1,300 written words in German over the seven weeks and 800 to 1,200 English words (ranging from 10 to 1,410, averaging 809 total). The average results are well under our expected goal of 500 words per task per group, yet some students went above. For a better understanding, we review those participants who reached our goal (see Table 2.2 for details). Christine (ACTFL Score: Advanced Mid) was one of the most proficient language speakers and had recently returned from a year-long study abroad, hence she was highly motivated and capable of participating in the exchange. Ivo (level estimate: Advanced Low) and Achim (ACTFL score: Intermediate Mid) also reached the average 500 words per task; however, both only completed the first three tasks with their partner. Most students on average produced between 300 and 350 words per task.

Table 2.1. Language production

	n	Average total German output	Average total English output	Average total output combined	Average percentage target language	Average output per task
Spoken (minutes)	2	60	53	113	54.5	16
Written (words)	18	922	809	1,731	52.6	315

Table 2.2. Case study subjects' language production

	Tasks completed	Average total German output	Average total English output	Average total output combined	Average percentage target language	Average output per task
Christine	6	2,931	586	3,517	83	586
Ivo	3	1,386	1,271	2,657	52	886
Achim	3	496	1,033	1,529	32	510

While students were expected to equally split their contributions between languages, this was not the case in all groups. The target language use percentage ranged from 20% to 98% with most students ranging between 40% and 60%. There were five outliers in target language use, three below the average and two above. There was no clear pattern that could explain the difference from the norm. Interestingly, inspired by the telecollaboration, three of the five outliers Christine (83% target language), Achim (32% TL), and Christian (20% TL) ended up participating in a year-long study program abroad in the partner city.

In summary, most of the students fell short of the language skill goals and language production goals. While these results may be discouraging, it should also be noted that students were linguistically able to complete the tasks without major miscommunications during their interactions with their partners. Furthermore, it should be noted that in addition to the fact that the telecollaboration inspired several students to go abroad to study, several other students continued their interactions with their telecollaboration partner after the class was over. Moreover, students clearly enjoyed the telecollaboration and saw it as beneficial. This is to say, the measures used did not accurately capture the learning potential and the potential delayed effects of learning. While this is only anecdotal evidence, it appears that in comparison to previous iterations of the course without the telecollaboration, more students were inspired to engage with the target community beyond the class through either long-term study abroad or continued interactions with their telecollaboration partners – both presumably contributing to further language learning and therefore a potential delayed effect.

Intercultural Competence Development

To assess the intercultural competence of the students as expressed in the telecollaboration, two teachers rated each task by each participant using the AACU rubric on IC (2010). The total possible score was 24: 2 x 4 points (i.e., 8 points) per category: (1) Knowledge (i.e., self-awareness of own culture and knowledge of cultural principles), (2) Skills (i.e., empathy with people who are different from oneself and verbal and nonverbal communication across communities and cultures), and (3) Attitudes (i.e., curiosity about other people and cultures and openness to interacting with others). The expectation was that students would reach 2 in each subcategory, totaling 12 points (2 points x 2 subcategories x 3 categories = 12). The teachers compared the instrument with the course goals listed in the course handbook (Goertler & Lesoski, 2015) to decide on goal scores on the AACU rubric. Level 4 of the rubric appears impossible to demonstrate in just one set of intercultural interactions, especially since it is implied that a learner can demonstrate such competence across multiple (i.e., more than two) cultures (e.g., "interprets intercultural experience from the perspectives of own and more than one worldview ...").

Students generally scored low regardless of the rater, averaging 9 points from rater 1 and 7 points from rater 2. Tasks that asked questions about culture lent themselves better for students to demonstrate their intercultural competence. Task 2 elicited interactions that generally resulted in higher scores (with the highest class average of 9.58) than task 4 (with the lowest class average score of 7.05). In the two task descriptions (see Table 2.3), one can see the explicit invitation to discuss cultural differences in task 2 and no mention of culture in task 4, which is likely why students were more able to demonstrate intercultural competence in their discussions on task 2 than in task 4.

Table 2.3. Comparison between prompts in tasks 2 and 4

Task 2: Stereotypes and cultural diversity	Task 4: Technology-mediated communication and learning
1. Share three beliefs/impressions you have about your partner's culture and ask your partner to do the same for your culture. What can you say about the truth of these observations? Where do they come from? Do these observations hold true or are they stereotypes? 2. Look at your concrete surroundings (i.e., the city that you live in). Tell your partner about the (sub)cultures in your direct surroundings. Are you influenced by these? 3. Discuss the role of language(s) (e.g., What role do they play in communicating across cultures?).	1. This semester you experienced various forms of technology-mediated communication and learning. What have you experienced for the first time this semester? What were already familiar media for you? 2. Reflect on the influence of the medium on the communication and/or learning process. 3. Discuss different modes that can be used for language learning and language use. Which modes do you use and why? Which modes are suitable for the language learning context and why? What are the potentials/drawbacks of the different modes?

There were no recognizable trends over time and while most students scored fairly consistently across tasks, others did not. It was initially hoped that students' scores would increase over time to show development of IC, but as mentioned in the discussion above, the tasks themselves may not have made it possible to demonstrate learning. Most students stayed within a 3-point range, typically scoring the lowest on task 4. Around one-third of the students had score ranges more than 3 points apart across the seven tasks (Christine 7–12; Daniel 6–11; Fritz 9–14; Ivo 6–12; Julian 6–12.5). It should be noted that the students with the greater variation included the two who completed the tasks orally (Fritz and Julian) as well as the two highest scorers (Christine and Fritz). It could be hypothesized that a higher range of scores in an individual is indicative of a better overall IC, with the lower scores being due to the tasks not providing scope for students to demonstrate this competence. The most consistent scores across tasks were received by Egon and Georg with typical scores around 7. These two students were the most neutral about the telecollaboration. This could be seen as further evidence that a smaller range of scores is indicative of lower overall IC, since these students did not receive higher scores on the tasks that were overall found to promote demonstration of IC. In the category of attitude, the rubric that evaluates whether learners are willing to engage with others, Georg and Egon had a minimalist approach in their communications, which may have resulted in lower scores in those subcategories and may explain or be explained by their lower enthusiasm for the telecollaboration in contrast to their peers, based on the reflective course evaluations at the end of the semester.

Only Fritz was able to reach the desired average score of 12 (rater 1's scores for Fritz averaged 13 and rater 2's averaged 11). Achim (average 13 and 9) also scored high across tasks, but only completed the tasks on which students typically scored higher. Christine (average 11 and 8), Friederike (average 10 and 7), and Julian (average 10 and 7) were approaching the goal according to the scores given by rater 1, but not rater 2. Fritz and Julian were the only students who completed their tasks orally. This might indicate that, using this measure, IC is more easily demonstrated in an oral communication format. Both Christine and Fritz met the language production expectations. This could mean that more language production per task and across time is necessary to demonstrate and/or develop IC. It should also be noted that Christine, Friederike, and Julian had had extensive experience abroad including living in Germany for a year or more prior to participation in this telecollaboration, hence a higher IC could be predicted. This was not the case for Fritz; he likely was able to demonstrate his IC more effectively because he completed all tasks consistently, his language output almost met the expectations in quantity, and he selected an oral communication format.

The main instructor and the course assistant served as the two raters who scored all tasks by all students; score differences of greater than 1 point were considered as a disagreement. Even allowing raters to disagree by a point, inter-rater reliability was very low at 45%, ranging from 0% to 83% agreement by student. In discussions about the different ratings, both raters expressed that sublevels were needed because the instrument was not fine-grained enough. This meant that it was easier to agree on low-performing students and harder to assess students who demonstrated higher ICC. Rater 2 tended to score students' performance lower and on a smaller range of scores, which led to disagreements in the case of higher-scoring students.

Discussion

Answers to the Research Questions

To answer research question 1, students did appear to reach the learning outcomes as outlined in the syllabus, achieving high scores in the class and on class assignments. However, when assessing their learning as exhibited in the telecollaboration transcripts, (1) most students stayed below the expectation for language output; and (2) most students scored lower than expected on the IC measure. Since most students did not complete their telecollaborations in the expected length, from an interactionist perspective (Gass, 1997) it is assumed that they decreased their language learning opportunities. The goal of the telecollaboration was to help students have more opportunities for language learning, since in the past years it was found that many students did not reach the expected Advanced Low level (Goertler et al., 2016). Unfortunately, most students still did not reach this level, which included the most successful telecollaborator, Fritz, whose ease in speaking German improved according to his own report and observations in the telecollaboration and in class. His ACTFL rating was still far below Advanced Low with an Intermediate Low. As for the culture learning goals, only Fritz met the expectations. It is possible that only long and especially synchronous oral exchanges make it possible for students to demonstrate and/or develop the expected IC levels. The other students, who scored above average on the IC measure, had had extensive previous experience in Germany. This still leaves the question of why students appeared to meet the learning outcome goals, as measured with class assignments and teacher scores, but did not meet the language production and IC goals. It is possible that the teachers rated students too favorably in class assignments or that class assignments were scored on several constructs combined and IC and language performance were no longer isolated from each other or from other elements such as task completion and content knowledge. It could also be that because the assignments were scored by the teachers during the course with the names of the students, the teachers experienced a stronger bias than when they scored the telecollaborations from a researcher perspective six months later with pseudonyms assigned.

Research questions 2 and 3 both addressed the validity of the instruments. Due to the conflicting results in response to research question 1, research question 2, whether different measures intended to measure the same construct would produce similar results, can clearly be answered No. That being said, in their end-of-semester reflective essays, blog entries, and in an exit survey, students generally reported feeling that they learned a lot from the telecollaboration and that it helped them improve their language proficiency and intercultural competence. Thus, teacher assessments and students' perceptions were in agreement, yet the research instruments did not show the same result despite the fact that both raters were also teachers in the course.

In response to research question 3, which asked whether raters assigned similar scores on the research measures, inter-rater reliability was well below acceptable levels for the IC research instrument (AACU, 2010). These results highlight the need for finding better instruments, establishing inter-rater reliability, and measuring a construct with more than one instrument to establish construct validity. These problematic findings will be discussed in the following subsection.

Explanation of the Results

Both in previous research and in the study reported here, several issues arose in implementing reliable and valid assessment instruments for telecollaborative exchanges. There were three problems with assessment in this study: (1) students scored lower on research instruments than expected based on course goals, (2) lack of correlation between measures, and (3) low inter-rater reliability. The two goals of the course in focus here were language development and intercultural competence development. While students met and exceeded expectations in course assignments scored with the grading criteria for the course, they did not meet score expectations on the research instruments, and correlation and inter-reliability were also low. There are several possible explanations: (1) familiarity effect, (2) isolation factor, (3) absence, (4) task design, (5) answer length, (6) mode of communication, (7) partnership, (8) development, (9) inter-rater reliability, and

(10) researcher-teacher double role. Each of these suggests recommendations for improved methods of assessment.

Familiarity effect: Teachers score their students more favorably as student success is connected to their own success. In this case both research raters were also the two teachers, hence the effect should have carried over to the research scoring. However, the later research scoring with students assigned pseudonyms may have been enough distance to decrease the familiarity effect in this scoring. For greater accuracy in classroom assessment, we suggest blind grading, with second ratings done whenever possible. At least written online assignments have the advantage that students could participate using pseudonyms, which would approximate blind review. At the end of the semester the grades assigned to pseudonyms could be assigned to the students under their real names.

Isolation factor: For classroom purposes the three learning outcome constructs were scored together; whereas for research purposes, language production and IC were assessed separately. It is possible that if each construct had been assigned a separate score during the course evaluation phase, there would have been a correlation across assignments and during the research phase. Additionally, the classroom grading criteria contained too many components that were effort- rather than skill-based. We recommend that constructs be scored separately on each grading assignment so that correlations between the same constructs across assignments and assignment types can be measured. While effort is less important from a research perspective, it often plays a role in classroom grading.

Absence: One of the most problematic issues with the data in this study is that it is impossible to say that lack of language production or evidence for a particular feature of IC in the datasets means that learners are not capable of performing at the required levels of language proficiency and IC. It simply means that in the record there was an absence of such skills. In the future, the telecollaboration records, which are open-ended language productions, should be triangulated with actual competence measures, which is why we included official ACTFL ratings where available.

Task design – prompt questions: Since there were differences by task, but not across time, it can be concluded that task design plays a role in allowing students to demonstrate IC and likely the same can be said about language proficiency. Besides factors like the tandem partner and the chosen mode of communication, the tasks' prompts play a crucial role: it was clear that tasks that specifically asked students to explore and discuss cultural differences resulted in the possibility of higher scores. Students who followed the instructions explored cultural issues and were generally able to reach higher scores in intercultural competence. If the prompt does not include elements that call for advanced level language and IC skills, there is no need for the learner to produce these skills though they still might, which goes back to the issue of absence. We recommend analyzing each task prompt to make sure that it specifically asks students to produce language at the intended proficiency level and the intended IC level (see Goertler, 2016 for the revised tasks). This can be ensured by integrating task prompts that trigger a reflective exchange.

Answer length: Students were told that they were expected to spend about 1 hour per week for the telecollaboration. This was done intentionally initially, since some students need more words than others to explain a concept and because we wanted to encourage participants to produce as much as possible within a reasonable time commitment. This resulted in a range of language production amounts per task. Even though assessing students only based on fulfilling certain length requirements as done in many other studies (Ware & Kramsch, 2005; Weasenforth et al., 2002) may not be the best approach, assigning a specific length may be necessary in order to be able to compare students' contributions. Participants with longer interactions scored higher on IC. But it is not clear if they scored higher because their interaction was longer and thereby had more room to demonstrate skills, or if they were able to have a longer conversation because they had higher IC skills. For research comparability, it might be necessary to only pick equal length segments across participants.

Mode of communication: Another choice that was made based on previous research was to allow students to select a communication tool they were familiar with and that was authentic to their preferred mode of communication. It was quickly clear during rating the assignments that students who completed the discussions synchronously had a higher success rate than those who used asynchronous tools. Furthermore, oral/video tools were more successful than text-based tools. While oral/video and synchronous formats did not always lead to higher scores, the students who met or got close to our expectations were those who used oral/video and/or synchronous formats of communication.

Partnerships: Based on previous research which outlined problems in telecollaboration due to unequal participation (Basharina, 2007; Schenker & Poorman, 2017), we made every effort to integrate the telecollaboration in both classes, which should have increased willingness to participate on both sides. We followed O'Rourke's (2007) recommendation to randomly match partners to avoid possible problems in the selection process. Most partnerships were productive for the entire semester, all but one in which the German student discontinued the conversation. Naturally some partnerships like that of Fritz and Christine worked better than those of others such as for example Klaus and Georg who were in a group of three. In response to several tasks Klaus and Georg made clearly ethnocentric and racist remarks and eventually, the German partner stopped communicating with them. In this case, the lack of further interaction from the German partner could be seen as an effect of low IC on the part of Klaus and Georg, but it could have been unrelated. Moreover, it is difficult to assign a grade to students whose partner stopped responding. Interestingly, partners who talked about a lot of topics unrelated to the tasks received higher scores than others. The most notable example here is once again Fritz and Christine, who consistently talked more off-topic than on-topic and had the longest overall interactions. Hence, Fritz had more opportunities to negotiate meaning and learn than others, if one argues from an interactionist perspective. Based on this research, we created conversation tips for students in subsequent telecollaboration projects (Goertler, 2016). From a pedagogical standpoint, teacher intervention in communication breakdown may seem useful, especially when the project involves young learners (Müller-Hartmann, 2007). But there have been mixed results on the effects of teacher interventions during communication breakdown in telecollaboration, and this intervention has not always proven to support student participation (Mazzolini & Maddison, 2003). It also poses a dilemma when part of the research focus is to assess how students are able to independently engage in intercultural communication.

Development: From a research standpoint, it cannot be ascertained whether students developed skills as a result of the telecollaboration or not. The class contained many other elements and learning could have occurred as a result of any or all of them. Since there were no notable trends across time in IC score or language production, it can be hypothesized that there were no measurable gains over time. Even though students in the surveys and course reflections attributed their learning to the telecollaboration, we cannot assume so. Since the IC top scorers were mostly experienced intercultural communicators, Fritz's case study is interesting because he was neither a language major, nor did he have a high language proficiency; also he had not lived abroad before. In his case, there is some evidence of development and of reaching course goals. Based on this finding, the second iteration of our telecollaboration specifically focuses on students like Fritz and their learning potential. From his case, we can hypothesize that synchronous and oral interactions might be more conducive to negotiations and thereby IC and language proficiency development. More positive effects of synchronous CMC over asynchronous CMC have also been suggested in previous research (Abrams, 2003), even though synchronous oral CMC brings many challenges and may result in less negotiation of meaning routines than synchronous written CMC (Van der Zwaard & Bannink, 2014). When clear trends over time are not visible for the whole group, case studies can be insightful. More research and replications are needed to evaluate the hypothesis.

Inter-rater reliability: The lack of correlation between measures and the low levels of inter-rater reliability point to issues with the instruments and/ or the raters. During the rating process, and during the discussion of the many samples where inter-rater reliability was low, the raters reported that the instruments were not fine-grained enough to truly capture the differences between students. Rater 1 proceeded to more generously interpret the score descriptions to show the differences between participants, whereas rater 2 stayed with the actual descriptions, which led to a smaller range of scores that did not accurately capture differences between students. The AACU criteria were selected for their relevance in the US college context and because they are based on the most prevalent definitions of IC in our field. The criteria are likely best used to measure change over a longer period of time or in more intensive contexts such as long-term study abroad. For shorter research or classroom projects, we recommend creating sublevels by taking the existing score sheet and applying it to existing data allowing subscores, and then taking a closer look at those sublevels to write new sublevel descriptors. Another way to improve assessment of telecollaboration would be to involve students more actively in the assessment process. In Schuetze's (2008) English-German discussion project students were given a list of ten processing criteria used for grading and assessment, for example. This can help students participate more effectively in the exchange, as they know what aspects of the project are most important and how exactly their participation is being evaluated. Students could even be included in the design of the assessment rubrics, if time permits.

Teacher-researcher role: One of the conflicts in conducting classroom research is that best practices for research do not always coincide with best practices for teaching, such as the aforementioned interventions in case of communication breakdown. This is also true for assessing telecollaboration: for course grades, effort and task completion might be most important; but for research purposes, those pieces for assessment might be less relevant. For example, in the current study task completion was a significant component of the scoring rubrics from the classroom perspective but was not a component of the research scoring rubrics. As teachers, we sent a message to our students with a scoring rubric and tried to motivate students to give maximum effort; as researchers, however, our primary focus was to establish whether students were able to demonstrate competencies in the outlined areas. In relation to language development and language skills, both sets of measurements should yield the same results. However, for IC the situation is more complicated. Specifically, as teachers we felt uncomfortable making IC a significant part of the course grade – even though it was part of the course goals – because of the ethical question of requiring someone to change their perspective in order to receive full points. As researchers, however, IC was one of our primary foci. Hence, we continue to support our approach of having different criteria and instruments for teaching and for research purposes in cases like ours where the goals for assessment are different from a research and a teaching standpoint. More research is needed to find instruments suited for each purpose but that correlate with each other when the outcome goals for the course and the ones to be measured from a research perspective are the same. Regardless of the situation, research results should inform teaching and teaching results should inform research.

Conclusion

Telecollaboration projects present several challenges and opportunities in assessing language skills and IC. The clearest and biggest advantage is that they offer an opportunity to assess IC in real-life situations, even in a foreign language context, and are often perceived very positively by learners. Furthermore, the interaction with native speakers is also a chance for learners to demonstrate higher language skills. The unique challenges of assessing language and IC in telecollaboration are communication records, the tasks, the partnerships, and the format. The communication records can be incomplete due to technical difficulties or not show evidence of the skills in focus. The tasks need to be explicitly and clearly outlined and designed to push participants to display the skills in focus. The partnerships – no matter how carefully prepared and guided – are not controllable and yet can influence the telecollaboration and then the data. The same is true for the format (asynchronous or synchronous; oral or written). Our recommendations for evaluating telecollaboration are: (1) to use several instruments and at least two raters; (2) to use existing assessment tools that have proved successful in previous research or teaching; (3) to have many sublevels of scoring; (4) to give students specific expectations for language production in telecollaboration; (7) to use additional data points independent of the telecollaboration records; (8) to assess learning in telecollaboration multi-dimensionally; and (9) to carefully design prompts. More research is needed to validate existing assessment tools or develop new tools to evaluate language and intercultural competence learning in telecollaboration.

About the Authors

Senta Goertler is Associate Professor of Second Language Studies and German at Michigan State University, where she coordinates Second-Year German. Her research focuses on technology-mediated language learning.

Theresa Schenker is a Senior Lector II and Director of the Language Program in the German department at Yale University. She is also the co-editor of Die Unterrichtspraxis. Her research focuses on technology-mediated language learning and community language programs.

Carly Lesoski is a doctoral candidate in German Studies at Michigan State University. Her research focuses on identity and telecollaboration.

Sonja Brunsmeier is an independent researcher, who has been affiliated with Universities of Education in Germany and Austria. Her research focuses on telecollaboration.

References

Abrams, Z. I. (2003). The effect of synchronous and asynchronous CMC on oral performance in German. *The Modern Language Journal*, 87(2), 157–167. https://doi.org/10.1111/1540-4781.00184

Abrams, Z. (2013). Say what?! L2 sociopragmatic competence in CMC: Skill transfer and development. *CALICO Journal*, 30(3), 423–445. https://doi.org/10.11139/cj.30.3.423-445

Akiyama, Y., & Saito, K. (2016). Development of comprehensibility and its linguistic correlates: A longitudinal study of video-mediated telecollaboration. *The Modern Language Journal*, 100(3), 585–609. https://doi.org/10.1111/modl.12338

Association of American Colleges and Universities. (2010). *Interculutral Knowledge and Competence Rubric*. https://www.aacu.org/value/rubrics/intercultural-knowledge

Arnold, N., & Ducate, L. (2006). Future foreign language teachers' social and cognitive collaboration in an online environment. *Language Learning & Technology*, 10(1), 42–66.

Basharina, O. (2007). An activity theory perspective on student-reported contradictions in international telecollaboration. *Language Learning & Technology*, 11(2), 82–103.

Beatty, K. (2010). *Teaching and Researching Computer-Assisted Language Learning* (2nd ed.). Harlow: Pearson.

Belz, J. A. (2002). Social dimensions of telecollaborative foreign language study. *Language Learning & Technology*, 6(1), 60–81.

Belz, J. A. (2007). The development of intercultural communicative competence in telecollaborative partnerships. In R. O'Dowd (ed.), *Online Intercultural*

Exchange: An Introduction for Foreign Language Teachers (pp. 127–167). Clevedon: Multilingual Matters Ltd.

Bennett, M. J. (2008). Transformative training: Designing programs for culture learning. In M. A. Moodian (ed.), *Contemporary Leadership and Intercultural Competence: Understanding and Utilizing Cultural Diversity to Build Successful Organizations* (pp. 95–110). Thousand Oaks, CA: Sage.

Bohinski, C. A., & Leventhal, Y. (2015). Rethinking the ICC framework: Transformation and telecollaboration. *Foreign Language Annals*, 48(3), 521–534. https://doi.org/10.1111/flan.12149

Bueno-Alastuey, M. C. (2010). Synchronous-voice computer-mediated communication: Effects on pronunciation. *CALICO Journal*, 28(1), 1–20. https://doi.org/10.11139/cj.28.1.1-20

Byram, M. (1997). *Teaching and Assessing Intercultural Communicative Competence*. Clevedon, UK: Multilingual Matters.

Byram, M. (2008). *From Foreign Language Education to Education for Intercultural Citizenship*. Clevedon, Buffalo, and Toronto: Multilingual Matters.

Cardoso, T., & Matos, F. (2013). Learning foreign languages in the twenty-first century: An innovating teletandem experiment through Skype. In A. Moreira, O. Benavides, & A. J. Mendes (eds.), *Media in Education: Results from the 2011 ICEM and SIIE Joint Conference* (pp. 87–95). New York: Springer.

Castillo-Scott, A. (2015). Pan-American teletandem language exchange project. *The EUROCALL Review*, 23(1), 36–40. https://doi.org/10.4995/eurocall.2015.4661

Chun, D. M. (2011). Developing intercultural communicative competence through online exchanges. *CALICO Journal*, 28(2), 392–419. https://doi.org/10.11139/cj.28.2.392-419

Dooly, M., Masats, D., Müller-Hartmann, A., & De Rodas, B. C. (2008). Building effective, dynamic online partnerships. In M. Dooly (ed.), *Telecollaborative Language Learning: A Guidebook to Moderating Intercultural Collaboration Online* (pp. 45–77). Bern: Peter Lang.

Fantini, A. E. (2006). Exploring and assessing intercultural competence. *World Learning Publications*, 1–74.

Felix, U. (2003). Pedagogy on the line: identifying and closing the missing links. In U. Felix (ed.), *Language Learning Online: Towards Best Practice* (pp. 147–171). Lisse: Swets & Zeitlinger.

Gass, S. (1997). *Input, Interaction, and the Second Language Learner*. Mahwah, NJ: Lawrence Erlbaum.

Gass, S., & Mackey, A. (2007). Input, interaction, and output in second language acquisition. In B. VanPatten & J. Williams (eds.), *Theories in Second Language Acquisition* (pp. 175–200). London: Erlbaum.

Goertler, S. (2016). *GRM 420: Course Handbook*. https://sentagoertler.files.wordpress.com/2012/09/2016-grm-420-course-handbook.pdf

Goertler, S., & Lesoski, C. (2015). *GRM 420: Course Handbook*. https://sentagoertler.files.wordpress.com/2012/09/2015-2016-grm-420-course-handbook.pdf

Goertler, S., Kraemer, A., & Schenker, T. (2016). Setting evidence-based language goals. *Foreign Language Annals*, 49(3), 434–454. https://doi.org/10.1111/flan.12214

Guth, S., & Helm, F. (2012). Developing multiliteracies in ELT through tele-collaboration. *ELT Journal*, 66(1), 42–51. https://doi.org/10.1093/elt/ccr027

Hauck, M. (2007). Critical success factors in a tridem exchange. *ReCALL*, 19(2), 202–223. https://doi.org/10.1017/S0958344007000729

Helm, F. (2015). The practices and challenges of telecollaboration in higher education in Europe. *Language Learning & Technology*, 19(2).

Jin, L. (2013). Language development and scaffolding in a Sino-American tele-collaborative project. *Language Learning & Technology*, 17(2), 193–219.

Kabata, K., & Edasawa, Y. (2011). Tandem language learning through a cross-cultural keypal project. *Language Learning & Technology*, 15(1), 104–121.

Kern, R. G. (1996). Using e-mail exchanges to explore personal histories in two cultures. In M. Warschauer (ed.), *Telecollaboration in Foreign Language Learning: Proceedings of the Hawai'i Symposium* (pp. 105–121). Honolulu: University of Hawai'i Press.

Kitade, K. (2006). The negotiation model in asynchronous computer-mediated communication (CMC): Negotiation in task-based email exchanges. *CALICO Journal*, 23(2), 319–348.

Kötter, M. (2002). *Tandem Learning on the Internet. Learner Interactions in Virtual Online Environments (MOOs)* (Vol. 6). Frankfurt a.M.: Peter Lang.

Kötter, M. (2003). Negotiation of meaning and codeswitching in online tandems. *Language Learning & Technology*, 7(2), 145–172.

Kramsch, C., & Thorne, S. L. (2002). Foreign language learning as global communicative practice. In D. Block & D. Cameron (eds.), *Globalization and Language Teaching* (pp. 83–101). London: Routledge.

Lee, L. (2007). One-to-one desktop videoconferencing for developing oral skills: Prospects in perspective. In R. O'Dowd (ed.), *Online Intercultural Exchange: An Introduction for Foreign Language Teachers* (pp. 281–286). Clevedon: Multilingual Matters Ltd.

Lee, L. (2008). Focus-on-form through collaborative scaffolding in expert-to-novice online interaction. *Language Learning & Technology*, 12(3), 53–72.

Lee, L., & Markey, A. (2014). A study of learners' perceptions of online intercultural exchange through Web 2.0 technologies. *ReCALL*, 26(3), 281–297. https://doi.org/10.1017/S0958344014000111

Liaw, M.-L. (2006). E-learning and the development of intercultural competence. *Language Learning & Technology*, 10(3), 49–64.

Lomicka, L., & Lord, G. (2012). A tale of tweets: Analyzing microblogging among language learners. *System*, 40(1), 48–53. https://doi.org/10.1016/j.system.2011.11.001

Mahfouz, S. M. (2010). A study of Jordanian university students' perceptions of using email exchanges with native English keypals for improving their writing competency. *CALICO Journal*, 27(2), 393–408. https://doi.org/10.11139/cj.27.2.393-408

Makaramani, R. (2015). 21st century learning design for a telecollaboration project. *Procedia – Social and Behavioral Sciences*, 191, 622–627. http://dx.doi.org/10.1016/j.sbspro.2015.04.567

Mazzolini, M., & Maddison, S. (2003). Sage, guide or ghost? The effect of instructor intervention on student participation in online discussion forums. *Computers & Education*, 40(3), 237–253. https://doi.org/10.1016/S0360-1315(02)00129-X

Menard-Warwick, J. (2009). Comparing protest movements in Chile and California: Interculturality in an Internet chat exchange. *Language and Intercultural Communication*, 9(2), 105–119. https://doi.org/10.1080/14708470802450487

Müller-Hartmann, A. (2007). Teacher role in telecollaboration: Setting up and managing exchanges. In R. O'Dowd (ed.), *Online Intercultural Exchange: An Introduction for Foreign Language Teachers* (pp. 167–193). Clevedon: Multilingual Matters Ltd.

O'Dowd, R. (2006). *Telecollaboration and the Development of Intercultural Communicative Competence* (Vol. 13). München: Langenscheidt.

O'Dowd, R. (2010). Issues in the assessment of online interaction and exchange. In S. Guth & F. Helm (eds.), *Telecollaboration 2.0* (Vol. 1, pp. 337–361). Bern: Peter Lang.

O'Dowd, R., & Ritter, M. (2006). Understanding and working with "failed communication" in telecollaborative exchanges. *CALICO Journal*, 23, 1–20.

O'Rourke, B. (2007). Models of telecollaboration (1): eTandem. In R. O'Dowd (ed.), *Online Intercultural Exchange: An Introduction for Foreign Language Teachers* (pp. 41–62). Clevedon: Multilingual Matters Ltd.

Perez, L. C. (2003). Foreign language productivity in synchronous versus asynchronous computer-mediated communication. *CALICO Journal*, 21(1), 89–104.

Peterson, M. (2009). Learner interaction in synchronous CMC: A sociocultural perspective. *Computer Assisted Language Learning*, 22(4), 303–321. https://doi.org/10.1080/09588220903184690

Polat, N., Mancilla, R., & Mahalingappa, L. (2013). Anonymity and motivation in asynchronous discussions and L2 vocabulary learning. *Language Learning & Technology*, 17(2), 57–74.

Rafieyan, V., Sharafi-Nejad, M., Khavari, Z., Eng, L. S., & Mohamed, A. R. (2014). Pragmatic comprehension development through telecollaboration. *English Language Teaching*, 7(2), 11–19. https://doi.org/10.5539/elt.v7n2p11

Satar, H. M., & Özdener, N. (2008). The effects of synchronous CMC on speaking proficiency and anxiety: Text versus voice chat. *The Modern Language Journal*, 92(4), 595–613. https://doi.org/10.2307/25173104

Sauro, S. (2012). L2 performance in text-chat and spoken discourse. *System*, 40(3), 335–348. http://dx.doi.org/10.1016/j.system.2012.08.001

Schenker, T. (2012). Intercultural competence and cultural learning through telecollaboration. *CALICO Journal*, 29(3), 449–470. https://doi.org/10.11139/cj.29.3.449-470

Schenker, T. (2015). Telecollaboration for novice language learners – Negotiation of meaning in text chats between nonnative and native speakers. In E. Dixon & M. Thomas (eds.), *Researching Language Learner Interactions Online: From Social Media to MOOCs* (Vol. 13, pp. 237–259). San Marcos: CALICO.

Schenker, T. (2016). Syntactic complexity in a cross-cultural e-mail exchange. *System*, 63, 40–50. https://doi.org/10.1016/j.system.2016.08.012

Schenker, T., & Poorman, F. (2017). Students' perceptions of telecollaborative communication tools. In C. Ludwig & K. v. d. Poel (eds.), *Collaborative*

Language Learning and New Media: Insights into an Evolving Field (pp. 59–75). Frankfurt am Main: Peter Lang.

Schuetze, U. (2008). Exchanging second language messages online: Developing an intercultural communicative competence? *Foreign Language Annals*, 41(4), 660–673. https://doi.org/10.1111/j.1944-9720.2008.tb03323.x

Shang, H.-F. (2007). An exploratory study of e-mail application on FL writing performance. *Computer Assisted Language Learning*, 20(1), 79–96. https://doi.org/10.1080/09588220601118479

Sotillo, S. M. (2000). Discourse functions and syntactic complexity in synchronous and asynchronous communication. *Language Learning & Technology*, 4(1), 82–119.

Spencer-Oatey, H., & Franklin, P. (2009). *Intercultural Interaction. A Multi-disciplinary Approach to Intercultural Communication.* New York: Palgrave Macmillan.

Stickler, U., & Emke, M. (2011). Literalia: Towards developing intercultural maturity online. *Language Learning & Technology*, 15(1), 147–168.

Stockwell, G., & Levy, M. (2001). Sustainability of e-mail interactions between native speakers and nonnative speakers. *Computer Assisted Language Learning*, 14(5), 419–442. https://doi.org/10.1076/call.14.5.469.5770.001

Taki, S., & Ramazani, Z. (2011). Improving reading skills through e-mail: The case of Iranian EFL students. *International Journal of Instructional Technology & Distance Learning*, 8(4).

Thomé-Williams, A. C. (2016). Developing intercultural communicative competence in Portuguese through Skype and Facebook. *Intercultural Communication Studies*, 15(1), 213–233.

Thorne, S. L. (2003). Artifacts and cultures-of-use in intercultural communication. *Language, Learning & Technology*, 7(2), 38.

Tian, J., & Wang, Y. (2010). Taking language learning outside the classroom: Learners' perspectives of eTandem learning via Skype. *Innovation in Language Learning and Teaching*, 4(3), 181–197. https://doi.org/10.1080/17501229.2010.513443

Toyoda, E., & Harrison, R. (2002). Categorization of text chat communication between learners and native speakers of Japanese. *Language Learning & Technology*, 6(1), 82–99.

Tudini, V. (2003). Using native speakers in chat. *Language Learning & Technology*, 7(3), 141–159.

Van der Kroon, L., Jauregi, K., & Jan, D. t. T. (2015). Telecollaboration in foreign language curricula: A case study on intercultural understanding in video communication exchanges. *International Journal of Computer-Assisted Language Learning and Teaching*, 5(3), 20. https://doi.org/10.4018/IJCALLT.2015070102

Van der Zwaard, R., & Bannink, A. (2014). Video call or chat? Negotiation of meaning and issues of face in telecollaboration. *System*, 44(0), 137–148. http://dx.doi.org/10.1016/j.system.2014.03.007

Vogt, K. (2006). Can you measure attitudinal factors in intercultural communication? Tracing the development of attitude in e-mail projects. *ReCALL*, 18(2), 153–173. https://doi.org/10.1017/S095834400600022X

Wang, Y. (2006). Negotiation of meaning in desktop videoconferencing-supported distance language learning. *ReCALL*, 18(1), 122–145. https://doi.org/10.1017/S0958344006000814

Ware, P. (2005). "Missed" communication in online communication: Tensions in a German-American telecollaboration. *Language Learning & Technology*, 9(2), 64–89.

Ware, P., & Kessler, G. (2014). Telecollaboration in the secondary language classroom: Case study of adolescent interaction and pedagogical integration. *Computer Assisted Language Learning*, 1–24. https://doi.org/10.1080/09588221.2014.961481

Ware, P., & Kramsch, C. (2005). Toward an intercultural stance: Teaching German and English through telecollaboration. *The Modern Language Journal*, 89(2), 190–205. https://doi.org/10.1111/j.1540-4781.2005.00274.x

Weasenforth, D., Biesenbach-Lucas, S., & Meloni, C. (2002). Realizing constructivist objectives through collaborative technologies: Threaded discussions. *Language Learning & Technology*, 6(3), 58–86.

Witte, A. (2014). *Blending Spaces: Mediating and Assessing Intercultural Competence in the L2 Classroom*. Boston and Berlin: De Gruyter.

Woodin, J. (2001). Tandem learning as an intercultural activity. In M. Byram, A. Nichols, & D. Stevens (eds.), *Developing Intercultural Competence in Practice* (pp. 189–203). Clevedon: Multilingual Matters Ltd.

Wu, W.-C. V., Marek, M., & Chen, N.-S. (2013). Assessing cultural awareness and linguistic competency of EFL learners in a CMC-based active learning context. *System*, 41(3), 515–528. http://dx.doi.org/10.1016/j.system.2013.05.004

Yang, Y.-F. (2011). Learner interpretations of shared space in multilateral English blogging. *Language Learning & Technology*, 15(1), 122–146.

Yanguas, I. (2012). Task-based oral computer-mediated communication and L2 vocabulary acquisition. *CALICO Journal*, 29(3), 507–531. https://doi.org/10.11139/cj.29.3.507-531

Zakir, M. A., Funo, L. B. A., & Telles, J. A. (2016). Focusing on culture-related episodes in a teletandem interaction between a Brazilian and an American student. *Innovation in Language Learning and Teaching*, 10(1), 21–33. https://doi.org/10.1080/17501229.2016.1134861

3 Assessing the Effect of Pedagogical Interventions on Success Rates and on Students' Perceptions of Connectedness Online

Victoria Russell*

Introduction

Currently, more than 7 million post-secondary students in the United States take at least one class online, and the growth rate for online enrollments continues to outpace traditional enrollments (Allen et al., 2016). However, not all students are successful in the online learning environment and attrition rates in online courses are considerably higher than in traditional courses (Herbert, 2006; Heyman, 2010). Given the high attrition rates in online courses in general and the unique challenges to teaching a world language online, it is important to identify pedagogical techniques that may be effective with online language learners and to define assessment practices to measure their efficacy. To that end, this study was funded with a pedagogical innovation grant that was awarded by the IDEA Center at Valdosta State University (VSU).

In response to the problems of declining enrollments, low retention rates among underclassmen, and the loss of faculty lines at the present institution, several pedagogical innovation grants were awarded by the VSU IDEA Center to help improve success rates in core curriculum courses with high rates of D, F, and W grades. The College of Arts and Sciences, in particular, experienced the largest decline in enrollment over a three-year period (2012–2015) compared to all other colleges at VSU, which resulted in a loss of over 30 faculty lines in 2015. After the loss of these faculty, several departments began to reconsider whether the foreign language requirement was necessary and some perceived it as a barrier to students' successful

* Valdosta State University, USA; varussell@valdosta.edu

completion of their majors. For example, the language requirement was either significantly reduced or removed from Criminal Justice – the largest major in the College of Arts and Sciences – and from Philosophy and Religious Studies. At the present institution, students are only required to take a foreign language if it is dictated by their major because there is no university-wide requirement for foreign language study. However, foreign language study can be used to fulfill one core curriculum requirement for all majors. Nonetheless, the loss of students – due to declining enrollments, low retention rates, and the removal of the foreign language requirement by some majors – points to an uncertain future for foreign language study at the present institution.

Given that online courses typically have significantly higher attrition rates than traditional (brick-and-mortar) classes across all disciplines (Herbert, 2006; Heyman, 2010), the need to identify pedagogical techniques and strategies that could improve outcomes in online language classes is particularly urgent. Equally important is the need to assess these interventions to determine whether they are effective for improving final course grades, retention rates, and language learning outcomes. It is also important to identify and assess other factors that may negatively impact students' performance in a language class, such as language anxiety and false beliefs about language learning (Onwuegbuzie, Bailey, & Daley, 2000; Chen & Chang, 2004; Horwitz, 1986, 1987 , 2001; Horwitz, Horwitz, & Cope 1986; Russell & Curtis, 2013; Sparks & Ganschow, 2007; Young, 1999). While these are likely not the only two factors at play, the research that is reviewed below suggests that they may influence language learning and final course outcomes; therefore, it is important to implement valid and reliable assessments for measuring these constructs. The problems of declining enrollments, high attrition rates in online classes, and the uncertain future of foreign languages at the university level are not unique to the present institution. In order for researchers, practitioners, and scholars to tackle these significant issues, assessment will play a vital role in determining which pedagogical techniques and strategies are effective for improving outcomes in online language classes.

Social Isolation and Disconnectedness

A number of researchers have documented that online learning may lead to feelings of social isolation (Haythornthwaite et al., 2000; Kanuka & Jugdev, 2006; Rovai, 2002; Shieh, Gummer, & Niess, 2008) and the high attrition rate in online courses may be due to students' perceptions of disconnectedness in the online learning environment (Angelino, Williams, & Natvig, 2007; Kanuka & Jugdev, 2006). Furthermore, online learning may lead to feelings of both psychological and physical (space and time) isolation for learners. Shin (2003) claimed that the psychological presence of peers, the instructor, and the institution has a positive effect on many aspects of the online learning environment including success and attrition rates. Angelino et al. (2007) supported this assertion by stating that relationships with peers and/or cohorts are instrumental for the successful completion of an online course.

In order to combat feelings of social isolation, several scholars have suggested creating learning communities within the online course (Bibeau, 2001; DiRamio & Wolverton, 2006; Palloff & Pratt, 2007). Similarly, DiRamio and Wolverton (2006) suggested that learning communities are effective for reducing the dropout rate in online courses. According to Bolliger and Inan (2012), students who feel connected to their peers are more likely to participate in course activities and to engage with others in the course. They asserted that connectedness refers to a sense of acceptance and belonging as well as to students' beliefs that they have a relationship with at least one other person in the course. Moreover, they claimed that there are four measureable domains that comprise students' perceptions of connectedness: (1) Comfort, (2) Community, (3) Facilitation, and (4) Interaction & Collaboration. While no study thus far has linked language learners' perceptions of connectedness with their success rates in online courses, there is evidence from other disciplines that students' perceptions of the presence of their peers, their teachers, and the institution are a significant predictor of success (Shin, 2003). Therefore, research is needed that measures students' perceptions of connectedness in an online language class. Furthermore, there is a need to explore how feeling of connectedness may impact learning outcomes for online language students. In the present study, the four domains listed above were examined to help determine whether the pedagogical interventions were effective in fostering perceptions of learner connectedness by the end of the course.

Factors Unique to Language Teaching

While high attrition rates and feelings of social isolation and disconnectedness are factors that affect online courses across disciplines, there are some unique factors to language learning that may exert an influence on students' learning outcomes, as measured by final course grades, in both traditional and online courses. Namely, students' levels of foreign language anxiety and their beliefs about language learning may impact their sense of self-efficacy and/or their motivation to continue with the online course.

Foreign Language Anxiety

Language anxiety can be debilitating for some students and research has shown that language anxiety may negatively impact students' performance in a language class (Aida, 1994; Chen & Chang, 2004; Horwitz, 1986, 2001; Onwuegbuzie et al., 2000; Sparks & Ganschow, 2007; Young, 1999). According to Horwitz et al. (1986: 128), language anxiety is "a distinct complex of self-perceptions, beliefs, feelings, and behaviors related to classroom language learning arising from the uniqueness of the language learning process." In order to assess a learner's level of language anxiety, Horwitz et al. (1986) created the Foreign Language Classroom Anxiety Scale (FLCAS), which incorporated three related anxieties: (1) communication apprehension, (2) test anxiety, and (3) fear of negative evaluation.

With respect to online language learning, Pichette (2009) compared classroom and online learners and found that among intermediate and advanced language students, there was no difference in perceived levels of language anxiety between classroom and online learners as measured by the FLCAS. However, he found slightly increased levels of language anxiety among online learners who were beginners compared to their counterparts who took their introductory language course in a traditional environment. Pichette suggested that although online language learners perceive similar or slightly higher levels of anxiety than traditional language learners, they may not feel as comfortable expressing their anxiety because there are fewer opportunities for synchronous interaction between the student and the professor in an online language class. He claimed that many instructors falsely believe that the online learning environment mitigates students' perceived levels of language anxiety. Therefore, Pichette cautioned online language instructors to be aware that anxiety is a concern for both traditional and online students.

In the present study, language anxiety was a topic covered in the peer support group discussions (one of the two pedagogical interventions) and learners' perceived levels of anxiety were measured using the FLCAS at the beginning and at the end of the course to determine whether the intervention had a positive impact on learners' anxiety levels.

Beliefs about Language Learning

Horwtiz (1985, 1988, 1989, 1990) asserted that responses on the Beliefs about Language Learning Inventory (BALLI) indicate whether an individual's beliefs about foreign language learning are comparable with what scholars know about how people learn foreign languages. The BALLI measures beliefs about language learning in the following five areas: (1) Foreign Language Aptitude, (2) Difficulty of Language Learning, (3) Nature of Language Learning, (4) Learning and Communication Strategies, and (5) Motivation and Expectation.

With respect to foreign language aptitude, Horwitz (1985) claimed that when individuals perceive themselves as lacking an innate ability for languages, they may have lower expectations of themselves. Regarding the difficulty of language learning, Horwitz (1985: 336) asserted that when some languages are perceived as being more difficult than others, individuals could become frustrated when they have difficulty learning an "easy language." For example, it is not uncommon for language students in the United States to perceive Spanish as an easy language compared to other languages that may be offered at universities such as Arabic, Chinese, French, German, Latin, or Portuguese. However, when students experience difficulty learning Spanish, which they perceive to be an easy language, then they may become frustrated because they fail to recognize that adult learners typically experience significant challenges learning any foreign language to which they have had little to no exposure previously. With respect to the nature of language learning, Horwitz claimed that when individuals believe that foreign language learning is different than learning other academic disciplines, they are less likely to perceive grammar instruction and/or translation as a key feature of language learning. In the area of learning and communication strategies, when instructors and students adhere to behaviorist theories regarding error correction, they are less likely to engage in communicative activities for fear of making mistakes. The final category, motivation and expectation, examines learners' level of motivation for learning the target language as well as their perception of the impact that language learning has on their future job prospects.

While the BALLI was originally developed for use with pre-service teachers who take foreign language methods classes, it has also been used to uncover the beliefs of in-service teachers and foreign language students across various levels (Kern, 1995; Peacock, 2001; Rifkin, 2000; Samimy & Lee, 1997; Siebert, 2003; White, 1999). Russell and Curtis (2013) found that online language students have strong beliefs about the language acquisition process, which may be erroneous. Furthermore, they found that students' false beliefs about language learning may hamper their satisfaction with their online language learning experience. The researchers suggested that it would be beneficial for online language instructors to share the rationale behind their pedagogical decisions in order to correct learners' false beliefs, which could help create an environment that is more conducive to learning. Russell and Curtis's findings support Horwitz's (1987) assertion that erroneous beliefs or misconceptions by learners may undermine their success in language learning.

In the present study, the constructs measured by the BALLI provided the discussion topics for one of the pedagogical interventions (the online peer support groups). The BALLI was used to measure students' beliefs about language learning prior to and following their participation in the intervention. Therefore, the BALLI measured whether students' beliefs were false at the beginning of the course and whether their beliefs shifted by the end of the course.

Research Questions

The present study attempted to increase students' success rates, as measured by final course grades, by implementing two pedagogical interventions that were designed to: (1) increase student-content and student-student interaction in the course, (2) decrease students' foreign language anxiety, and (3) correct students' false beliefs about language learning. To that end, the following research questions were posed:

1. What are the effects of the pedagogical interventions on success rates as measured by final course grades?
2. Do students' perceived foreign language anxiety levels and beliefs about language learning change from the beginning to the end of the course?
3. What are students' perceived levels of connectedness in the areas of Comfort, Community, Facilitation, and Interaction & Collaboration at the end of the course?

Method

Participants

Participants in the experimental group included 33 students who enrolled in an intermediate-level online Spanish course during the fall of 2015. There were 17 males and 16 females and their ages ranged from 18 to 52, with a mean age of 22.53. Of the 33 participants, six students were flagged as being at risk of failure by the institution based on their SAT scores and on their prior academic performance. The remaining 25 students were in good academic standing.

The same instructor had taught this online course twice previously and all other factors were the same except for the pedagogical interventions. The classes from the previous two semesters were used as a control group: 37 students completed the course during the spring of 2015 (7 students were flagged as at risk of failure) and 32 students completed the course during the spring of 2014 (9 students were flagged as at risk of failure).

At the present institution, the majority of students who take third-semester Spanish do so because it is a requirement for their major. Students who take the course online do so voluntarily and many take the course online for convenience. However, there are some students who take online language courses because they live outside of the state or country. The present study did not inquire about students' motivation for taking the course online.

Online Course

All sections of the online course examined in this study were delivered asynchronously and the instructor provided weekly lectures that were recorded and captioned on the learning management system (LMS), which was BrightSpace D2L. There was one mandatory synchronous online orientation session and four optional synchronous exam review sessions. If students could not attend the live exam review sessions, they were able to view the recordings at a later time. Therefore, the course was designed for anytime, anyplace learning. The course text was *Plazas* by Cengage and all sections of the course had the same weekly homework assignments that were completed on Cengage's iLrn platform. The homework assignments required students to practice using the target language in the three modes of communication: presentational speaking and writing, interpretive listening and reading, and interpersonal communication. The homework activities were infused with the target language culture and there were also assigned homework activities that focused specifically on aspects of the target language culture(s). In addition to the weekly homework assignments, which were identical for the experimental and control groups, there were four chapter exams, one final exam, three quizzes, and three compositions. The assignments and their weights for the experimental and control groups are listed in Table 3.1. Of note, for the experimental group, each pedagogical

Table 3.1. Course assignments and weights for the experimental and control groups

Group	Assignment	Weight
Experimental	Chapter exams	30%
	Homework	25%
	Quizzes	10%
	Compositions	10%
	Peer support discussions	10%
	Talk abroad	10%
	Final exam	5%
Control	Chapter exams	40%
	Homework	35%
	Quizzes	10%
	Compositions	10%
	Final exam	5%

intervention was worth 10% of the final course grade and the interventions were graded for completion rather than for accuracy. The pedagogical rationale behind this decision was to encourage students to participate in the two interventions.

Pedagogical Interventions

Online peer support groups: Seven peer support groups, comprised of 5 or 6 students each, were created at the beginning of the course. Group members were required to interact with each other through structured discussions (in English) that occurred at two-week intervals throughout the semester. These discussions were asynchronous, text-based discussions. The groups were designed to provide an online peer support network and a space for students to discuss their thoughts and beliefs about the online language learning process. The discussion topics were as follows: (1) online learning strategies, (2) language anxiety, (3) foreign language aptitude and difficulty of language learning, (4) nature of language learning and strategies for learning and communication, and (5) motivation and language learning. All of the aforementioned topics – except for online learning strategies and language anxiety – are constructs that are examined by the BALLI.

The instructor created the question prompts for each discussion. After students discussed each topic initially, the instructor provided information concerning second language research findings related to each topic. After reading the research summaries, group members were prompted to discuss the topic again and to state whether their beliefs changed after learning about the research findings. The purpose of this intervention was to increase student-student interaction, to help alleviate students' foreign language anxiety, and to correct students' false beliefs about language learning.

Synchronous conversations with native speakers: Students participated in four synchronous conversations with native speakers of Spanish via the TalkAbroad videoconferencing platform. The conversations took place approximately every four weeks and each conversation lasted 30 minutes. Students could schedule the conversations for the days and times that were convenient for their schedules and they had the option of choosing the same partner for all four conversations or using different partners. Both the students and their conversation partners were provided with conversation topics and question prompts in advance, which were created by the instructor. The topics and question prompts for each conversation related directly to the grammatical structures and vocabulary items that were covered in the course. All of the conversations were recorded and they were graded for completion rather than for accuracy to help alleviate students' language anxiety. This intervention was designed to increase students' interaction with the course content. (For more information on the TalkAbroad application, visit: https://talkabroad.com/index/story#home)

Instruments and Procedures

MLAT: As conceptualized by Carroll and Sapon (1959), the Modern Language Aptitude Test (MLAT) is a norm referenced test that is often used by the military and government agencies to measure foreign language learning aptitude. Schools and guidance counselors also use the MLAT to determine if a student has a foreign language learning disability. The test has five parts; however, only Part 4 (Words in Sentences) was used for the present study. This portion of the test measures grammatical sensitivity and research has shown that grammatical sensitivity is the number-one predictor of successful language learning in classroom settings (Carroll & Sapon, 1959, 2002; Child, 1998; Ehrman, 1998; McGuire & Scott, 2005). This test was delivered via the LMS. Students were required to complete it as part of the "Getting Started" module during the first week of classes. Students with high and low scores on Part 4 of the MLAT were distributed evenly among the seven online peer support groups. In addition, students who were at risk of failure were also distributed evenly among the seven groups.

FLCAS: The FLCAS has 33 items that are rated on a 5-point Likert scale ranging from 1 (strongly disagree) to 5 (strongly agree). An anxiety score is derived by summing the ratings on the 33 items; thus, FLCAS scores range from 33 to 165. When statements are negatively worded, responses are reversed and recoded so that a high score represents high anxiety. Students' perceived foreign language anxiety levels were measured using the FLCAS at the beginning (pre-test) and at the end of the course (post-test). The FLCAS was delivered via the Qualtrics survey platform.

BALLI: The BALLI contains 34 items that are rated on a 5-point Likert scale ranging from 1 (strongly disagree) to 5 (strongly agree). Five constructs were measured as follows: (1) nine items measured beliefs about foreign language aptitude; (2) six items measured difficulty of language learning; (3) six items measured the nature of language learning; (4) eight items measured learning and communication strategies; and (5) five items measured motivation and expectation. The BALLI was delivered as a pre- and post-test via the Qualtrics survey platform.

Online Student Connectedness Survey (OSCS): The OSCS was developed by Bolliger and Inan (2012) as a summative evaluation instrument. Because the survey items inquire about learners' experiences by the end of a course or program, it is not possible to use this instrument as a pre-test. There are 25 items rated on a 5-point Likert scale ranging from 1 (strongly disagree) to 5 (strongly agree). There are four subscales of the OSCS: Comfort, Community, Facilitation, and Interaction & Collaboration. Comfort refers to students' perceptions of security, contentment, and comfort with the learning environment and course technologies – eight items measure this construct. Six items measure Community, which is a learner's emotional attachment to others in the course. Facilitation is measured by six items, and it refers to students' perceptions of the level of teacher presence in the course. Five items measure Interaction & Collaboration, which are students' perceptions of the depth of their interactions with their peers and with their instructor to complete course assignments and projects. The OSCS was administered as a post-test to determine students' perceptions regarding their level of connectedness by the end of the course. It was administered via the Qualtrics survey platform.

Analyses

Success rates: Final course grades were examined to determine the percentage of D/F/W grades. These were compared to D/F/W rates in the previous two semesters that the same instructor taught this course online without using the two pedagogical interventions. Grades of W were included in the analysis because students who withdraw from a course are unsuccessful and the W grade may have a negative impact on their future academic success.

In order to determine if the difference in success rates between the experimental and control groups was statistically significant, data were subjected to a Chi-Square (X^2) Test of Independence. There were two factors in the analysis: (1) group (experimental and control), and (2) D/F/W grades. The Chi-Square Test of Independence was employed because both variables are categorical.

Language anxiety: Mean FLCAS scores from the beginning and from the end of the course were subjected to a dependent samples *t*-test to determine if there were statistically significant differences in students' mean anxiety scores from pre- to post-test.

Beliefs about language learning: BALLI results were examined descriptively and students' responses on each item were compared at the beginning and at the end of the course. In other words, the percentage of participants that either agreed or strongly agreed, neither agreed or disagreed, or disagreed or strongly disagreed were examined both pre- and post-test across the five constructs measured by the BALLI. Horwtiz (1985) did not intend for the BALLI to yield a composite score; rather, each item was intended to be used for descriptive purposes and to stimulate class discussions. BALLI topics were covered in the peer support group discussions, and when students' beliefs were false, follow-up discussions focused on the research findings related to the construct examined in an attempt to correct learners' false beliefs. Thus, the BALLI was used in this study as the author intended; namely, it was employed as a tool to identify and to help correct students' false beliefs about language learning.

Perceptions of connectedness: Descriptive statistics on the four subscales of the OSCS were examined to determine students' mean level of connectedness. Mean scores higher than 3.5 were interpreted to indicate a high level of connectedness, mean scores of 2.5 to 3.5 were interpreted to indicate a medium level of connectedness, and mean scores lower than 2.5 were interpreted to indicate a low level of connectedness for each subscale.

Results

Success Rates

Research Question 1 examined the effect of the two pedagogical interventions on success rates as measured by students' course grades. Figure 3.1 shows the D/F/W rates for the experimental group (Fall 2015) and the D/F/W rates for two previous semesters with the same instructor (the control groups).

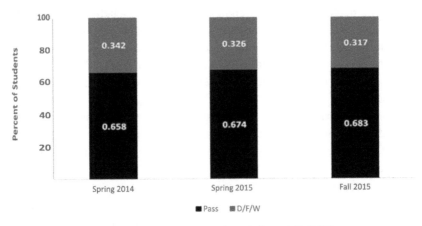

Figure 3.1. Percentage of Pass vs. Drop/Fail/Withdrawal (D/F/W) rates across three semesters of SPAN 2001

A visual examination of Figure 3.1 reveals that the rate of D/F/W grades appears to be declining across the three semesters examined. In order to determine if the difference in D/F/W rates between the experimental (Fall of 2015) and control groups (former semesters) was statistically significant, data were subjected to a Chi-Square Test of Independence. The analysis did not reveal a statistically significant difference, $X^2(1) = 0.033, p > 0.05$.

Language Anxiety

Research Question 2 compared students' perceived levels of anxiety at the beginning and at the end of the course. While 30 students completed the FLCAS at pre-test, only 7 completed it at post-test. Results were analyzed using a dependent (paired) samples t-test. This analysis revealed a significant difference in mean levels of anxiety observed at the two times of testing, $t(6) = -3.59, p < 0.05$. Mean anxiety scores were significantly lower at post-test (M = 98.14, SD = 27.79) than at pre-test (M = 118.14, SD = 22.53). The observed difference between the mean scores was 20.00 and the 95% confidence interval for the difference between the means extended from 6.39 to 33.61. The effect size was computed as $d = 2.10$, which is a very large effect size.

Table 3.2. Beliefs about language learning inventory results: Sample items for survey

Survey items	Agree or Strongly Agree (%)		Neither Agree nor Disagree (%)		Disagree or Strongly Disagree (%)	
	Pre	Post	Pre	Post	Pre	Post
Item 2: Some people have a special ability for languages.	83	100	10	0	7	0
Item 3: Some languages are easier to learn than others.	82	100	14	0	4	0
Item 20: The most important part of learning a foreign language is learning the grammar.	71	66	11	33	18	0
Item 19: If beginning students are permitted to make errors in Spanish, it will be difficult for them to speak correctly later on.	36	17	17	0	47	83
Item 27: If I learn to speak Spanish very well, I will have better opportunities for a good job.	85	83	11	17	4	0

Beliefs about Language Learning

Research Question 2 also examined students' beliefs about language learning at the beginning and at the end of the course across the five areas measured by the BALLI. While 28 students completed the BALLI at the beginning of the course, only 6 students completed it at the end of the course. Presented in Table 3.2 is the most salient item from each category of the BALLI, as follows: Foreign Language Aptitude (Item 2), Difficulty of Language Learning (Item 3), Nature of Language Learning (Item 20), Learning and Communication Strategies (Item 19), and Motivation and Expectations (Item 27). *Note:* The sample items listed in Table 3.2 for each category are representative of all of the responses for the category. The items that demonstrated either the most or the least change in beliefs for each category from pre- to post-test are included in Table 3.2.

Connectedness

Research Question 3 investigated students' perceived levels of connectedness at the end of the course as measured by the OSCS. While all of the

Table 3.3. Mean online student connectedness scores and standard deviations

Construct	Mean (Range 1–5)	SD	Min.	Max.
Comfort	4.33	0.82	3.0	5.0
Community	2.50	0.84	1.0	3.0
Facilitation	4.67	0.52	4.0	5.0
Interaction & Collaboration	3.50	0.84	3.0	5.0

Note: n = 6

students in the course consented to participate in the study, only 6 students completed the OSCS. Mean scores and standard deviations are presented in Table 3.3.

Table 3.3 reveals that the highest mean score was for Facilitation and the lowest mean score was for Community. Of note, the mean score for Comfort (M = 4.33) was also high.

Discussion

Outcomes

The first research question examined the effect of the pedagogical interventions on students' learning outcomes as measured by final course grades. No significant differences were found when D/F/W grades were compared between the experimental and control groups. It appears that the interventions were not effective for improving success rates. A deeper examination of the other constructs that were measured in this study may shed light on why the two interventions were not effective.

Results from the FLCAS indicated that students' anxiety levels were significantly lower at the end of the course compared to the beginning of the semester. However, given the small sample size for the FLCAS, the results must be interpreted with caution. In the present study, it is impossible to determine whether the synchronous conversations with native speakers, or the online peer support groups, or both, were responsible for this outcome because the interventions were not examined in isolation. The synchronous conversations were graded for completion rather than for accuracy; therefore, students may have become less anxious with each low-stakes conversation with a native speaker. In addition, two of the required discussion prompts from the online peer support groups were related to language anxiety. It is possible that foreign language anxiety may have exerted an influence on students' decision to withdraw from the course, especially for those who withdrew early on in the semester when anxiety levels were higher. More research is needed in this area; in particular, studies that investigate the relationship between language anxiety and other outcomes such as oral and written proficiency gains, success rates, and attrition rates.

An examination of the BALLI results showed that students' beliefs about language learning were, by and large, resistant to change, which may help explain why the interventions did not yield significant decreases in D/F/W grades. Participants' beliefs changed little in the areas of language aptitude, difficulty of language learning, nature of language learning, and motivation and expectations, even though they were prompted to discuss research findings related to these constructs in the online peer support groups. Some erroneous beliefs appeared to persist throughout the course; for example, students' false belief that learning grammar is the most important factor for language learning was resistant to change. This may be due to the nature of language teaching in the U.S., where traditional, grammar-based instruction is the dominant paradigm (Wong & VanPatten, 2003). Moreover, the course textbook – like the majority of texts that are available on the postsecondary market – has a heavy emphasis on grammar.

Students' beliefs did not appear to change regarding motivation and expectation – they began and ended the course believing that learning Spanish will provide them with better opportunities for a good job. One area where learners' beliefs appeared to shift more significantly was in the area of learning and communication strategies. False beliefs regarding errors and error correction appeared to diminish by the end of the course. The peer support discussions included information on overgeneralization errors in first and second language acquisition, the role of correction, and the types of errors that are impervious to correction. It appears that students were more receptive to this topic compared to the other research topics that they discussed. Their interactions with native speakers may have contributed to their beliefs about error correction because during the TalkAbroad conversations, only errors that impeded communication tended to receive correction through the negotiation of meaning. Overall, the online peer support/ discussion groups did not appear to be effective for changing students' false beliefs about language learning. However, the results must be interpreted with caution due to the small sample size. More research is needed on how beliefs about language learning may impact outcomes in online courses.

Students' perceptions of connectedness were measured by the OSCS at the end of the course and the subscale with the lowest mean score was Community. This subscale assessed whether the learners felt an emotional connection with each other. The low score in this area (M = 2.5) indicated that students felt that they did not get to know their peers on a personal level in the course. OSCS scores ranged from 1 (Strongly Disagree) to 5 (Strongly Agree). Since the support groups and discussion prompts were created by the instructor, it is possible that the students simply viewed this intervention as another course task rather than as an opportunity to connect more deeply with their peers. Furthermore, Interaction & Collaboration scores were only slightly above average. This subscale assessed how well learners discussed ideas, shared work, and collaborated with each other. The mean score for this subscale (M = 3.5) indicates that there is room for improvement in this area.

Facilitation was the subscale with the highest mean score (M = 4.67). This subscale assessed the instructors' ability to facilitate the online class. The respondents' high scores in this area demonstrated that they perceived their instructor to be highly responsive – and present – in the course while providing frequent feedback. Comfort was the subscale with the second highest mean score (M = 4.33). This subscale measured learners' comfort with the online learning environment and with using the course technologies. Participants' high scores indicated that they were comfortable expressing their thoughts and opinions and asking for help when needed.

The results of the OSCS suggest that while students perceived a connection to the instructor and felt comfortable using the course technologies to express themselves, they did not appear to feel a sense of emotional attachment to each other. The two pedagogical interventions did not appear to be beneficial for stimulating learners' perceptions of connectedness in the areas of Community and Interaction & Collaboration. These results may help explain why there were no significant differences in success rates between the experimental and control groups in the present study as a result of implementing the two pedagogical interventions.

Three Types of Presence

Garrison, Anderson, & Archer (2010) asserted that three types of presence are necessary for an effective, efficient, and satisfying online teaching and learning experience: social presence, teaching presence, and cognitive presence. Social presence allows individuals to connect with each other based on their uniqueness as individuals, which includes their family relationships, their hobbies, lifestyle, and interests. Teaching presence is "the sum of all the behaviors faculty use to direct, guide, and design the learning experiences" (Boettcher & Conrad, 2016: 46). Teaching presence includes directing, guiding, and mentoring students throughout the course. Finally, cognitive presence refers to guiding students' intellectual growth and supporting their development of knowledge, skills, and understandings. It is possible that the online peer support groups only engaged students on an intellectual rather than on a social level with each other, which may help explain the findings of the present study. Furthermore, social presence may be the mediating variable between cognitive and teaching presence (Garrison, Cleveland-Innes & Fung, 2010; Shea & Bidjerano, 2009). Future research should explore pedagogical interventions that include both social and intellectual interactions among learners to determine their impact on language learning and final course outcomes as well as on attrition rates.

Assessment in Online Language Education and Suggestions for Future Research

In order to determine which pedagogical techniques and strategies are the most effective for online language instruction, researchers and classroom practitioners need to seek out and employ a variety of assessments that are valid and reliable. In the present study the FLCAS, the BALLI, and the OSCS were used to assess language anxiety, beliefs about language learning, and learners' perceptions of connectedness, respectively. The former two instruments have been widely used in traditional language classrooms and substantial evidence of their validity and reliability have been collected (Aida, 1994; Horwtiz, 1985, 1988, 1989, 1990; Horwitz et al., 1986). Given that Pichette (2009) found that online language students' perceived anxiety levels are similar to those of traditional classroom-based language learners, more research is needed in this area. Studies that examine the impact of language anxiety on attrition rates and language learning outcomes are needed, and the FLCAS is an appropriate instrument to use for studies of this nature.

The results of this study indicate that the majority of students' false beliefs about language learning appeared to be resistant to change even though they were directly addressed though the peer support discussions. Given that erroneous beliefs may undermine students' success in language learning (Horwitz, 1987) and that false beliefs may diminish students' satisfaction with their online language learning experience (Russell & Curtis, 2013), examining the impact of false beliefs about language learning on learning outcomes and student satisfaction is another area that is in need of future research. Because the BALLI was designed as a tool to measure and correct students' false beliefs, this assessment is useful for both researchers and online language educators.

While this is the first study in the field of online language education to employ the OSCS, this instrument has been used across a wide variety of other disciplines, and its creators have provided ample evidence of its validity and reliability (Bolliger & Inan, 2012). The results of this study indicate that future research needs to seek out and assess techniques and strategies that facilitate students' perceptions of social connectedness. The OSCS is a valuable assessment measure for studies of this nature. Future studies may also attempt to determine if there is a correlation between students' perceptions of connectedness across the four domains measured by the OSCS and attrition rates in online language classes.

Future research should attempt to measure the constructs examined in this study (language anxiety, beliefs about language learning, and students' perceptions of connectedness) with larger-scale studies as a means of determining how to help language learners be more successful in online learning environments. Moreover, future studies could examine how these constructs may contribute to language learning outcomes by measuring proficiency gains in the three modes of communication – interpretive, presentational, and interpersonal (ACTFL, 2017) – as a result of exposure to the pedagogical techniques.

Limitations

Many participants failed to complete the FLCAS, the BALLI, and the OSCS at the end of the course even though they were offered extra credit to do so. This may be due to the time constraints that all students face at the end of the semester, or the fact that the majority of students (68.3%) passed the course with a C or higher and did not perceive a need to spend time on extra credit assignments. In addition, it is possible that those who did not pass the course (31.7%) may have completely disengaged from the online learning environment by the end of the semester. In future studies, researchers may need to collect data over multiple semesters or they may need to offer greater incentives for participants to complete the study.

In addition, the grading between the experimental and control groups was not equal because the two pedagogical interventions were worth 10% of the course grade each for the experimental group, but the control groups did not have these items included in the final course grade. Moreover, the interventions were graded for completion only as an incentive for students in the experimental group to participate in them. While this pedagogical decision may have resulted in greater participation by students, at least initially, it is difficult to compare the final course grades between the groups due to this difference.

Conclusion

While the two pedagogical interventions described in this chapter did not have a beneficial effect on success rates as measured by final course grades, the other constructs that were examined in this study may help explain why they were not effective in doing so. Namely, the FLCAS revealed that anxiety levels were high at the beginning of the course (which may have caused withdrawals early on), the BALLI results showed that some false beliefs about language learning remained largely unchanged, and the OSCS results revealed that the interventions did not appear to help students build an emotional connection to each other. Given the high attrition rates in online courses across the nation (Herbert, 2006; Heyman, 2010), it will be important for future research to seek out and assess pedagogical interventions that help online language students build a stronger sense of community and improve their learning outcomes.

About the Author

Victoria Russell is an Associate Professor of Spanish and Foreign Language Education at Valdosta State University. She earned a PhD in Second Language Acquisition and Instructional Technology from the University of South Florida, and her research interests include online language pedagogy, foreign language teacher preparation, and pragmatics. Her work has appeared in journals such as *Foreign Language Annals*, *The Internet and Higher Education*, and *Dimension*.

References

ACTFL (2017). *World Readiness Standards for Learning Languages* [Electronic version]. Retrieved June 5, 2017 from: https://www.actfl.org/publications/all/world-readiness-standards-learning-languages/standards-summary

Aida, Y. (1994). Examination of Horwitz, Horwitz, and Cope's construct of foreign language anxiety: The case of students of Japanese. *Modern Language Journal*, 78(2), 155–168. https://doi.org/10.2307/329005

Allen, E. I., Seaman, J., Poulin, R., & Straut, T. T. (2016). Online report card: Tracking online education in the United States. *Babson Survey Research Group Report* (pp. 1–57). The Sloan Consortium.

Angelino, L. M., Williams, F. K., & Natvig, D. (2007). Strategies to engage online students and reduce attrition rates. *Journal of Educators Online*, 4(2), 1–14. https://doi.org/10.9743/jeo.2007.2.1

Bibeau, S. (2001). Social presence, isolation and connectedness in online teaching and learning: From the literature to real life. *Journal of Instruction Delivery Systems*, 15(3), 35–39.

Boettcher, J., & Conrad, R. M. (2016). *The Online Teaching Survival Guide: Simple and Practical Pedagogical Tips* (2nd ed.). San Francisco: Jossey-Bass.

Bolliger, D. U., & Inan, F. A. (2012). Development and validation of the online student connectedness survey. *The International Review of Research in Open and Distance Education*, 13(3), 41–65. https://doi.org/10.19173/irrodl.v13i3.1171

Carroll, J. B., & Sapon, S. (1959). *The Modern Language Aptitude Test*. San Antonio, TX: The Psychological Corporation.

Carroll, J. B., & Sapon, S. (2002). *Modern Language Aptitude Test: Manual 2002 Edition*. N. Bethesda, MD: Second Language Testing, Inc.

Chen, T., & Chang, G. (2004). The relationship between foreign language anxiety and learning difficulties. *Foreign Language Annals*, 37(2), 279–289. https://doi.org/10.1111/j.1944-9720.2004.tb02200.x

Child, J. R. (1998). Language aptitude testing: Learners and applications. *Applied Language Learning*, 9, 1–10.

DiRamio, D., & Wolverton, M. (2006). Integrating learning communities and distance education: Possibility or pipedream? *Innovative Higher Education*, 31(2), 99–113. https://doi.org/10.1007/s10755-006-9011-y

Ehrman, M. (1998). The Modern Language Aptitude Test for Predicting Learning Success and Advising Students. *Applied Language Learning*, 9(1&2), 32–71.

Garrison, D. R., Anderson, T., & Archer, W. (2010). The first decade of the community of inquiry framework: A retrospective. *The Internet and Higher Education*, 13, 5–9. https://doi.org/10.1016/j.iheduc.2009.10.003

Garrison, D. R., Cleveland-Innes, M., & Fung, T. S. (2010). Exploring causal relationships among teaching, cognitive, and social presence: Student perceptions of the community of inquiry framework. *The Internet and Higher Education*, 13, 31–36. https://doi.org/10.1016/j.iheduc.2009.10.002

Haythornthwaite, C., Kazmer, M. M., Robins, J., & Shoemaker, S. (2000). Community development among distance learners: Temporal and technological dimensions. *Journal of Computer-Mediated Communication*, 6(1): 0. https://doi.org/10.1111/j.1083-6101.2000.tb00114.x

Herbert, M. (2006). Staying the course: A study in online student satisfaction and retention. *Online Journal of Distance Learning Administration*, 9(4): 0.

Heyman, E. (2010). Overcoming student retention issues in higher education online programs. *Online Journal of Distance Learning Administration*, 13(4).

Horwitz, E. K. (1985). Using student beliefs about language learning and teaching in the foreign language methods course. *Foreign Language Annals*, 18(4), 333–340. https://doi.org/10.1111/j.1944-9720.1985.tb01811.x

Horwitz, E. K. (1986). Preliminary evidence for the reliability and validity of a foreign language anxiety scale. *TESOL Quarterly*, 20(3), 559–564. https://doi.org/10.2307/3586302

Horwitz, E. K. (1987). Surveying student beliefs about language learning. In A. Wenden & R. Rubin (eds.), *Learner Strategies in Language Learning* (pp. 119–129). London: Prentice Hall International.

Horwitz, E. K. (1988). The beliefs about language learning of beginning university students. *Modern Language Journal*, 72(3), 283–294. https://doi.org/10.2307/327506

Horwitz, E. K. (1989). Facing the blackboard: Student perceptions of language learning and the language classroom. *ADFL Bulletin*, 20(3), 61–64. https://doi.org/10.1632/adfl.20.3.61

Horwitz, E. K. (1990). Attending to the affective domain in the foreign language classroom. In S. Sieloff Magnan (ed.), *Shifting the Instructional Focus to the Learner* (pp. 15–33). Middlebury, VT: Northeast Conference Reports.

Horwitz, E. K. (2001). Language anxiety and achievement. *Annual Review of Applied Linguistics*, 21, 112–126. https://doi.org/10.1017/s0267190501000071

Horwitz, E. K., Horwitz, M., & Cope, J. (1986). Foreign language classroom anxiety. *Modern Language Journal*, 70(2), 124–132. https://doi.org/10.1111/j.1540-4781.1986.tb05256.x

Kanuka, H., & Jugdev, K. (2006). Distance education MBA students: An investigation into the use of an orientation course to address academic and social integration issues. *Open Learning*, 21(2), 153–166. https://doi.org/10.1080/02680510600715578

Kern, R. G. (1995). Students' and teachers' beliefs about language learning. *Foreign Language Annals*, 28(1), 71–92. https://doi.org/10.1111/j.1944-9720.1995.tb00770.x

McGuire, J. M. & Scott, S. S. (2005). Review of Carroll, J. B. & Sapon, S. M. (2002 ed.), Modern Language Aptitude Test (MLAT). *Journal of Psychoeducational Assessment*, 23, 96–104. https://doi.org/10.1177/073428290502300109

Onwuegbuzie, A. J., Bailey, P., & Daley, C. E. (2000). The validation of three scales measuring anxiety at different stages of the foreign language learning process: The input anxiety scale, the processing anxiety scale, and the output anxiety scale. *Language Learning*, 50(1), 87–117. https://doi.org/10.1111/0023-8333.00112

Palloff, R. M., & Pratt, K. (2007). *Building Online Learning Communities: Effective Strategies for the Virtual Classroom* (2nd ed.). San Francisco: Jossey-Bass.

Peacock, M. (2001). Pre-service ESL teachers' beliefs about second language learning: A longitudinal study. *System*, 29(2), 177–195. https://doi.org/10.1016/s0346-251x(01)00010-0

Pichette, F. (2009). Second language anxiety and distance language learning. *Foreign Language Annals*, 42(1), 77–93. https://doi.org/10.1111/j.1944-9720.2009.01009.x

Rifkin, B. (2000). Revisiting beliefs about foreign language learning. *Foreign Language Annals*, 33(4), 394–408. https://doi.org/10.1111/j.1944-9720.2000.tb00621.x

Rovai, A. P. (2002). Development of an instrument to measure classroom community. *The Internet and Higher Education*, 5(3), 197–211. https://doi.org/10.1016/s1096-7516(02)00102-1

Russell, V., & Curtis, W. (2013). Comparing a large- and small-scale online language class: An examination of teacher and learner perceptions. *The Internet and Higher Education*, 6, 1–13. https://doi.org/10.1016/j.iheduc.2012.07.002

Samimy, K. K., & Lee, Y. A. (1997). Beliefs about language learning: Perspectives of first year Chinese learners and their instructors. *Journal of the Chinese Language Teachers Association*, 32(1), 40–60.

Shea, P., & Bidjerano, T. (2009). Community of inquiry as a theoretical framework to foster "epistemic engagement" and "cognitive presence" in online education. *Computers and Education*, 52(3), 543–553. https://doi.org/10.1016/j.compedu.2008.10.007

Shieh, R. S., Gummer, E., & Niess, M. (2008). Perspectives of the instructor and the students. *TechTrends*, 52(6), 61–68.

Shin, N. (2003). Transactional presence as a critical predictor of success in distance learning. *Distance Education*, 24(1), 69–86. https://doi.org/10.1080/01587910303048

Siebert, L. (2003). Student and teacher beliefs about language learning. *ORTESOL Journal*, 21, 7–40.

Sparks, R., & Ganschow, L. (2007). Is the foreign language classroom anxiety scale measuring anxiety or language skills? *Foreign Language Annals*, 40(2), 260–287. https://doi.org/10.1111/j.1944-9720.2007.tb03201.x

White, C. (1999). Expectations and emergent beliefs of self-instructed language learners. *System*, 27, 443–457. https://doi.org/10.1016/s0346-251x(99)00044-5

Wong, W., & VanPatten, B. (2003). The evidence is IN: Drills are OUT. *Foreign Language Annals*, 36(3), 403–423. https://doi.org/10.1111/j.1944-9720.2003.tb02123.x

Young, D. J. (1999). Giving priority to the language learner first. In D. J. Young (ed.), *Affect in Foreign and Second Language Learning*. Boston: McGraw-Hill.

4 Language MOOCs: Assessing Student Knowledge and Comprehension of Clinical Terminology

Carrie DEMMANS EPP,* Rae Mancilla,**
and Valerie Swigart***

Introduction

Research into massive open online courses (MOOCs) has focused on student retention and attrition, regardless of instructional domain, with disappointingly high drop-out rates being reported (Davis et al., 2017; Gasevic et al., 2014; Kizilcec & Halawa, 2015; Kizilcec, Piech, & Schneider, 2013). Recent work has begun to move beyond this basic attrition and retention model to characterize student behaviors within MOOCs (Baikadi et al., 2016; Geigle & Zhai, 2017; Ramesh et al., 2014) and occasionally tie those behaviors to student learning (Koedinger et al., 2015; Wang et al., 2015) or learning strategies (Kizilcec, Pérez-Sanagustín, & Maldonado, 2016). However, existing work is in the early stages, and there has been little investigation of how learner activities specifically relate to language learning.

Within the broader domain of MOOCs, those that support language learning are called LMOOCs. These online language courses are characterized by their "unrestricted access and potentially unlimited participation" (Martín-Monje & Bárcena, 2015: 1). They present an opportunity to support a greater breadth and number of learners. However, their use to support language learning has received little scholarly attention, with LMOOCs representing less than one percent of all MOOCs (Bárcena & Martín-Monje, 2015). The first book about LMOOCs (Murray & Vazirabad, 2015) recently

*   University of Pittsburgh, USA; cdemmans@pitt.edu
**   University of Pittsburgh, USA; ram199@pitt.edu
***   University of Pittsburgh, USA; valerie@pitt.edu

presented theoretical considerations for designing these online courses. It also detailed the potential of these online courses for supporting learners of additional or foreign languages across skills (e.g., pronunciation or composition). LMOOCs could be used to help prepare professionals in English for Specific Purposes (ESP) contexts (Godwin-Jones, 2014) through the explicit instruction of specialized vocabulary, registers, or language varieties (Coxhead, 2013).

To prepare professionals for the language that is specific to their context, some LMOOCs foreground the central role of vocabulary in language development and use (Henriksen et al., 2008) as it interfaces with career readiness. A French for Specific Purposes MOOC (*Travailler en Français*) exposed learners to the specialized vocabulary needed for seeking employment (Martín-Monje & Bárcena, 2015), while *Professional English* provides the only example of an ESP MOOC (Ventura & Martín-Monje, 2016). These initiatives have mainly employed multimodal resources to support task-based learning (Ellis, 2009), emphasizing the use of authentic language to learn by completing tasks (e.g., preparing resumes). Although few investigations document how learner activities within MOOCs facilitate language acquisition, student self-reports (e.g., questionnaires, interviews) from *Professional English* suggest students' specialized vocabulary knowledge improved following course completion (Ventura & Martín-Monje, 2016), but they did not measure student knowledge.

Assessment of student knowledge in MOOCs has relied on peer evaluation and automated quizzes where learners receive system-generated corrective feedback (Baikadi et al., 2016; Chandrasekaran et al., 2017), with the aim of triggering their noticing and correction of errors (Schmidt, 1990). Some LMOOCs require students to attain a minimum average score (e.g., 60%) on quizzes before proceeding to more difficult tasks. Others ask them to apply an instructor-supplied rubric to peers' final projects (Martín-Monje & Bárcena, 2015). Nonetheless, ties between common assessment practices in LMOOCs and student learning outcomes (Martín-Monje & Bárcena, 2015) have not been empirically studied or validated, leading to calls for research in this area (Dixon & Fuchs, 2015).

The present study empirically investigates an ESP MOOC that aims to scaffold healthcare practitioners' (e.g., nurses') learning of American clinical terminology and prepare them for communicating effectively in clinical settings. This LMOOC uses explicit instruction, context-rich exposure, and learning by testing (Anderson, 2010; Roediger & Karpicke, 2006) to facilitate specialized vocabulary learning. While new to MOOCs, such methods for building vocabulary knowledge have a history of success in computer-assisted language learning (Levy, 2009). In addition to these common techniques, this LMOOC's design draws from situated learning (Gee, 2006) and the Community of Practice framework (Lave & Wenger, 2011). Like all situated learning, this LMOOC considers learning a contextual process where learners establish meaningful associations among new knowledge, skills, and experience (Choi & Hannafin, 1995). Similarly, learners are encouraged to share and reflect on their experiences within the LMOOC forum so they can build a community to help them learn from one another's contexts. These approaches are infrequently employed within MOOCs, which tend towards instructivist approaches.

This study examines how LMOOC participation relates to vocabulary knowledge, how student vocabulary knowledge changed, and the differences in these measures between student groups. It asks (RQ1) To what extent does student knowledge of clinical terminology change?, (RQ2) How are students' activities within the MOOC related to their performance?, and (RQ3) How does MOOC completion influence their comprehension of clinical terminology when entering clinical settings?

Method

This study used a mixed-methods explanatory design (Creswell & Plano Clark, 2011) that combined observational data, student self-reports, and assessments of vocabulary knowledge to explore student performance within the LMOOC and changes in their knowledge of clinical terminology. In this design, qualitative data are used to explain quantitative results. This combination enabled the triangulation of several data types to better explain student learning and achievement.

Clinical Terminology: An ESP MOOC

Like most MOOCs, LMOOCs tend towards instructivist approaches, where information is transmitted to learners through instructor-developed content and activities. In this model, learner interaction sometimes occurs through discussion forums and assessment tends to be automated. Lecture watching and easily gradable work (i.e., multiple-choice quizzes) are common learning activities (Baikadi et al., 2016; Chandrasekaran et al., 2017). Like these MOOCs, the development of an LMOOC by the University of Pittsburgh School of Nursing in 2012 followed an instructivist approach. This LMOOC, *Clinical Terminology for International and U.S. Students* (http://www.coursera.org/learn/clinical-terminology), was offered through

Coursera and developed by a nursing professor, an instructional design team, and language learning experts.

This LMOOC aims to prepare health professionals new to American clinical sites to communicate effectively with clinical staff because a lack of facility with commonly-used medical terms and abbreviations is disabling to practitioners. Accurate understanding of clinical terms and abbreviations is essential to effective communication and patient safety (Leonard, Graham, & Bonacum, 2004). However, the Greek and Latin etymology of clinical terminology makes it difficult to acquire both for those who speak English as a first language and for those who speak it as an additional language (Stephens & Moxham, 2016). Moreover, English-language learners (ELLs) are additionally stressed by the fast-paced nature of communication in clinical settings (Ferguson, 2012; Olson, 2012). The fast-paced nature of clinical communication, its deep integration within clinical settings, and its etymology make it necessary for nursing programs to offer language training to all students (Long & Uscinski, 2012). This training typically involves students memorizing lists of vocabulary. Diverging from these pedagogical practices, this course emphasized situating learning within medical contexts alongside learning-by-testing approaches.

This six-week course was organized around five clinical topics. It began with videos and readings presenting simple topics and progressed through various emergency situations. The final week integrated previously covered materials. Videos leveraged virtual realia from clinical settings (Martín-Monje & Bárcena, 2015) with students receiving a clinical-unit tour, seeing photos of equipment in use, reading clinical notes, and interpreting patient records (see Figure 4.1 for examples of video stills). Students were encouraged to complete course activities in the sequence in which they were presented and to use a clinical terminology dictionary (see www.clinical-terminology.org) to support their learning. Students were also encouraged to join a community of practice (Lave & Wenger, 2011) through their participation in the discussion forum. Like their participation in the discussion forum, students controlled their use of LMOOC resources: they could perform course activities in whichever order they wanted.

Audiovisual case studies with interactive decision-making points emphasized the embedded nature of vocabulary learning to exploit the extended mapping principle (Carey, 2010). This principle states that we increase our understanding of vocabulary each time we encounter a word being used in context. Each week's lectures embedded ungraded practice quizzes and that week's situated learning experiences were followed by a quiz assessing students' knowledge of the terminology that was covered in those materials. Like the rest of the LMOOC content, these quizzes were developed by

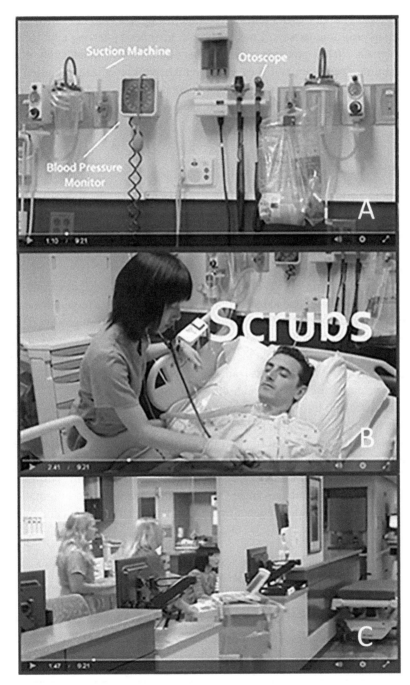

Figure 4.1. Video stills demonstrating clinical settings with photos of equipment in use. (A) is introducing targeted clinical terminology through annotations. (B) shows a nurse interacting with her patient. (C) shows part of the clinical context.

a team of domain experts and instructional designers who consulted with language learning experts. Consistent with learning-by-testing approaches (Anderson, 2010), students received their quiz scores immediately after submitting their quiz and they could retake weekly quizzes as often as desired. Since the quizzes are a fundamental part of the data being analyzed, additional details are provided in the Instruments and Data Collection subsection.

Participants

When learners agree to Coursera's end-user licensing agreement, they consent to their data being used to study learning. Of the 15,198 people registered in the Spring 2015 offering of this LMOOC, only 9,442 logged in and participated in the course, which is consistent with the enrollment and course completion patterns typical of MOOCs (Jordan, 2014).

Only a subset (n = 1,264) of these students were included in this study. To be included students had to have completed the five quizzes required to earn a certificate from the LMOOC. From these 1,264 learners, a group of 103 nursing students were required to complete this LMOOC to prepare them for clinical practicums within their nursing degree programs; these students are herein referred to as NurseTrainees. The remaining 1,162 LMOOC students are called MOOConly, and serve as a comparison group.

Demographic information was collected from the NurseTrainees group when they completed the pre-test. At the time, Coursera used a web form to collect demographic information from students. Coursera only provides demographic data for a portion of the students enrolled in a course. In this case, the demographic data from 100 students was provided. However, these data-sharing practices meant the provided demographic information was not always from the students whose data were analyzed. This limitation

Table 4.1. Demographic information as a percentage of those belonging to the entire LMOOC (n = 100) and the subset of NurseTrainees (n = 103)

| Learners | Female | ELL | Age | | | Industry | | |
			Under 30	30–40	Over 40	Health	Education	Other
LMOOC	58	53	59	19	22	40	14	46
NurseTrainees	93	10	100	0	0	100	0	0

Note: Only a portion of the demographic data from the LMOOC is represented due to the constraints that Coursera has on access to full demographic datasets. The total LMOOC participation was 9,442.

of Coursera's demographic data prohibits our ability to analyze student performance based on ELL status. These Coursera-provided demographics are reported in Table 4.1 because they provide a sense of who enrolled in this LMOOC. Table 4.1 also shows the demographics of the NurseTrainees group to enable comparison between the MOOC learners for whom we have information and the nursing students.

Instruments and Data Collection

Three data sources were analyzed to determine the relationships among LMOOC activities, learner knowledge of clinical terminology, and the later use of those terms in real-world settings. A delayed self-report and pre- and post-tests were collected from the NurseTrainees to measure learning. The pre-test was administered before these students began the LMOOC. The post-test and self-report were administered following LMOOC completion. These data were not collected from all LMOOC students because students enrolled in MOOCs are not accessible before or after a session offering.

The delayed self-report was administered approximately four months after the NurseTrainees completed the LMOOC. This self-report collected information about students' experiences during their first three weeks working in clinical settings. The self-report was a questionnaire that posed three open-ended questions designed to elicit information about Nurse Trainees' experiences in clinical contexts. Questions asked participants to describe how their comprehension of clinical terminology influenced their affective state, their ability to contribute to the clinical work environment, and their understanding of what was happening around them. These open-ended responses were used to help interpret the results of the quantitative analyses.

Logs of student interactions with the LMOOC and their quiz results were available for all participants because Coursera automatically records individual student activities within each course. This logging includes when learners accessed resources (i.e., videos, ungraded quizzes, discussion forums, and graded quizzes), the number of each resource type accessed (i.e., the number of videos viewed or quizzes attempted), and the number of times they watched the videos or submitted the quizzes (i.e., number of quiz attempts and lecture views). See Veeramachaneni (2014) and Manning (2014) for details on Coursera's features and logging procedures.

All LMOOC quizzes and pre-/post-tests asked learners to define and interpret terms that had been included in the LMOOC learning materials. To assess their knowledge of terminology, each term was presented within a specified clinical context. The content of both test types was consistent, came from the materials students were expected to have studied, and used

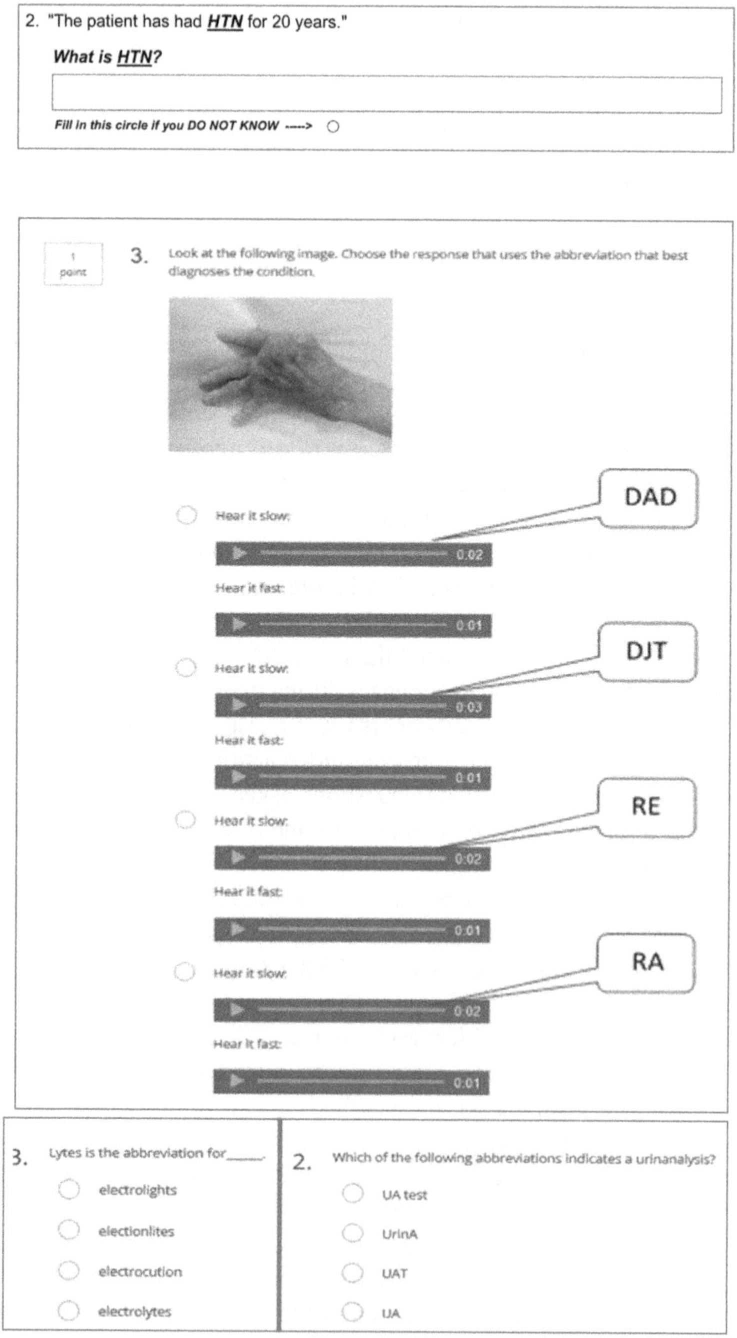

2. "The patient has had **_HTN_** for 20 years."

What is _HTN_?

Fill in this circle if you DO NOT KNOW -----> ○

---

3. 1 point Look at the following image. Choose the response that uses the abbreviation that best diagnoses the condition.

○ Hear it slow: ▶ .... 0:02 — DAD

Hear it fast: ▶ 0:01

○ Hear it slow: ▶ .... 0:03 — DJT

Hear it fast: ▶ 0:01

○ Hear it slow: ▶ .... 0:02 — RE

Hear it fast: ▶ 0:01

○ Hear it slow: ▶ .... 0:02 — RA

Hear it fast: ▶ 0:01

---

3. Lytes is the abbreviation for_____.

○ electrolights
○ electionlites
○ electrocution
○ electrolytes

2. Which of the following abbreviations indicates a urinanalysis?

○ UA test
○ UrinA
○ UAT
○ UA

Figure 4.2. Sample items from the assessments. An audio example with annotated responses (middle) and text-based examples (top and bottom).

similar question prompts. However, the affordances of the online platform and testing environments resulted in two fundamental differences between the online LMOOC quizzes and the paper-based pre- and post-tests.

First, the 30-item pre- and post-tests used the same test form, which asked learners to define a term or expand an acronym within a particular context (see Figure 4.2, top); they were productive rather than receptive like the 10-item multiple-choice LMOOC quizzes (rest of Figure 4.2).

Second, the LMOOC quizzes included usage-based items and incorporated audio and visual stimuli rather than only using text-based stimuli. This difference in test-item delivery was intended to more closely align with the eventual usage environment of course materials. These differences were also due to the aims of the assessments: pre- and post-tests were meant to measure changes in student knowledge, and LMOOC quizzes were meant to measure knowledge of clinical terminology while supporting learning of vocabulary that had been covered during the lessons. These differences also made the tests more difficult, resulting in a lower expected learning-score gain.

Analysis

Descriptive statistics were calculated for assessments of learner knowledge (i.e., LMOOC quizzes and tests) and their activities within the LMOOC: median (Mdn), inter-quartile range (IQR), minimum (Min), and maximum (Max) are provided. Evidence of learning was also sought through the analysis of student responses on the self-report and pre- and post-test. Proportional learning-score gains are used to characterize changes in learner knowledge (RQ1). Non-parametric methods (e.g., Wilcoxon signed-ranks) were used to test for differences between groups as well as between assessments for the NurseTrainees group (RQ1). Non-parametric tests were used because data were not normally distributed. Effect sizes (e.g., r) are reported to quantify these differences. The relationships between these activities and learner knowledge were determined using Pearson correlations (RQ2).

Thematic analysis of the open-ended responses from the delayed self-report was conducted by one of the authors and reviewed by another (RQ3). Differences were settled through discussion using a consensus-based approach. Student responses from the post-test and self-reports were similarly analyzed to identify which elements of clinical terminology had been learned by the NurseTrainees (RQ1).

Findings

RQ1: To what extent does student knowledge of clinical terminology change?

For testing, NurseTrainees experienced a median learning-score gain of 22% (IQR = 20, Min = 0, Max = 71) from the pre-test (Mdn = 7%, IQR = 7, Min = 0, Max = 67) to post-test (Mdn = 30%, IQR = 17, Min = 7, Max = 83). This gain describes the NurseTrainees' significantly higher post-test score ($Z = -8.78$, $p < 0.001$, $r = 0.86$). For quizzes, students' first and final attempt scores, averaged across all receptive LMOOC quizzes, show significant improvement between the first and final attempt for both groups, with large effect sizes (Table 4.2).

Student learning-score gains on these receptive assessments (Table 4.3) are larger than those observed from the pre-test to the post-test, which coincides with the increased cognitive demands of production over recognition (Jones, 2004). When considered alongside the gains observed from the pre-test to the post-test, these results suggest the LMOOC partially achieved its goal of supporting learning through testing.

Proportional learning-score gains describe changes in student scores over the course of their reattempting the graded quizzes (Table 4.3). As shown in Table 4.3, 69% of NurseTrainees and 94% of MOOConly students

Table 4.2. The results of the Wilcoxon signed-ranks tests and student scores on the language assessments performed through the MOOC platform

Quizzes	First attempt				Final attempt				Wilcox		
	Mdn	IQR	Min	Max	Mdn	IQR	Min	Max	Z	p	r
NurseTrainees	92	12	36	100	100	6	80	100	7.34	<0.001	0.72
MOOConly	92	10	0	100	98	8	30	100	24.37	<0.001	0.72

Table 4.3. Students' learning gain scores and the number of times that they attempted each quiz

Quizzes	Learning gain score					No. of submissions				
	n	Mdn	IQR	Min	Max	n	Mdn	IQR	Min	Max
NurseTrainees	71	100	0	50	100	103	1	1	1	5
MOOConly	1,087	67	100	0	100	1,161	1	1	1	17

Note: Not all students took each quiz more than once, meaning they may not have a gain score for each quiz.

rewrote at least one quiz, with learners taking advantage of this learning-by-testing approach through different combinations of quizzes. While all learners who took the quiz more than once appear to have learned through these assessments, the NurseTrainees experienced higher learning gains ($U = 19770.50$, $p < 0.001$, $r = 0.20$) while attempting the quizzes fewer times ($U = 45892.00$, $p < 0.001$, $r = 0.11$). Five of the NurseTrainees also admitted to having "skipped right to the quizzes" because they did not "feel like [the lessons] were helpful," possibly as a result of their prior clinical experiences.

The delayed self-reports provide further evidence of student knowledge of course terminology. As one student correctly explained, "I overheard a nurse say a patient could not be OOB meaning out of bed." Another correctly explained that she "knew that an 'NG' tube was a nasogastric tube and [she] knew it went from the nose to the gastrointestinal tract." In addition to defining terms, students occasionally showed they had begun to integrate terms into their communication practices. For example, when completing the self-report about her comprehension of terminology used in clinical settings, one nursing student wrote the term vitals instead of vital signs: "our instructor asked us to input vitals into the EMR." Using vitals as a shorthand for vital signs was one of the learning objectives within this LMOOC.

For the NurseTrainees, there was no relationship between the number of times they attempted a graded quiz and the score on their first attempt ($p = 0.269$). However, one was found for the MOOConly group ($r = 0.23$, $p < 0.001$) and a weak relationship was found between their scores on the first attempt at a quiz and the number of ungraded quizzes they attempted ($r = 0.32$, $p < 0.001$). The presence and absence of these relationships bolsters the argument that the LMOOC supported learning through testing for those who relied on it to learn clinical terminology. However, NurseTrainees sometimes found "it hard to differentiate whether the terminology... was from this course..., but reading lab values was easier in the EMR." This quote also demonstrates learner integration of course materials into her communication practices, where instead of writing electronic medical record, she wrote its abbreviation (EMR).

While both groups improved from their first to final attempt at a quiz, small but significant differences were observed between groups: NurseTrainees, on average, had higher First Attempt scores ($U = 383.00$, $p < 0.001$, $r = 0.08$). No differences were found between groups for their Final Attempt scores ($p = 0.598$). In addition to these differences, a relationship ($r = 0.22$, $p < 0.001$) between MOOConly's average First Attempt score and the number of video lectures watched was found, demonstrating that these quizzes assessed or reinforced the information that was contained in the materials.

RQ2: How are students' activities within the MOOC related to their performance?

The ostensible difference in final grades between NurseTrainees and MOOConly appears to be due to chance ($U = 58014.00$, $p = 0.597$, $r = 0.01$), with students from both groups receiving high grades (Table 4.4). Grades earned by NurseTrainees ($r = 0.22$, $p = 0.025$) and MOOConly students ($r = 0.18$, $p < 0.001$) showed weak relationships to the number of ungraded quizzes that they completed, and both groups' discussion forum activities were low: 2% of students from the NurseTrainees group and 20% of those from the MOOConly group posted. Rather than interacting with one another, students in this LMOOC spent most of their time interacting with course materials.

As can be seen in Table 4.4, students in the MOOConly group watched videos more than once (the number of views is greater than the number of videos viewed), whereas those from the NurseTrainees group watched most videos once even if they re-watched the occasional video. In the self-report data, two of the 11 NurseTrainees who did not watch videos admitted they "didn't do any of the lessons" which consisted of the videos and ungraded quizzes, while others "really liked how there were practice questions using the videos because they helped [students] learn and apply the knowledge."

Table 4.4. Learner grades and LMOOC activities for NurseTrainees and MOOConly

Measures	NurseTrainees				MOOConly			
	Mdn	IQR	Min	Max	Mdn	IQR	Min	Max
MOOC grade	100	6	80	100	98	6	36	100
Number of posts	0	0	0	2	0	0	0	34
Lecture videos								
No. views	29	36	0	76	61	35	0	248
No. viewed	28	34	0	67	51	21	0	67
Quizzes (ungraded)								
No. attempts	132	180	5	341	203	119	5	698
No. attempted	22	25	5	36	34	17	5	37

Note: No. views is the number of times a learner began to watch a video. No. viewed is the total number of videos the learner began to watch. No. attempts is the number of times ungraded quizzes were submitted. No. attempted is the total number of ungraded quizzes the learner submitted at least once.

This difference in student re-watching habits was significant ($U=$ 25718.50, $p < 0.001$, $r = 0.27$). The NurseTrainees watched fewer lecture videos ($U = 29874.00$, $p < 0.001$, $r = 0.26$), attempted fewer ungraded quizzes ($U = 46240.50$, $p < 0.001$, $r = 0.11$), and performed fewer retesting activities ($U = 45892.00$, $p < 0.001$, $r = 0.11$) than students in the MOOConly group. These lower activity levels may reflect differences in group composition, with the NurseTrainees group consisting of fewer second-language learners and more healthcare professionals, with presumably greater background knowledge. NurseTrainees may have also had the support of an American clinical community of practice outside the LMOOC.

For those in the MOOConly group, the number of times they attempted ungraded quizzes had a moderately strong relationship with the number of videos they viewed ($r = 0.68$, $p < 0.001$) and a moderate relationship with the number of times they viewed those videos ($r = 0.43$, $p < 0.001$). This implies these students were re-watching the videos and redoing the ungraded quizzes as part of a review process rather than redoing the graded quiz as soon as possible following an incorrect response (i.e., 30 minutes later). Students in the NurseTrainees group showed similar relationships ($r = 0.82$, $p < 0.001$) between the number of ungraded quizzes that they attempted (Table 4.4, No. attempted row) and the number of videos they watched (No. viewed row). However, the relationship between the number of ungraded quizzes attempted by the NurseTrainees and the number of times they viewed videos was stronger ($r = 0.60$, $p < 0.001$) than that found for MOOConly students, suggesting these students took a more active approach to their learning.

RQ3: How does MOOC completion influence students' comprehension of clinical terminology when entering clinical settings?

Student self-reports indicate the Clinical Terminology LMOOC seemed to accomplish its goal of supporting vocabulary acquisition and transfer to real-world settings. This learning resulted in better comprehension and improved affect for NurseTrainees. Student claims that they were "able to follow … without having to look up what [teachers] were referring to when using abbreviations," especially "when entering clinical and lectures in the beginning of Fall semester," show the near transfer of knowledge (Cree & Macaulay, 2000) to instructional settings. Students also mentioned their ability to recognize the aural ($n = 23$) or written ($n = 29$) forms of abbreviations, providing evidence that the LMOOC prepared them for joining the nursing community of practice.

Twenty-three of the Nurse Trainees stated, knowing "more terminology … made the transition less overwhelming" and made "going into clinical less stressful" because they had "a clearer understanding of clinical terminology" and were not "scared that [they] wouldn't understand and … have to constantly ask what things mean." For those without prior medical experience, this meant they "could add to the conversation more," demonstrating higher levels of self-efficacy regarding clinical language use in speech (MacIntyre & Gregersen, 2012).This builds on prior work by showing that reducing listening anxiety (Elkhafaifi, 2005) improves student self-efficacy, which influences linguistic performance (Wang, Kao, & Liao, 2016).

Student perceptions were mixed when they had prior medical experience. One student credited the LMOOC with helping familiarize her "with a lot of common abbreviations … which made [her] feel like [she] at least knew something going into clinical." This familiarity with clinical discourse was also reported to help learners understand "what the other nurses were talking about and not having to ask the nurse about every abbreviation helped reduce stress." In contrast, some students with previous medical experience claimed they "don't remember specifically what [they] learned through the LMOOC or just picked up somewhere else." Some students also reported they could not "recall utilizing any skills taken from the course" and said, "if I recognized a term it was from a different source." These students may have acquired familiarity with some LMOOC vocabulary from prior experiences (e.g., hospital visits). Other students dismissed the course because they "already knew a lot of the language" and "don't constantly have to ask what things mean." These comments reflect the beginner-level nature of the course that did not account for pre-existing learner knowledge.

Conclusions

Those who completed the LMOOC demonstrated knowledge of the usage and meaning of targeted clinical terminology (RQ1). Moreover, those who were enrolled in a nursing program generally felt the LMOOC fostered their ability to understand the studied terminology when it was encountered in classroom and clinical settings (RQ3). While all students showed learning gains following multiple attempts at the graded quizzes (RQ2), comparing the LMOOC quiz performance and behaviors between those who were only enrolled in the online course and those who were also enrolled in a nursing program revealed several differences that ranged from LMOOC resource usage to domain-specific background training and language proficiency. These differences, student learning contexts outside of the LMOOC, and the LMOOC's assessment practices help to explain why both groups earned similar grades even though those in the nursing program did less and improved their scores to a greater extent from one quiz to the next. However, this online course's aim of having all learners acquire similar levels of vocabulary knowledge meant that enabling repeated attempts at learning and assessment was more important than being able to differentiate who learned clinical terminology the fastest or with the least effort. If greater differentiability were needed, additional assessment in clinical settings may have revealed differences in students' knowledge of how to use clinical terminology. The assessments that were employed and the delayed self-report provide evidence that LMOOCs and other online courses can support vocabulary learning when situated instructivist approaches are used. As a next step, the influence of this LMOOC on students' language usage in clinical settings could be explored to better detail the extent to which acquired knowledge transfers to real-world settings.

This study provides evidence for the potential of MOOCs to support language learning when these online courses focus on lower-level language skills that include vocabulary or listening comprehension. However, the state of current automated grading tools (Litman et al., 2016; Rahimi et al., 2017) means that higher-level skills, such as oral communication, cannot yet be meaningfully assessed in the types of large-scale environments that MOOCs aim to support. These types of tasks will need to remain the purview of smaller-scale online courses, where assessment of pragmatics and other elements of oral or written communication can be reliably assessed in a theoretically grounded way.

As the learning gains and experiences of the nursing students show, these scalable online courses can be used in conjunction with face-to-face programs to enable blended learning experiences that help to prepare learners for language use in professional settings (Swigart & Liang, 2016). These types of LMOOCs should also be integrable within online learning programs to provide supplementary instruction and allow learners to assess their knowledge in a low-stakes setting. The ability to perform ungraded LMOOC quizzes and re-attempt graded quizzes following a cooling-off period seems to have been an effective technique for supporting vocabulary learning because it increased learner exposure to vocabulary in context. The use of ungraded quizzes also forced a more active approach to processing learning materials and helped to prepare students for the graded quizzes, which is evidenced by the relationships between these activities and the scores earned by those who were only taking the course online.

The lack of difference between both groups' final LMOOC scores alongside their similar quiz-taking behaviors indicates the employed learning-by-testing approach can support specialized vocabulary training when test items are highly contextualized. Online language learning materials should therefore integrate assessment by contextualizing quiz items to take advantage of the fast and extended mapping principles (Carey, 2010). However, the LMOOC's provisioning of feedback that highlights correct and incorrect student responses may enable students to game the system and achieve higher scores without learning the content. Therefore, care must be taken when designing quizzes and online learning environments to ensure student learning. A combination of graded and non-graded quizzes should be used to ensure online courses effectively support vocabulary development. Immediate feedback is likely most appropriate for ungraded quizzes, with delayed feedback being more appropriate for graded quizzes. Gaming detectors can also be integrated into LMOOC or other computer-assisted language learning platforms to reduce the impact of gaming or other negative student behaviors (Baker et al., 2008). Alternatively, features could be developed that ask students to redo questions they had answered incorrectly; part of this process could involve asking students to link their new response to the learning materials upon which the answer is predicated.

Given the high enrollment found in MOOCs, better assessment mechanisms are required. The current approaches seem to support student learning but additional mechanisms, including those suggested above, are needed if we are to use the assessments from these online courses for anything other than formative feedback. As this early empirical work shows, the ungraded and graded quizzes commonly employed within MOOCs can be used to support language learning. The learner-initiated repetition of these and other learning activities (e.g., watching videos) seems to enable this support when students' primary language learning activity is the online course. When students have other domain-specific learning support (e.g., face-to-face courses), their use of online resources is less indicative of their performance on the assessments that are embedded within online language for specific purposes courses. This expands our understanding of the role these assessments and online courses can play in supporting this type of language learning.

About the Authors

Carrie DEMMANS EPP is a Research Associate at the University of Pittsburgh where she studies language learning and the use of technology to support learning. Prior to this, Carrie completed her PhD in mobile-assisted language learning at the University of Toronto, and she earned her MSc (University of Saskatchewan) in computer science with a focus on applying artificial intelligence techniques within computer-assisted language learning. Her work focuses on how to effectively use technology in educational settings.

Rae Mancilla, EdD, is an Instructional Designer in the Center for Teaching and Learning at the University of Pittsburgh. She works in the division of online learning and has published in numerous SLA and CALL journals including *Applied Linguistics*, *Learning Languages Journal*, and *Language Learning and Technology*. Her research focuses on written syntactic complexity, technology-enhanced language learning, and professional development for Instructional Designers.

Valerie Swigart, PhD, MSN, MEd, CRNP, is a full Professor of Nursing at the University of Pittsburgh. Her academic career has focused on the interface of technology, healthcare, ethics, and human behavior. She has completed two NIH funded studies with large qualitative databases. Her research has supported better understanding of the processes of surrogate decision-making regarding life-sustaining technology, the impact of long-term mechanical ventilation, homeless persons' healthcare-seeking behaviors, Middle Eastern women's experience of sexual harassment and domestic abuse, and the use of MOOCs in the flipped classroom. Teaching interests include international research and collaboration, cross-cultural communication, and ethical/social justice issues. She is currently teaching a massive open online course about clinical terminology that has reached thousands of students over the globe.

References

Anderson, A. (2010). Why testing boosts learning. *Scientific American Mind*, 21(6), 13–13. https://doi.org/10.1038/scientificamericanmind0111-13a

Baikadi, A., Schunn, C. D., Long, Y., & Demmans Epp, C. (2016). Redefining "what" in analyses of who does what in MOOCs. In *9th International Conference on Educational Data Mining (EDM 2016)* (pp. 569–570). Raleigh, NC, USA: International Educational Data Mining Society (IEDMS).

Baker, R. S., Corbett, A. T., Roll, I., & Koedinger, K. R. (2008). Developing a generalizable detector of when students game the system. *User Modeling and User-Adapted Interaction (UMUAI)*, 18(3), 287–314. https://doi.org/10.1007/s11257-007-9045-6

Bárcena, E., & Martín-Monje, E. (2015). Language MOOCs: An emerging field. In E. Martín-Monje & E. Bárcena (eds.), *Language and MOOCs: Providing Learning, Transcending Boundaries* (pp. 1–15). Warsaw and Berlin: De Gruyter Open Ltd.

Carey, S. (2010). Beyond fast mapping. *Language Learning and Development*, 6(3), 184–205. https://doi.org/10.1080/15475441.2010.484379

Chandrasekaran, M. K., Demmans Epp, C., Kan, M.-Y., & Litman, D. (2017). Using discourse signals for robust instructor intervention prediction. In *Thirty-First AAAI Conference on Artificial Intelligence (AAAI)* (pp. 3415–3421). San Francisco, CA, USA.

Choi, J.-I., & Hannafin, M. (1995). Situated cognition and learning environments: Roles, structures, and implications for design. *Educational Technology Research and Development*, 43(2), 53–69.

Coxhead, A. (2013). Vocabulary and ESP. In B. Paltridge & S. Starfield (eds.), *The Handbook of English for Specific Purposes* (pp. 115–132). Malden, MA: John Wiley & Sons Inc.

Cree, V. E., & Macaulay, C. (eds.). (2000). *Transfer of Learning in Professional and Vocational Education*. London and New York: Routledge.

Creswell, J. W., & Plano Clark, V. L. (2011). *Designing and Conducting Mixed Methods Research* (2nd ed). Los Angeles: Sage Publications.

Davis, D., Jivet, I., Kizilcec, R. F., Chen, G., Hauff, C., & Houben, G.-J. (2017). Follow the successful crowd: Raising MOOC completion rates through social comparison at scale. In *Proceedings of the Seventh International Learning Analytics & Knowledge Conference* (pp. 454–463). New York, NY, USA: ACM. https://doi.org/10.1145/3027385.3027411

Dixon, E., & Fuchs, C. (2015). Face to face, online, or MOOC: How the format impacts content, objectives, assignments, and assessments. In E. Dixon & T. Michael (eds.), *Researching Language Learner Interactions Online: From Social Media to MOOCs* (pp. 89–105). San Marcos, Texas: CALICO.

Elkhafaifi, H. (2005). Listening comprehension and anxiety in the Arabic language classroom. *The Modern Language Journal*, 89(2), 206–220. https://doi.org/10.1111/j.1540-4781.2005.00275.x

Ellis, R. (2009). *Task-Based Language Learning and Teaching* (7th impression). Oxford: Oxford University Press.

Ferguson, G. (2012). English for medical purposes. In B. Paltridge & S. Starfield (eds.), *The Handbook of English for Specific Purposes* (pp. 243–261). Malden, MA: John Wiley & Sons.

Gasevic, D., Kovanovic, V., Joksimovic, S., & Siemens, G. (2014). Where is research on massive open online courses headed? A data analysis of the MOOC Research Initiative. *The International Review of Research in Open and Distributed Learning*, 15(5). Retrieved from http://www.irrodl.org/index.php/irrodl/article/view/1954

Gee, J. P. (2006). *Situated Language and Learning: A Critique of Traditional Schooling* (reprint). New York: Routledge.

Geigle, C., & Zhai, C. (2017). Modeling MOOC student behavior with two-layer hidden Markov models. In *Proceedings of the Fourth (2017) ACM Conference on Learning @ Scale* (pp. 205–208). New York, NY, USA: ACM. https://doi.org/10.1145/3051457.3053986

Godwin-Jones, R. (2014). Global reach and local practice: The promise of MOOCs. *Language Learning & Technology*, 18(3), 5–15.

Henriksen, B. (2008). Declarative Lexical Knowledge. In D. Albrechtsen, K. Haastrup, & B. Henriksen (eds.), *Vocabulary and Writing in a First and Second*

Language: Processes and Development (pp. 22–66). New York: Palgrave Macmillan UK. https://doi.org/10.1057/9780230593404_2

Jones, L. (2004). Testing L2 vocabulary recognition and recall using pictorial and written test items. *Language Learning and Technology*, 8(3), 122–143.

Jordan, K. (2014). Initial trends in enrolment and completion of massive open online courses. *The International Review of Research in Open and Distributed Learning*, 15(1), 133–160. http://dx.doi.org/10.19173/irrodl.v15i1.1651

Kizilcec, R. F., & Halawa, S. (2015). Attrition and achievement gaps in online learning. In *Proceedings of the Second (2015) ACM Conference on Learning @ Scale* (pp. 57–66). New York, NY, USA: ACM. https://doi.org/10.1145/2724660.2724680

Kizilcec, R. F., Pérez-Sanagustín, M., & Maldonado, J. J. (2016). Recommending self-regulated learning strategies does not improve performance in a MOOC. In *Third Annual ACM Conference on Learning at Scale (L@S)* (pp. 101–104). New York, NY, USA: ACM.

Kizilcec, R. F., Piech, C., & Schneider, E. (2013). Deconstructing disengagement: Analyzing learner subpopulations in massive open online courses. In *Learning Analytics and Knowledge (LAK)* (pp. 170–179). New York, NY, USA: ACM. https://doi.org/10.1145/2460296.2460330

Koedinger, K. R., Kim, J., Jia, J. Z., McLaughlin, E. A., & Bier, N. L. (2015). Learning is not a spectator sport: Doing is better than watching for learning from a MOOC. In *Learning @ Scale* (pp. 111–120). New York, NY, USA: ACM. https://doi.org/10.1145/2724660.2724681

Lave, J., & Wenger, E. (2011). *Situated Learning Legitimate Peripheral Participation* (24th impression). Cambridge: Cambridge University Press.

Leonard, M., Graham, S., & Bonacum, D. (2004). The human factor: The critical importance of effective teamwork and communication in providing safe care. *Quality and Safety in Health Care*, 13(suppl. 1), 185–190. https://doi.org/10.1136/qshc.2004.010033

Levy, M. (2009). Technologies in use for second language learning. *The Modern Language Journal*, 93, 769–782. https://doi.org/10.1111/j.1540-4781.2009.00972.x

Litman, D., Young, S., Gales, M., Knill, K., Ottewell, K., van Dalen, R., & Vandyke, D. (2016). Towards using conversations with spoken dialogue systems in the automated assessment of non-native speakers of English. In *Proceedings of the 17th Annual Meeting of the Special Interest Group on Discourse and Dialogue* (pp. 270–275). Los Angeles: Association for Computational Linguistics. Retrieved from http://www.aclweb.org/anthology/W16-3635

Long, M. K., & Uscinski, I. (2012). Evolution of languages for specific purposes programs in the United States: 1990–2011. *The Modern Language Journal*, 96, 173–189. https://doi.org/10.1111/j.1540-4781.2012.01303.x

MacIntyre, P., & Gregersen, T. (2012). Affect: The role of language anxiety and other emotions in language learning. In S. Mercer, S. Ryan, & M. Williams (eds.), *Psychology for Language Learning* (pp. 103–118). London: Palgrave Macmillan UK. Retrieved from http://link.springer.com/10.1057/9781137032829_8

Manning, J. (2014, April 14). Comparing MOOC platform features [Academic]. Retrieved March 6, 2017, from https://teachingcommons.stanford.edu/ teaching-talk/comparing-mooc-platform-features

Martín-Monje, E., & Bárcena, E. (2015). *Language MOOCs: Providing Learning, Transcending Boundaries*. Retrieved from http://www.degruyter.com/isbn/ 9783110422504

Murray, L., & Vazirabad, A. F. (2015). Language MOOCs: Providing learning, transcending boundaries. *ReCALL*, 27(3), 358–361. https://doi.org/10.1017/ S0958344015000051

Olson, M. A. (2012). English-as-a-Second Language (ESL) nursing student success: A critical review of the literature. *Journal of Cultural Diversity*, 19(1), 26–32.

Rahimi, Z., Litman, D., Correnti, R., Wang, E., & Matsumura, L. C. (2017). Assessing students' use of evidence and organization in response-to-text writing: Using natural language processing for rubric-based automated scoring. *International Journal of Artificial Intelligence in Education*, 1–35. https://doi. org/10.1007/s40593-017-0143-2

Ramesh, A., Goldwasser, D., Huang, B., Duamé III, H., & Getoor, L. (2014). Learning latent engagement patterns of students in online courses. In *Twenty-Eighth AAAI Conference on Artificial Intelligence* (pp. 1272–1278). Retrieved from http://www.aaai.org/ocs/index.php/AAAI/AAAI14/paper/view/8571

Roediger, H. L., & Karpicke, J. D. (2006). Test-enhanced learning: taking memory tests improves long-term retention. *Psychological Science*, 17(3), 249–255. https://doi.org/10.1111/j.1467-9280.2006.01693.x

Schmidt, R. W. (1990). The role of consciousness in second language learning. *Applied Linguistics*, 11(2), 129–158. https://doi.org/10.1093/applin/11.2.129

Stephens, S., & Moxham, B. J. (2016). The attitudes of medical students toward the importance of understanding classical Greek and Latin in the development of an anatomical and medical vocabulary. *Clinical Anatomy (New York, N.Y.)*, 29(6), 696–701. https://doi.org/10.1002/ca.22700

Swigart, V., & Liang, Z. (2016). Digital resources for nursing education: Open courseware and massive open online courses. *International Journal of Nursing Sciences*, 3(3), 307–313. https://doi.org/10.1016/j.ijnss.2016.07.003

Veeramachaneni, K. (2014). Setting up the Coursera-MOOCdb transformation scripts [Academic]. Retrieved December 2, 2015, from http://moocdbdocs. readthedocs.io/en/latest/Coursera.html

Ventura, P., & Martín-Monje, E. (2016). Learning specialised vocabulary through Facebook in a massive open online course. *New Perspectives on Teaching and Working with Languages in the Digital Era*, 117.

Wang, X., Yan, D., Wen, M., Koedinger, K., & Rosé, C. P. (2015). Investigating how student's cognitive behavior in MOOC discussion forums affect learning gains. In *8th International Conference on Educational Data Mining (EDM)* (pp. 226–233). Madrid, June 26–29.

Wang, Y.-H., Kao, P.-F., & Liao, H.-C. (2016). The relationship of vocabulary learning strategies and self-efficacy with medical English and terminology. *Perceptual and Motor Skills*, 122(1), 47–66. https://doi.org/10.1177/0031512516628377

PART TWO

ASSESSING ONLINE TEACHERS

5 Issues and Challenges in the Assessment of Online Language Teacher Performance

Barbara Lafford,[*] Carmen King de Ramírez,[**] and James Wermers[***]

Introduction

In recent years there has been a surge in scholarship focused on the development of quality online second/foreign language (S/FL) instruction, including work on designing effective online courses and teacher preparation (e.g., Compton, 2009; Ernest et al., 2013; Hampel & Stickler, 2005; Hubbard & Levy, 2006; Kessler, 2006; Meskill & Anthony, 2007). However, at the same time that there has been a growing focus on developing quality online language education (e.g., distance courses, blended courses, learning management systems [LMSs] use in face-to-face [f2f] courses), there has been a relative dearth of scholarship on how to best assess language faculty performance in online environments. Some valuable studies touching on this topic have been published in the last ten years (e.g., Arnold et al., 2009; Compton, 2009; Hampel & Stickler, 2005; Lai, Zhao, & Li, 2008); however, several factors still complicate the assessment of online language teaching.

This chapter will focus on four issues involved in the assessment of online language teaching: uneven training/uneven institutional expectations, faculty resistance to online teaching and to their assessment as online instructors, diverse backgrounds among online instructors, and instruments used to assess the performance of online faculty. It will set out the challenges these factors present for carrying out such assessments, and possible solutions for meeting each of those challenges. The chapter will also

* Arizona State University, USA; blafford@asu.edu
** University of Arizona, USA; carmenking@email.arizona.edu
*** Arizona State University, USA; jwermers@asu.edu

include brief findings from a pilot study that provided a rationale for the focus on these four issues associated with online instructor assessment.

Issue #1: Uneven Training, Uneven Institutional Expectations

As surveys from Allen and Seaman (2008) and Parker, Lenhart, and Moore (2011) have shown, universities are increasingly relying upon online learning to help fulfill their academic and economic goals; this is a trend that includes, but is not limited to, a growing number of online FL courses. However, at the same time there is good evidence to suggest that faculty across disciplines remain wary of online (and other technologically mediated) instruction. According to a survey from Inside Higher Education (2016: 19) on faculty attitudes on technology, a majority of university faculty surveyed remain skeptical that "online courses can achieve student learning outcomes that are at least equivalent to those of in-person courses." This skepticism may stem from the lack of research comparing learning outcomes in these two environments. The dearth of these types of studies is due to the fact that extraneous variables (e.g., different instructors, different student pool, varying time on task) compromise comparative studies of student outcomes in f2f vs. online environments. Furthermore, while faculty surveyed overwhelmingly believe that "meaningful training" is essential to ensure high-quality online education, a majority feel there is inadequate institutional support for imparting online courses.

Behind both instructor concern for the quality of online courses across the disciplines and the quality of support offered to those teaching these courses, lies the reality that teaching online requires a monumental shift in how educators understand their craft. As Major (2015: 1) noted: "Teaching online means altering the ways in which we conceive of our work as teachers. It means rethinking our views and our abilities. It means developing new knowledge about teaching and media, new forms of pedagogy. ... It means rethinking how we develop materials as well as how we spend our time." Unpacking this concern further, Major (2015: 9) remarked that "When teaching online, technologies do not simply serve as functional instruments that can assist with instructional work. Instead, they serve to mediate our realities and, in so doing, become part of them." Major also proposed that teaching online requires that educators rethink everything they know about the theory and practice of teaching, and that they take on a variety of roles, including that of designer, media creator, content teacher, evaluator, etc.

There are a number of studies (e.g., Keengwe & Kidd, 2010; Ko & Rossen, 2010; Major, 2015; Tschida, Hodge, & Schmidt, 2016) that both chronicle the complexity of online teaching and provide insight on how educators, including FL educators, can best prepare to meet the demands of the online environment. However, despite a growing body of literature in the past 20 years, robust training that prepares faculty to both efficiently administer online courses and to rethink the practice of teaching for digital spaces (e.g., training that prepares faculty to thoughtfully engage socially mediated digital culture in their courses) remains the exception and not the norm (Major, 2015; Ko & Rossen, 2010). As Ko and Rossen (2010: 16) put it, "While more prevalent than in the early years of online education, still scarce is the availability of reliable and effective training for online instructors." All too often the mantra has become "do no harm" rather than "achieve excellence"; this is reflected in the persistent and troubling tendency to discuss "moving" or "porting" f2f classes into online environments – discussions that elide the complex shift identified by Major (2015) and Ko and Rossen (2010).

Another issue related to the lack of training in online pedagogy was articulated by Tobin, Mandernach and Taylor (2015: 14), "… Instructors who may or may not have been trained in pedagogical techniques are evaluated by peers and administrators who may or may not have a scholarly vocabulary (or the technical background) to be able to evaluate their online teaching practices." Unless this situation is resolved, online educators, and among them language teachers, will not be effectively evaluated and will not receive focused, expert feedback on their online teaching performance so they can improve. This is not to say that no work has been done on these issues. Scholars working on teaching FL online (Compton, 2009; Hubbard & Levy, 2006) have encouraged the kind of rich engagement with online pedagogy suggested by Major (2015) and others, but more such scholarship is needed in order to move the field of the assessment of online FL teaching forward.

There is no simple solution for the issues that arise when teaching online is treated as an extension of teaching in the classroom (e.g., when faculty assume that the way they may use an LMS in an online class is necessarily analogous to the way they may use it in an online course). That said, there are a few things educators can do to move in the right direction. First and foremost, FL educators need to keep in mind that teaching in online environments requires rethinking long-held beliefs. Many educators have no direct training in online pedagogy; even when training is provided, it is often focused on tools at the expense of a more robust understanding of digital pedagogy (Baran, Correia, & Thompson, 2011; Tschida, Hodge, & Schmidt, 2016). For example, instructors may receive special training to use a particular piece of software like an LMS (e.g., Blackboard, Angel,

Moodle, D2L, etc.), or other online courseware, but will not receive training that allows them to ground the use of that tool, and its potential limitations, in a rigorous understanding of digital pedagogies. In order to effectively move from f2f spaces and into online spaces, educators must recognize that the ways they have done things in the past – policies and practices rooted in decades of f2f education – may have to be revised or replaced in online environments (e.g., unseating the centrality of the professor [and the lecture format] in favor of socially mediated interaction).

Second, FL educators must be stakeholders in all aspects of online course design, administration, and evaluation. Many universities, including the large state universities at which the authors of this chapter work, have separated out the tasks of instructional design and online teaching and in the process have created a chasm between the individuals who develop FL courses (individuals whose training is more often than not in instructional design and not the specific subject area of a course) and the people teaching those courses (who are subject area experts). While there is ostensible practical value in such an arrangement, as faculty do not need to become technology experts and thus are free to focus on the business of teaching, these arrangements too often lead to situations where faculty are critically unaware of how digital environments shape student expectations, experiences, and performances, and of how to capitalize on emerging digital technologies to help students meet course outcomes (e.g., faculty may be unaware of how the LMS must effectively replace the physical architecture of the brick-and-mortar classroom in ways that both engage students and do not overtax cognitive load). Making FL faculty stakeholders in, and whenever possible responsible for, instructional design and its theoretical underpinnings would allow FL faculty to more effectively make the leap from f2f to online learning in ways that benefit both themselves and their students by pushing them to understand what is unique in online classes. This, in turn, would provide faculty with the requisite skills both to navigate existing online environments and to rethink those environments in ways that fuse their unique disciplines with the ever-expanding affordances of digital technologies (e.g., faculty could move away from replicating the physical classroom online and work to develop new ways of engaging students). This is, to be sure, something that would require an increased time commitment from faculty along with an increased financial commitment from colleges and universities, but it would be well worth the investment.

Third, as some FL scholars have suggested (Compton, 2009; Hubbard & Levy, 2006), institutions must work to provide high-quality training and support for online instructors – training and support that go beyond simple technology workshops. The kinds of mindfulness and design responsibility outlined above require a great deal of time and effort on the part of faculty. These efforts can be helped along at an institutional level by providing robust training for online faculty, high-quality support services, and compensation in keeping with these demands. This type of training is also crucial for instructors and administrators who need to evaluate online faculty, as the latter may resist being evaluated in a new teaching environment and their diverse backgrounds pose other challenges to the assessment process.

Issue #2: Faculty Resistance to Online Teaching and to Their Assessment as Online Instructors

Factors that may contribute to faculty resistance to online teaching, and their concomitant resistance to being assessed as pedagogues in virtual environments, include the loss of autonomy, the perception that online teaching is peripheral to their professional goals, lack of institutional incentives and support, the substantial time commitment involved, and their reluctance to reinvent themselves as pedagogues.

Language teachers at or above the level of Graduate Teaching Assistants (TAs) are usually accustomed to some degree of autonomy over curricular issues and the design/format of the course they teach, and may resist giving up that control. Unlike in other university departments (e.g., history, math, art), which utilize TAs mostly for ancillary tasks (e.g., attendance-taking, grading, leading small discussion groups instead of the primary lectures), FL departments give much autonomy to their graduate TAs, who are used to being responsible for teaching individual sections of a course (e.g., classroom instruction, creating classroom materials, dealing with student issues, serving as instructors of record for those sections). As a result, this expectation of a significant degree of pedagogical autonomy forms part of the FL instructor's disciplinary culture.

Online programs, including FL programs, vary in the amount of autonomy given to instructors at various levels; some online programs require faculty to take over a course that has already been created and may not give them authority to edit the content or the shell, while other programs allow changes to be made by individual instructors or by a team of pedagogues and course designers. Tenured/Tenure-track (T/TT) faculty often have complete autonomy over the initial creation of the course content and design of the course shell. However, in some institutions (e.g., Arizona State University, University of Arizona) faculty may also have to undergo training in best practices of online teaching before they can offer their courses in online environments and have their course shells approved by a central online authority before they can be offered.

As the expectations of various language faculty positions vary greatly, entering into online teaching and training may be seen as peripheral to the professional goals of faculty in certain ranks. For example, T/TT positions are evaluated largely on research production with little incentive for undertaking new pedagogical endeavors (Zhao & Cziko, 2001). The lack of incentives that the system offers to T/TT faculty interested in pedagogical innovation is compounded by the fact that novice online instructors must invest a considerable amount of time in familiarizing themselves with course materials, digital platforms, and resources provided by ancillary staff such as instructional designers and web programmers (Bartolic-Zlomislic & Bates, 1999; Stone & Perumean-Chaney, 2011). In addition, FL classes (as opposed to many online courses in other disciplines) require instructors to spend time interacting with students online (especially in courses that build basic communication skills). The significant number of hours required for interaction with individual students makes online FL teaching an extremely time-intensive commitment to undertake.

Thus, T/TT faculty coming up for tenure and/or promotion may be reluctant to engage in online teaching and training due to the lack of institutional incentives and the substantial time commitment it requires, especially when first creating online courses. Unless a T/TT faculty member's research is directly related to online pedagogy, spending time learning to create and teach courses online is seen as an activity that is not rewarded, as it is perceived as being marginal to their research-focused position. In addition, contract faculty who have heavy teaching loads or serve as Language Program Directors also have limited time to be trained and teach successfully online. The distractions from academic research and administrative duties presented by participating in online teaching may explain why part-time and adjunct faculty are more frequently assigned online teaching assignments than full-time faculty (Seaman, 2009).

While many T/TT faculty are reluctant to teach online, there are several advantages to the flexibility that online instruction allows. Experienced online professors have reported an increase in productivity as virtual instruction allowed them to spend more time on service or research (Meyer, 2012). In order to promote online courses as an attractive teaching option, faculty mentorship programs can be established. Such programs pair an experienced online instructor with a novice to mitigate fears associated with online instruction and share best practices (Gabriel & Kaufield, 2008; Zhao & Cziko, 2001).

Mentorships should be accompanied by formal department-sponsored workshops that highlight specific pedagogical tools used across course curricula. The authors of the current chapter have found that the most successful workshops for online FL faculty at their institution were those led by colleagues, as opposed to technology specialists who do not necessarily have experience in the classroom. Topics covered in workshops designed to transition f2f instructors to an online environment should concentrate on increasing instructors' knowledge of tools that are already available to them. For example, course management systems (CMSs), which are used by the majority of universities across the United States, are most frequently implemented as student tracking systems, as opposed to an effective interactive learning tool (Kim & Bonk, 2006). Workshops that encourage instructors to explore tools integrated into a CMS platform that they already use can enhance current f2f instruction as well as introduce techniques for student interactions in the virtual classroom. While these tools will vary according to the CMS program used at each university, some tools that can be used for FL instruction include VoiceThread for asynchronous oral presentations and discussions, and Adobe Connect for synchronous partner chats, breakout rooms, and tutoring.

Faculty resistance to online teaching also may be brought about by their reluctance to re-invent themselves as FL pedagogues (Strambi & Bouvet, 2003). Effective online courses require new approaches to the content and design of classes that instructors may have taught for years in a f2f environment. This resistance may be exacerbated when instructors who have taught extensively in face-to-face environments are asked to undergo training to become effective online language teachers. When experienced faculty who have been successful in traditional classrooms see themselves as accomplished professionals, they may perceive a threat to their self-image when told that they must substantially rethink and revise much of what they do in order to reflect best practices in online pedagogy. In addition, resistance to online instruction in a blended environment may partially stem from instructors' misperception of the function of the online component in the curriculum. For example, teaching assistants in Drewelow's (2013) study perceived the virtual portion of the blended class as a tutor to facilitate student communication in the f2f portion of the class. Their failure to understand their roles as moderators of communication in the online environment resulted in their perception that the online component "reduced their roles and presence in the classroom, becoming even an impediment to their teaching" (Drewelow 2013: 1015).

As instructors' self-perceptions of their success as virtual pedagogues (their self-knowledge that they are neophytes in this new environment) may cause them to resist assessments of their performance as online teachers, self-assessment (an integral part of in-depth qualitative assessments) becomes difficult. Instructors may not recognize that they need help and so their self-assessments may be very different than those of their supervisor. If professional and institutional factors change the conditions under which they are assessed, instructors may not be as initially successful at online teaching as they were in f2f environments. If instructors believe they are not being successful in this new environment they may opt out of the online instructor pool, which then reduces the number of instructors being evaluated. This reduced number of online FL instructors (and the concomitant drop in the number of subjects in studies of the evaluation of online language teaching) poses a threat of external validity to any generalizations that are made about online language instructors in assessment research.

Thus, in order to facilitate faculty buy-in to being evaluated as online language teachers there must be a cultural change within language departments so that online faculty training/assessment is considered equally important as f2f faculty training/assessment. This is best established by appointing a faculty member to advise online peers as well as hold them responsible for implementing best practices in the digital classroom. By identifying a point person for online coordination, efforts to develop online training and assessment tools are more likely to be continuous and address specific departmental needs. Furthermore, online coordinators may encourage changes in FL faculty's perspectives on digital pedagogies by inviting them to take part in the creation of new online rubrics and trainings. This buy-in to the online assessment process on the part of faculty will facilitate their willingness to participate in the evaluation process (e.g., thoughtful self-assessments, positive reception of feedback from supervisor assessments) and will, therefore, provide more meaningful assessments of online pedagogical performance. However, differences among faculty in their background training and online language teaching experience may complicate this buy-in process.

Issue #3: Training Instructor Populations with Diverse Experiences – A Pilot Study

While articles have been written on preparing language instructors to teach in online environments (Compton, 2009; Hubbard & Levy, 2006), there is little information about who these instructors are and what types of experiences they have as virtual pedagogues. One of the major challenges facing the assessment of online foreign language faculty is the diversity of instructor backgrounds (e.g., different levels of prior f2f and online FL teaching experience and concomitant perceptions of and attitudes toward online FL education, and differences in technological expertise, content knowledge of research in FL pedagogy, rank, perceptions of self-efficacy). These differences must be recognized in order for valid and reliable assessments of online FL teaching to take place. This section attempts to shed light on how the diversity of backgrounds affects the assessment of online language faculty. As the authors are not aware of publications that specifically analyze the relationship between background diversity and assessment in online FL instructors, they will provide a general overview of the issue and share brief findings of a pilot study they conducted with online FL faculty.

There are a number of studies that aim to establish faculty's perceptions of and experiences with online courses (Alodail, 2016; Bolliger, Inan, & Wasilik, 2014; Crews & Curtis, 2011; Stewart, Goodson, & Miertschin, 2010). Ozan, Wuensch, & Kishore (2011) is perhaps one of the most comprehensive studies published regarding faculty's perceptions of online education, with 46 institutions of higher education and 648 faculty represented. While this is a study that includes a large number of instructors from a variety of academic ranks (adjunct, lecturer, assistant/full professor), it fails to provide further background information that would clearly illustrate the multiple factors that contribute to faculty diversity (e.g., academic area of expertise, years of online experience, training in digital pedagogy).

The variation in backgrounds of online instructors was addressed by Koehler & Mishra (2009) who argued that very few of those faculty demonstrate equal competencies across the technology, pedagogy, and content knowledge (TPACK) spectrum. While in-depth studies dedicated to exploring the various facets of online faculty profiles have yet to be published, by piecing together faculty data found in studies of faculty perspectives and competencies (e.g., Ozan et al., 2011; Koehler & Mishra, 2009), it is clear that online instructors possess different levels of pedagogical experience, competencies, and academic ranking. This variation may also be reflected in a wide range of perceptions of self-efficacy among online instructors and may pose challenges for assessing those individuals. For example, experienced f2f instructors, who are comfortable with an established teaching style, may become more overwhelmed with online classes than novice teachers who are just beginning their career and are still developing an identity as pedagogues (Wolf, 2006). However, it could also be argued that veteran f2f instructors are more familiar with their institution's policies and resources and thus they hold an advantage over novice instructors, who are still adapting to their new career. In either case, an online instructor's sense of self-efficacy (formed, in part, through his/her self-assessment of their possession of TPACK elements) may ultimately influence his/her motivation for teaching online courses and may be influenced by the support received from colleagues and the administration (Gabriel & Kaufield, 2008; Meyer, 2012). A negative sense of self-efficacy may diminish the instructor's motivation to participate fully in the self-assessment process and lead to less effective evaluations of the instructor's abilities.

In order to understand more clearly how background diversity among online language instructors might affect the assessment process, the authors carried out a pilot study in 2013–2014. The pilot study found that language instructors varied greatly in their online expertise. The five Spanish instructors who participated in the study were teaching online during the period in which they participated in the online workshops and assessment process. All participants had extensive (10–15 years) face-to-face FL teaching experience but varied in their online teaching experience (0–6 years) and areas of academic expertise (i.e., linguistics, literature, education). Furthermore, of the five instructors, only two had received training in digital pedagogy before teaching their first online course.

Prior to the first online course they taught at the university, all of the instructors were provided a content populated LMS module, a detailed syllabus and an online course overview. At the end of the first year of online teaching, the coordinator evaluated the faculty with a basic rubric that represented the three categories of online tasks for which the instructors were responsible (course format, communication with students, instructor effort). In order to carry out the evaluation, the online coordinator entered each instructor's LMS to seek evidence for the criteria represented in the rubric. At the conclusion of the evaluation, the coordinator met with each instructor to discuss the evaluation outcome.

During the coordinator-instructor post-evaluation meeting, all five instructors expressed dissatisfaction with the evaluation system. For example, some instructors considered the language used in the rubric to be too vague while others claimed that the rubric contained technological jargon that was difficult to understand. Faculty members with previous online teaching experience voiced discrepancies between what past institutions had required and the present institution's expectations regarding virtual course design and instructor responsibilities. Novice online faculty especially struggled with trouble-shooting synchronous software used in their courses and a lack of assistance from university technical support. While some instructors struggled more with technology than others, all of the faculty members expressed some difficulties navigating the course LMS.

The grievances and discrepancies expressed in the first round of instructor evaluations pointed to variances in the instructors' online training, expectations, and initiative. In fact, in post-evaluation meetings, the biggest discrepancies between instructor and coordinator perspectives were among the two instructors who had several years of online teaching experience and formal online training. Despite the detailed materials and course overviews provided to instructors prior to their first online teaching experience, discrepancies were also found between self and coordinator evaluations of the three novice instructors. This first evaluation process made clear that despite an instructor's online teaching experience, it is imperative that a thorough training be led by each institution to ensure that instructors are up to speed with requirements specifically pertaining to the institution for which they are currently teaching. In order for trainings to be effective, language departments must present and adhere to a clear assessment tool that addresses the needs of all instructors.

The following semester, the same instructors began a 4-step evaluation process that included (1) presentation of a new rubric; (2) digital pedagogy workshops; (3) formal application of the rubric; (4) debriefing with the online coordinator. The revised rubric took into account additional skill sets suggested by scholars (Hampel & Stickler, 2005; Compton, 2009; Lai et al., 2008) and the development of functional computer literacy, critical literacy, and rhetorical literacy (Blake, 2013). Furthermore, the rubric facilitated differentiated assessment (Blaz, 2016) by measuring four levels of competency (novice, developing, accomplished, expert) across a variety of categories that represented the performance of a specific skill, changes in performance, the achievement standards, and individual effort.

In order to address differences in the faculty's backgrounds, the research participants were required to attend a series of eight digital pedagogy roundtables specifically designed for FL faculty. These roundtables, in which instructors could review and comment on the assessment tools by which they would be evaluated, were facilitated by the FL faculty member who designed the online Spanish-language curriculum and the department's digital humanities coordinator. These roundtables provided transparency in the evaluation process and promoted a collaborative approach to assessment that encourages accountability and emphasizes each instructor's role in improving the academic program as a whole (Rickards & Stitt-Bergh, 2016). This type of transparent evaluation process for the assessment of online language teaching can help to mitigate the deep dissatisfaction that many faculty have associated with previous evaluation and standardization practices (Banta & Pike, 2012; Fryshman, 2007; Hales, 2013). The results of this pilot study suggest that faculty participation in the assessment process should not be limited to the pre-evaluation stage but should extend through all stages of the evaluation process.

The required monthly roundtables addressed specific categories represented in the rubric (i.e., technology in online FL teaching, instructor facilitation, course structure, evaluation of online learners, professional development) as well as encouraged the discussion of and suggestions for the rubric revisions. Aside from familiarizing instructors with the assessment rubric, the roundtables also allowed experienced and novice instructors alike to discuss best practices in online education, express concerns about their own courses, and share ideas. The roundtable facilitators also aimed to ensure that online instructors worked from a common base of pedagogical knowledge by specifically addressing key concepts that would form part of their online instructor evaluation. In fact, specific categories represented in the online instructor rubric were presented at the roundtable sessions and faculty members' feedback was taken into consideration when adjustments were made to the rubric.

Toward the end of the semester, the instructors were given a copy of the rubric and asked to conduct a self-evaluation. In addition to assigning themselves a number on a 1–4 evaluation scale (novice, developing, proficient, expert), instructors were asked to provide evidence from within their LMS module that substantiated their self-rating. By having instructors provide observable components of their LMS as evidence, the coordinator was able to navigate more easily each instructor's LMS in order to locate information pertinent to the evaluation process. Not only did this step expedite the evaluation process but it also prepared both the coordinator and the instructor to approach the last step of the process (debriefing) with a greater awareness of the most salient strengths and weaknesses of the course/instructor.

The individual debriefing sessions lasted an average of 45 minutes and were primarily focused on discussing the instructor's experience with the course and setting professional and pedagogical goals for subsequent semesters. These sessions required both instructors and evaluators to reflect on and justify the assessment outcomes. These structured discussions were perhaps the most informative portion of the evaluation process as they provided specific feedback as well as an individualized action plan that took into account the different backgrounds and needs of each online instructor.

In the debriefing sessions and post-evaluation survey, instructors expressed much higher satisfaction with the 4-step collaborative evaluation than with the previous online teaching assessment conducted independently by the coordinator. The instructors attributed the success of the revised evaluation process to the solidarity they found among their online colleagues. Four of the five instructors indicated that they found their colleagues to be more helpful than the designated instructional technology expert in trouble-shooting virtual course issues.

The findings from this pilot study demonstrate that the challenges to ped-agogical assessment posed by diversity in instructors' pedagogical training, attitudes, and expectations can be effectively mitigated through a multi-step evaluation process that builds a community of practice that prepares instructors to effectively engage in the online environment. This evalua-tion process encourages the use of specific and varied assessment activi-ties, in keeping with current research on performance evaluation (Baartman et al., 2007; Knight 2000; Schuwirth & van der Vlueten, 2011; van der Vleuten, 2016). In addition, this multi-step process not only encourages the formation of a regular learning community but also facilitates differentiated assessment through pre- and post-instructor reflections. Blaz (2016) argues that differentiated assessment takes several factors into account (i.e., indi-vidual's performance of a specific skill, style of learning, and level of cogni-tive ability) and should reflect growth (changes in performance/knowledge/ skills from beginning to end of the unit), achievement (actual standards-based performance), and effort. As with students, differentiated approaches to assessment address instructors' unique and varied backgrounds and thus positively influence a sense of self-efficacy (Bandura, 1994; Shohani et al., 2015).

Aside from variances in online language instructors' personal expe-riences, professional and institutional factors affect the success and suc-cessful assessment of individual virtual pedagogues (Eteokleous, 2008). While motivated, entrepreneurial instructors are more likely to delve into new online projects, the emphasis that institutions place on innovation as well as the accessibility of professional development opportunities factor into instructors' implementation and continued use of new technologies (Drent & Meelissen, 2008; Riel & Becker, 2008). Institutional factors that account for discrepancies among virtual pedagogues include academic cul-ture, infrastructure, peer and administrative support, student expectations, and curricular flexibility (Ching & Hursh, 2014; http://www.sciencedirect. com.ezproxy4.library.arizona.edu/science/article/pii/S0360131513003357-bib29; Mueller et al., 2008). It is, therefore, difficult to carry out compara-tive assessments of the success of online faculty at different institutions (or even in different departments in the same institution) if expectations, administrative support, training, and assessment tools differ significantly from context to context.

In order to gather more information on the motivations and backgrounds of online FL instructors and the institutional contexts in which they work, FL departments can begin to address online instructor diversity through surveys that solicit information regarding online faculty's training and academic backgrounds as well as institutional and personal expectations and reservations. Given the lack of current information on the diversity of digital pedagogues, the authors propose a national survey that will provide data regarding the personal, professional and institutional backgrounds of online FL faculty. This information can help to create a national dialogue and foster inter-institutional solutions to reform these assessment processes and create more appropriate and flexible assessment instruments to evaluate online FL teachers.

In addition, with this information on instructor backgrounds at hand, existing lacunae can be identified and addressed in departmental trainings. By adapting training models to address the needs of diverse instructors, instructor self-efficacy is likely to increase and standards for online courses are more likely to be met; this is especially important in sequenced FL courses in which students will progressively move through a series of online language courses in the same department. Instructor trainings must be followed up with formal assessments that hold instructors accountable for implementing the department's preferred online methods and tools. In order to do so, assessment tools must be adapted to reflect the instructor's progress as he/she moves through specific benchmarks established in departmental trainings. Assessment tools should also address faculty diversity by requiring instructors to reflect on their own progress and set goals for individual improvement. The following section provides a critical evaluation of various instruments that can be used for this type of assessment.

Issue #4: Instruments Used to Assess Online Language Faculty

Universities are required to carry out annual evaluations of all faculty who teach in f2f and online environments (Watanabe, Norris, & González-Lloret, 2009). Rubrics to evaluate f2f teaching are prevalent and form an integral part of classroom observation feedback to instructors. In quality language programs, they regularly undergo scrutiny and revisions to help the rubric keep up with changes in pedagogical practice (Lord, 2014). However, as noted by Tobin, Mandernach, and Taylor (2015), rubrics to evaluate f2f language teaching are inadequate to address the metrics by which online language teachers should be assessed. For instance, the interaction that takes place among students and between teachers and learners in f2f language courses would be evaluated using a rubric designed for classroom observations by peers or supervisors. When assessing the interaction that takes place in online language teaching environments, the evaluation of the instructor's strategic use of various virtual communication tools to facilitate interaction would need to form part of a revised evaluation rubric that includes questions relevant to that environment (e.g., choice of the best tools to encourage different types of interaction, availability of chosen tools to students, creativity of interactive tasks that take advantage of the affordances of the online environment). Moreover, when departments look to extant professional rubrics for guidance in assessing online teaching (e.g., Compton, 2009; Quality Matters, 2014; TESOL, 2008), they find that these rubrics vary greatly in what they assess (e.g., course organization, technological knowledge, pedagogical skills, record-keeping, feedback, evaluative skills), the assumptions they make, and how progress in teaching ability is determined.

Although all three of the aforementioned rubrics provide statements against which elements of online instruction can be evaluated, the focal points of these instruments are somewhat distinct. For instance, the Quality Matters (2014) rubric concentrates on setting standards for evaluating the design of the online course and instructional products. In contrast, both Compton (2009) and the TESOL Technology Standards Framework (2008) contain statements that refer to the abilities acquired by the instructor. However, while Compton's framework assesses general skills acquired by instructors in the areas of technology, pedagogy, and evaluation of online language teaching, the benchmarks contained in the TESOL Technology Standards Framework (2008) are much more developed. The TESOL Technology Standards contain four main goals, each with 3–4 standards beneath them. The four primary goals are centered on foundational knowledge and skills in technology, integration of pedagogical knowledge and skills with technology to enhance language teaching and learning, the application of technology in record-keeping, feedback and assessment, and the use of technology to improve communication, collaboration, and efficiency. As there are important elements of the evaluation of online instruction that are unique to each instrument, it may be necessary to utilize more than one of these three rubrics to assess fully the abilities of online language teachers.

Another drawback of using the aforementioned rubrics is that none of them consistently provides fine-grained scales that can gauge progress on individual skills. For instance, Compton (2009) recognizes three levels of expertise in online language teaching skills (novice, proficient, and expert teachers). However, the differences in these levels are determined additively, by the possession of certain skills at the novice level and additional (more complex) skills at the proficient and at the expert levels, and not by the determination of the extent to which the online teacher controls each ability at each level.

Similarly, the TESOL Technology Standards Framework (2008) distinguishes between performance indicators for a basic and more expert level of technology for most of its standards, but this evaluation model is also additive in nature. Finally, Quality Matters (2014) is focused primarily on the way in which online courses are constructed and the clarity with which course elements are communicated to students. The parts of this rubric that may reflect teacher expertise are focused on evaluating the instructor-created structure and products for the course (given different weightings) rather than on the assessment of the development of the expertise of the instructor. It is, therefore, imperative that the narrow focus of these rubrics on certain elements of an online course be recognized and that a more comprehensive rubric be created that accounts for all factors relevant to online language teaching.

Another challenge presented by the use of the three extant rubrics in question is the fact that the metrics are often very general and not applicable or relevant when evaluating faculty charged with teaching a course created by others (e.g., Teaching Assistants who do not have full or even partial control over the curriculum and/or course shell development). In addition, these rubrics do not overtly consider prior experience with online teaching in their application (e.g., requiring a certain level of novice instructors and a higher level for experienced faculty). Thus, it is difficult to use only one rubric to evaluate the skills of different faculty who vary greatly in the amount of online experience they have and their control over course content and format.

Another deficiency of these rubrics is that none of them requires in-depth self-reflection on the instructor's ability to teach successfully in an online environment. Of the three rubrics in question, only the TESOL Technology Standards Framework (2008: 32, 39) requires some type of self-reflection, e.g., "teachers demonstrate understanding of their own teaching styles," "review personal pedagogical approaches," and "regularly reflect on the intersection of professional practice and technological developments." However, this rubric seems to have been created primarily to assist supervisors with teacher evaluations rather than to provide an instrument for instructors to assess their own progress.

Thus, language departments are challenged to figure out how to measure expertise in online language teaching and to evaluate developmental progress (via formative and summative assessments) of online language teachers in a field where extant professional rubrics do not measure similar objectives, lack the ability to carry out a fine-grained approach to assessment, and lack flexibility in their application and options for self-assessment/ reflection.

In order to address these issues, applied linguists and language supervisors will need to create flexible rubrics to measure abilities related to online teaching. These rubrics would be modular in nature, so that online language teachers could be evaluated using appropriate modules based on their past experience with online teaching and the control they have over the course materials and course format creation. Before applying these assessment rubrics, evaluators (supervisors and peer-reviewers) would participate in a norming session in which terms are defined and operationalized, and evaluations of online teaching would be carried out individually (and then compared) to see where discrepancies occur in the application of the rubric. The fine-grained rubric would measure instructor progress using descriptors that distinguish at least 3–4 levels of competence for each metric evaluated. The new rubric would also require self-reflection so that instructors who have participated in the aforementioned norming sessions could gauge their own progress regarding their incorporation of best practices of online language instruction (spelled out in the new modular rubric) into their teaching (King de Ramírez, Lafford, & Wermers, 2017).

In addition to arranging for faculty peer reviews and observations (monitoring of shells and teacher-student interaction), feedback on teaching, and regular evaluation of online instructors, FL departments need to provide ongoing professional development opportunities for language instructors that invite their input on ways to improve their online teaching skills and implement the best practices of online language instruction. Without such institutional support, initial FL faculty resistance to teaching in online environments may thwart the efforts of universities hoping to capitalize on the demand for online FL education.

Conclusions

This chapter has addressed issues and challenges of online FL instructor assessment related to uneven training and uneven institutional expectations, faculty resistance to online teaching and to their assessment as online instructors, diverse backgrounds among online instructors, and instruments used to evaluate the performance of online language faculty. While these factors can inhibit the creation of a collegial community of online language practice, viable solutions to these challenges have been presented in this study.

In order to implement these solutions, language departments must promote the creation of a community of practice that encourages the use of innovative pedagogical approaches to address the evolving role of 21st-century educators. In doing so, professional development opportunities must be made available to faculty, and systems of accountability for integrating these technologies into departmental curricula must be implemented (Wermers, King de Ramírez, & Lafford, 2014, 2015). While standardization of required elements of online courses is key to online student success, allowing some flexibility in the creation and implementation of course content will address the diversity of expertise found among faculty members. Flexibility must also be built into evaluative instruments used to assess the performance of FL instructors in online language courses; those instruments must recognize the diversity of instructor experience and the roles that faculty play in the creation and implementation of online language courses. In addition, faculty should provide input into the creation of the evaluation rubrics used to assess their performance in order to allow them to perceive themselves as stakeholders in the evaluation process.

Faculty who feel part of a supportive community of practice that recognizes and values their expertise as pedagogues and scholars and who work with administrations that reward their participation in innovative online language teaching programs are more likely to participate willingly and enthusiastically in online pedagogical training and assessment procedures. This enthusiasm, combined with professional development and administrative support, could help to position a department as a leader in the field of online language teaching assessment.

About the Authors

Barbara Lafford is a Professor of Spanish in the College of Integrative Sciences & Arts at Arizona State University (ASU). Her research areas include Spanish sociolinguistics, second language acquisition, Spanish applied linguistics, computer-assisted language learning, and languages for specific purposes. Professor Lafford has served as Associate Editor for the Applied Linguistics section of *Hispania*, President of the Board for CALICO (the Computer-Assisted Language Instruction Consortium), and as Editor for the Monograph/Focus Issue Series of the *Modern Language Journal* from 2005 to 2014.

Carmen King de Ramirez is an Assistant Professor of Spanish at the University of Arizona. She has worked as an online coordinator of Spanish courses at two major state universities, where she designed and launched course content for new Spanish programs. She serves as a certified online course reviewer for Quality Matters and is engaged in developing online pedagogy training for foreign language (FL) faculty and graduate students. Her research interests/publications include Online FL Pedagogy, Language for Specific Purposes (LSP), and Service Learning.

James Wermers is the Digital Humanities Course Manager for the Languages & Culture faculty in the College of Integrative Sciences and a Faculty Fellow in the Center for the Study of Race and Democracy at Arizona State University. James coordinates training, development, and deployment of digital pedagogy and digital initiatives for a 50-member interdisciplinary faculty at ASU, teaches courses in composition, film, gender studies, literature, philosophy, and religious studies, and works on innovative and engaging community programs, including "Philosophy and Film Series" and "Words on Wheels."

References

Alodail, A. (2016). The instructors' attitudes toward the use of E-learning in classroom in college of education at Al Baha University. *TOJET: The Turkish Online Journal of Educational Technology*, 15(1), 126–135. Retrieved from http://files.eric.ed.gov/fulltext/EJ1086229.pdf

Allen, E. I., & Seaman, J. (2008). Staying the course: Online education in the United States. The Sloan Consortium. Retrieved from http://www.sloan-c.org/publications/survey/pdf/staying_the_course.pdf

Arnold, N., Ducate, L., Lomika, L., & Lord, G. (2009). Assessing online collaboration among language teachers: A cross-institutional wiki case study. *Journal of Technology and Teacher Education*, 8(2), 121–139. Retrieved from http://pdxscholar.library.pdx.edu/cgi/viewcontent.cgi?article=1011& context=ling_fac

Baartman, L. K. J., Prins, F. J., Kirschner, P. A., & van der Vleuten, C. P. M. (2007). Determining the quality of competence assessment programs: A self-evaluation procedure. *Studies in Educational Evaluation*, 33(3–4), 258–281. http://dx.doi.org/10.1016/j.stueduc.2007.07.004

Bandura, A. (1994). *Self-Efficacy: The Exercise of Control*. New York: John Wiley & Sons.

Banta, T. W., & Pike, G. R. (2012). Making the case against – one more time. In R. Benjamin (ed.), *The Seven Red Herrings about Standardized Assessment in Higher Education* (NILOA Occasional Paper No. 15, pp. 24–30). Urbana, IL: University of Illinois and Indiana University, National Institute for Learning Outcomes Assessment.

Baran, E., Correia, A. P., & Thompson, A. (2011). Transforming online teaching practice: Critical analysis of the literature on the roles and competencies of online teachers. *Distance Education*, 32(3), 421–439. http://dx.doi.org/10.1080/01587919.2011.610293

Bartolic-Zlomislic, S., & Bates, A. T. (1999). Investing in on-line learning: Potential benefits and limitations. *Canadian Journal of Communication*, 24(3). Retrieved from http://www.cjc-online.ca/index.php/journal/article/view/ 1111/1017

Blake, R. (2013). *Brave New Digital Classroom: Technology and Foreign Language Learning* (2nd ed.). Washington, DC: Georgetown University Press.

Blaz, D. (2016). *Differentiated Instruction: A Guide for World Language Teachers* (2nd ed.). New York: Routledge.

Bolliger, D. U., Inan, F. A., & Wasilik, O. (2014). Development and validation of the Online Instructor Satisfaction Measure (OISM). *Educational Technology & Society*, 17(2), 183–195. Retrieved from http://www.jstor.org/stable/jeductechsoci.17.2.183

Ching, C. C., & Hursh, A. W. (2014). Peer modeling and innovation adoption among teachers in online professional development. *Computers & Education*, 73, 72–82. http://dx.doi.org/10.1016/j.compedu.2013.12.011

Compton, L. K. L. (2009). Preparing language teachers to teach language online: A look at skills, roles, and responsibilities. *Computer Assisted Language Learning*, 22(1), 73–99. http://dx.doi.org/10.1080/09588220802613831

Crews, T. B., & Curtis, D. F. (2011). Online course evaluations: Faculty perspective and strategies for improved response rates. *Assessment & Evaluation in Higher Education*, 36(7), 865–878. http://dx.doi.org/10.1080/02602938.2010.493970

Drent, M., & Meelissen, M. (2008). Which factors obstruct or stimulate teacher educators to use ICT innovatively. *Computers & Education*, 51(1), 187–199. http://dx.doi.org/10.1016/j.compedu.2007.05.001

Drewelow, I. (2013). Exploring graduate teaching assistants' perspectives on their roles in a foreign language hybrid course. *System*, 41(4), 1006–1022. http://dx.doi.org/10.1016/j.system.2013.09.007

Ernest, P., Catasus, M. G., Hampel, R., Heisner, S., Hopkins, J., Murphy, L., & Stickler, U. (2013). Online teacher development: Collaborating in a virtual learning environment. *Computer Assisted Language Learning*, 26(4), 311–333. http://dx.doi.org/10.1080/09588221.2012.667814

Eteokleous, N. (2008). Evaluating computer technology integration in a central-ized school system. *Computers & Education*, 51(2), 669–686. http://dx.doi.org/10.1016/j.compedu.2007.07.004

Fryshman, B. (2007). Outcomes assessment: No gain, all pain. *Inside Higher Education*. Retrieved from https://www.insidehighered.com/views/2007/11/13/fryshman

Gabriel, M., & Kaufield, K. (2008). Reciprocal mentorship: An effective support for online instructors. *Mentoring & Tutoring: Partnership in Learning*, 16(3), 311–327. http://dx.doi.org/10.1080/13611260802233480

Hales, S. (2013, March 11). Who's assessing the assessors' assessors? *Chronicle of Higher Education*. Retrieved from http://chronicle.com/article/Whos-Assessing the-Assessors/137829

Hampel, R., & Stickler, U. (2005). New skills for new classrooms: Training tutors to teach languages online. *Computer Assisted Language Learning*, 18(4), 311–326. https://doi.org/10.1080/09588220500335455

Hubbard, P., & Levy, M. (eds.). (2006). *Teacher Education in CALL*. Amsterdam: John Benjamins.

Inside Higher Education (2016). *Quality Matters Standards from the QM Higher Education Rubric* (5th ed.). Retrieved from https://www.insidehighered.com/node/175121/download/0fa76a88cc33735c76f662735d86ee30

Keengwe, J., & Kidd, T. T. (2010). Towards best practices in online learning and teaching in higher education. *Journal of Online Learning and Teaching*, 6(2), 533–541. Retrieved from https://pdfs.semanticscholar.org/3494998f1c80c7745998d969686f394aaddb6735.pdf

Kessler, G. (2006). Assessing CALL teacher training: What are we doing and what we could do better? In P. Hubbard & M. Levy (eds.), *Teacher Education in CALL* (pp. 23–44). Philadelphia: John Benjamins.

Kim, K., & Bonk, C. J. (2006). The future of online teaching and learning in higher education: The survey says. *Educause Review*, 22–30. Retrieved from http://er.educause.edu/articles/2006/1/the-future-of-online-teaching-and-learning-in-higher-education-the-survey-says

King de Ramírez, C., Lafford, B., & Wermers, J. (2017). Evaluating online language instructors. Workshop given at the annual meeting of the Computer-Assisted Language Instruction Consortium (CALICO), Flagstaff, AZ, May 2017.

Knight, P. T. (2000). The value of a programme-wide approach to assessment. *Assessment & Evaluation in Higher Education*, 25(3), 237–251. http://dx.doi.org/10.1080/713611434

Ko, S., & Rossen, S. (2010). *Teaching Online: A Practical Guide* (3rd ed.). New York: Routledge.

Koehler, M. J., & Mishra, P. (2009). What is technological pedagogical content knowledge. *Contemporary Issues in Technology and Teacher Education*, 9(1), 60–70. Retrieved from https://citejournal.s3.amazonaws.com/wp-content/uploads/2016/04/v9i1general1.pdf

Lai, C., Zhao, Y., & Li, N. (2008). Designing a distance foreign language learning environment. In S. Goertler & P. Winke (eds.), *Opening Doors through Distance Language Education: Principles, Perspectives, and Practices*. CALICO Monograph Series Vol. 7 (pp. 85–108). Texas: Computer Assisted Language Instruction Consortium (CALICO).

Lord, G. (2014). *Language Program Direction: Theory and Practice*. Upper Saddle River, NJ: Pearson.

Major, C. H. (2015). *Teaching Online: A Guide to Theory, Research, and Practice*. Baltimore, MD: Johns Hopkins University Press.

Meskill, C., & Anthony, N. (2007). Learning to orchestrate online instructional conversations: A case of faculty development for foreign language educators. *Computer Assisted Language Learning*, 20(1), 5–19. http://dx.doi.org/10.1080/09588220601118487

Meyer, K. (2012). The influence of online teaching on faculty productivity. *Innovative Higher Education*, 37(1), 37–52. http://dx.doi.org/10.1007/s10755-011-9183-y

Mueller, J., Wood, E., Willoughby, T., Ross, C., & Specht, J. (2008). Identifying discriminating variables between teachers who fully integrate computers and teachers with limited integration. *Computers & Education*, 51(4), 1523–1537. http://dx.doi.org/10.1016/j.compedu.2008.02.003

Ozan, E., Wuensch, K., & Kishore, M. (2011). Instructors' attitudes on online education delivery systems: An analysis of a comprehensive study. International
Conference on Information Technology Based Higher Education. Retrieved
from http://ieeexplore.ieee.org/document/6018695/

Parker, K., Lenhart, A., & Moore, K. (2011). The digital revolution and higher
education: College presidents, public differ on value of online learning. Pew
Internet & American Life Project. Retrieved from http://www.pewsocialtrends.
org/2011/08/28/the-digital-revolution-and-higher-education

Quality Matters (2014). *Quality Matters Standards from the QM Higher Education
Rubric* (5th ed.). Retrieved (via subscription) from https://www.qualitymatters.
org/rubric.

Rickards, W. H., & Stitt-Bergh, M. (2016). Higher education evaluation, assessment, and faculty engagement. *New Directions for Evaluation*, 2016(151),
11–20. http://dx.doi.org/10.1002/ev.20200

Riel, M., & Becker, H. J. (2008) Characteristics of teacher leaders for information
and communication technology. In J. Voogt & G. Knezek (eds.), *International
Handbook of Information Technology in Primary and Secondary Education*
(pp. 397–417). New York: Springer.

Schuwirth, L., & van der Vleuten, C. P. M. (2011). Programmatic assessment:
From assessment of learning to assessment for learning. *Medical Teacher*, 33,
478–485. http://dx.doi.org/10.3109/0142159X.2011.565828

Seaman, J. (2009). *Online Learning as a Strategic Asset. Volume II: The Paradox
of Faculty Voices – Views and Experiences with Online Learning*. New York:
Association of Public and Land-Grant Universities. Retrieved from http://files.
eric.ed.gov/fulltext/ED517311.pdf

Shohani, S., Azizifar, A., Gowhary, H., & Jamalinesari, A. (2015). The relationship
between novice and experienced teachers' self-efficacy for personal teaching and external influences. *Procedia – Social and Behavioral Sciences*, 185,
446–452. http://dx.doi.org/10.1016/j.sbspro.2015.03.357

Stewart, B. L., Goodson, C., & Miertschin, S. L. (2010). Off-site faculty:
Perspectives on online experiences. *Quarterly Review of Distance Education*,
11(3), 187–191. Retrieved from https://www.learntechlib.org/p/53213/

Stone, M. T., & Perumean-Chaney, S. (2011). The benefits of online teaching
for traditional classroom pedagogy: A case study for improving face-to-
face instruction. *MERLOT Journal of Online Learning and Teaching*, 7(3),
393–400. Retrieved from http://jolt.merlot.org/vol7no3/stone_0911.htm

Strambi, A., & Bouvet, E. J. (2003). Flexibility and interaction at a distance: A
mixed-model environment for language learning. *Language Learning &
Technology*, 7(3), 81–102. Retrieved from http://llt.msu.edu/vol7num3/pdf/
strambi.pdf

TESOL (2008). *TESOL Technology Standards Framework*. Alexandria, VA:
TESOL. Retrieved from http://www.tesol.org/docs/default-source/books/
bk_technologystandards_framework_721.pdf

Tobin, T. J., Mandernach, B. J., & Taylor, A. H. (2015). *Evaluating Online Teaching:
Implementing Best Practices*. Boston: Wiley.

Tschida, C. M., Hodge, E. M., & Schmidt, S. W. (2016). Learning to teach online:
Negotiating issues of platform, pedagogy, and professional development. In

Teacher Education: Concepts, Methodologies, Tools, and Applications (pp. 1275–1296). Hershey, PA: IGI Global.

van der Vleuten, C. P. M. (2016). Revisiting "Assessing professional competence: From methods to programmes." *Medical Education, 50,* 885–888. http://dx.doi.org/10.1111/medu.12632

Watanabe, Y., Norris, N. & González-Lloret, M. (2009). Identifying and responding to evaluation needs in college foreign language programs. J. M. Norris, J. McE. Davis, C. Sinicrope, & Y. Watanabe (eds.), *Toward Useful Program Evaluation in College Foreign Language Education* (pp. 5–58). Honolulu: University of Hawai'i, National Foreign Languages Resource Center.

Wermers, J. E., King de Ramirez, C., & Lafford, B. (2014). Evaluating online foreign language faculty: Issues & Instruments. Paper presented at the annual meeting of the Computer Assisted Language Instruction Consortium (CALICO), Athens, OH, May 2014.

Wermers, J. E., King de Ramirez, C., & Lafford, B. (2015). A new instrument for evaluating online foreign language faculty. Paper presented at the annual meeting of the Computer Assisted Language Instruction Consortium (CALICO), Boulder, CO, May 2015.

Wolf, P. D. (2006). Best practices in the training of faculty to teach online. *Journal of Computing in Higher Education, 17*(2), 47–78. http://dx.doi.org/10.1007/BF03032698

Zhao, Y., & Cziko, G. A. (2001). Teacher adoption of technology: A perceptual control theory perspective. *Journal of Technology and Teacher Education, 9*(1), 5–30. Retrieved from http://leegreen.wiki.westga.edu/file/view/Teacher+adoption+of+technology-+A+perceptual+control+theory+perspective.pdf

6 Evaluating Teacher Tech Literacies Using an Argument-Based Approach

Jesse Gleason* and Elena Schmitt**

Introduction

Across the United States, the need for language teachers with technology-specific literacies is climbing, yet many teachers may be underprepared for such positions due to inadequate experience with or training in computer-assisted language learning (CALL) (Godsey, 2015; Lynch, 2016). What is more, language teacher education programs may struggle to equip teacher candidates with the tools they need to approach an ever-changing multi-modal landscape (Borthwick & Gallagher-Brett, 2014; Nami, Marandi & Sotoudehnama, 2016; Sehlaoui & Albrecht, 2009). In the Northeastern US, in a region with critical need for language teacher training, faculty in an MS Bilingual Education & TESOL program took up the challenge to train PK-12 teachers using state-of-the-art videoconferencing technology. The present study showcases data taken from one course in this program, and uses an argument-based approach to validity (Chapelle, Enright & Jamieson, 2008; Kane, 2006) to make the claims that teachers in this course (a) were able to transform their traditional face-to-face teaching practices to sophisticated technology-mediated teaching practices within a synchronous online environment and (b) had equivalent content learning opportunities to those in the on-ground courses.

Language Teacher Education and Technology

The language teaching profession has been a leader in the pedagogical application of technology since the emergence of the Audiolingual method

*   Southern Connecticut State University, USA; gleasonj8@southernct.edu
**   Southern Connecticut State University, USA; schmitte1@southernct.edu

in the 1950s (Brooks, 1964; Richards & Rodgers, 2014). This leadership continues today as evidenced by the multitude of professional associations (CALICO, IALLT, AAAL-TEC, etc.) and academic journals (e.g., *CALICO, Language Learning & Technology, System*, etc.) dedicated to the topic, as well by the growth of graduate programs that focus on language learning with technology. At present, the exploration of technology for language teacher education has sought to bring language instructors closer together by means of telecollaborative virtual exchange programs, videoconferencing (VC), and synchronous chats, among many other innovative curricular uses. As a result, teacher education programs must ensure that their candidates receive adequate opportunities to gain practice incorporating the emerging technological infrastructure into their overall curricular blueprints (Sehlaoui & Albrecht, 2009).

Language teacher preparation programs have a responsibility to develop technologically literate professionals. The International Technology Education Association (ITEA) defines *technological literacy* as "the ability to use, manage, assess, and understand technology" (ITEA, 2003: 9). Following Cope and Kalantzis (2015) and New London Group (1996), we would argue that the term "new literacies" or "multi-literacies" is more relevant as it highlights the multitude of multi-modal, technology-mediated spaces and environments in which we live and learn today. Under the premise that they must be apprenticed into the communities of practice of their disciplines (Walqui & van Lier, 2010), teachers must – at least in part – have the opportunity to develop their technological *literacies* (knowledge and skills) within specialized communities of practice. How do we ensure that teacher education programs accomplish this? As Darling-Hammond et al. (2005: 200) argue: "For teacher preparation institutions to ensure that teachers know how to use the technologies that are part of the professional communities of practice, these, too, need to be infused into the content pedagogical courses that teachers take, so that they are using the tools within the disciplines themselves, not just learning about them in the abstract."

Teachers must have the opportunity to use the tools in the discipline of language teaching within their graduate programs in TESOL and Bilingual Education. As Darling-Hammond et al. (2005) suggest, the first and necessary step to building teacher tech literacies involves apprenticing teachers into the specialized communities of practice that will allow them to experience the types of learning that they can carry on into their own classrooms at a later date. Therefore, teacher education programs must provide the appropriate spaces, assignments, assessments, and learning goals that not only allow them to try out emerging technologies for pedagogical purposes but also involve mentorship into communities of practice that utilize these technologies.

This chapter showcases how viewing the development of teacher tech literacies through an argument-based approach to validity can help ensure that graduate teacher education programs offer teacher candidates opportunities to take part in specialized communities of practice that prepare them to use technology in practical and innovative ways. This preparation will help them transform their teaching, which may consist primarily of traditional face-to-face (f2f) pedagogies, into instruction that involves sophisticated uses of technology in synchronous and asynchronous computer-mediated communication (CMC) environments.

An Argument-Based Approach to Validity

Evaluation of teacher tech literacies is inherently complex (Borthwick & Gallagher-Brett, 2014; Nami et al., 2016). With the goalpost of educational technology in constant motion, measurement of teacher tech literacies in terms of specific technological tools is liable to be quickly outdated. Therefore, we must assess teacher tech literacies beyond their use or facility with individual technological tools. In order to incorporate the multitude of ways and contexts in which language teachers may use technology with their own current or future students, we propose an argument-based approach to validity (hereafter "an argument-based approach").

An argument-based approach (Bachman & Palmer, 2010; Kane, 2006; Messick, 1989) provides a framework for evaluating teacher tech literacies that does not depend on any tool or program per se, but one which can use evidence from specific contexts as backing to support claims about teachers' readiness to engage with technology for teaching in multimodal environments. An argument-based approach entails the development of two types of argument: (a) an *interpretive argument*, which provides a conceptual roadmap for justifying the use and interpretation of some measure, and later (b) a *validity argument*, which entails a critical analysis of evidence to support the inferences of the interpretive argument. This approach is based on practical argument structure (Toulmin, 2003), which has been commonly applied in non-mathematical fields such as law, sociology, and literary analysis (Chapelle et al., 2008). An argument-based approach entails linking chains of reasoning (claims) together on the basis of data or observations (grounds). Figure 6.1 shows an example of this for the *domain definition* inference, the first step in an interpretive chain of reasoning, which, within this study, relates the skills of using technology in general to using technology for specific pedagogical tasks.

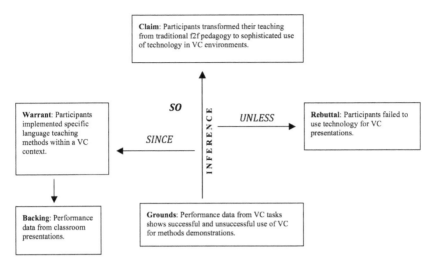

Figure 6.1. An example structure of the domain definition inference of an interpretive argument for teacher tech literacies

According to Jamieson et al. (2008), the assumptions underlying the domain definition inference include ensuring that the types of assessment tasks that take place in the classroom (pedagogical domain) are representative of the academic domains in which teachers will eventually work with their own students (target language use domain). In other words, in order to ascertain how teacher candidates might be expected to perform in the real-world domain (i.e., their classrooms), we first need to ensure that teachers are successfully executing learning tasks that assess their technology-specific literacies over the course of their professional development or graduate study.

Once a clear domain has been defined, the second inference called *evaluation* makes the claim that our observations of student performance on assessment tasks are evaluated in a way that allows us to provide observed scores that are reflective of the targeted abilities (Chapelle et al., 2008). Backing is provided in the form of equivalent scoring on the rubric used to evaluate teachers' effectiveness in delivering instruction using different language teaching methods across VC and on-ground courses. Observed teacher candidate performance is examined as a measure of tech-mediated teaching, which is highly relevant for determining the meaning of in-class practice for future authentic teaching performance. Figure 6.2 showcases five inferences of a possible interpretive/validity argument, specifically those of: *domain definition, evaluation, generalization, extrapolation,* and *utilization.* To support the first two inferences of an interpretive argument

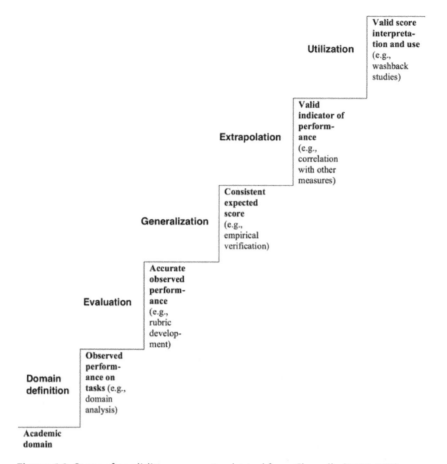

Figure 6.2. Steps of a validity argument, adapted from Chapelle (2008: 349)

(domain definition and evaluation), backing for this study is provided in the form of direct evidence of teachers using and being evaluated on their use of synchronous CMC for the demonstration of specific language teaching methodologies during a TESOL methods course taught entirely using VC.

As shown above, an argument-based approach allows us to construct a chain of reasoning that will determine our participants' facility with technologically infused pedagogies. It begins with the domain definition inference, which clearly lays out the context and the technologies used within this context as a prerequisite to further evaluation. Although domains for language teacher education may change as can the technologies within these contexts, clearly describing the domain in our context allows us to subsequently evaluate teachers' tech literacies for language instruction in our domain-specific environment. The second inference of the interpretive argument, evaluation, allows us then to assess context-specific teacher tech literacies to ensure comparability across on-ground and VC course modalities. Although a full interpretive and subsequent validity argument, as shown in Figure 6.2, is beyond the scope of the present chapter, we will show how the first and second inferences of an interpretive argument play a role in evaluating teacher candidates' tech literacies in a VC course environment.

Methods

Context and Participants

The data for our study were collected during the third semester of a required TESOL methods course in an MS in Bilingual, Multicultural Education and TESOL program at a medium-sized university in the Northeastern US. Courses in this program were taught in both on-ground formats as well as in a newly instated VC format, which included students who were on campus as well as those who connected to campus from a distant location, two hours from the university's main campus. Without the distant course option, English-to-speakers-of-other-languages (ESOL) teacher candidates, many of whom were practicing PK-12 teachers working full-time at schools across the state, could not have enrolled in the graduate program at this institution.

A total of 12 teacher candidates participated in this course: six were located at a distant location and six participated from the university's on-campus technology-equipped classroom. All the ESOL teacher candidates were matriculated graduate students. The off-campus group was located within two hours' drive from the university and gathered in the same classroom for a total of 2.5 hours of class weekly. Self-reported data indicated that only one of the ESOL teacher candidates had significant experience with technology prior to entering the MS TESOL program, and it was he who served as the tech liaison for his school district. The other ESOL teacher candidate participants reported a basic technological understanding and experience that included work-related use of computers, overhead projectors, video and audio equipment. All ESOL teacher candidates from the distant cohort had taken two prior courses in the graduate program using the same VC technology in the two semesters leading up to this study. Only half of the on-campus cohort had participated in a VC-technology-mediated synchronous online course prior to taking this class. Thus, the majority of students (75%) had experience using the particular state-of-the-art technology available in the videoconferencing classroom before the start of the semester.

The videoconferencing classroom on-campus was equipped with a Cisco Sx80 Telepresence system, two Precision 60 cameras, several Clear One Pendant microphones, three 70" HD monitors, a Touch Panel room controller, and a wireless Lavelier microphone for the instructor. The classroom used an SIP gateway to receive telepresence phone calls and also had the ability to use the BlueJeans telecollaboration service to which the university was subscribed. The distant videoconferencing classroom was also equipped with two monitors, but had none of the other state-of-the-art features, such as a touch screen or pendant microphones. Instead, the distant cohort had to rely on a more basic technological setup than the on-campus students.

Data Collection and Analysis

The data in our study were captured by videorecording 10 out of 15 total class meetings over the course of one semester. The videorecorded sessions focused on capturing the ESOL teacher candidates' teaching demonstrations using a variety of traditional and contemporary language teaching methodologies. These methodologies created a broad theoretical foundation upon which further development of more specialized techniques for teaching English learners (ELs) would be built during a second TESOL methods course the following semester. The rest of the time in the course, ESOL teacher candidates engaged in discussions about the connections between second language acquisition theory and language teaching methodologies. The researchers, faculty members in the MS TESOL graduate program, viewed the videorecordings of these class meetings and carefully selected three teaching demonstrations for qualitative multimodal analysis by two experienced and one inexperienced teacher candidates. This selection was guided by our goals to shed light on how ESOL teacher candidates' implementation of different pedagogical methodologies could be adapted to the VC environment as well as to determine whether ESOL teacher candidates were capable of successfully engaging with technology to implement their teaching demonstrations. Each of the three selected demonstrations included a different approach to language teaching: (a) a student-centered experiential methodology using Total Physical Response (c.f. Asher, 1982), (b) a teacher-directed methodology like the Audiolingual method (c.f. Brooks, 1964), and (c) a task-based methodology (c.f. Nunan, 2004; Willis & Willis, 2007).

In order to determine teacher candidates' success delivering language tasks using VC, an assessment rubric was used (Appendix A). This rubric was developed and implemented for a number of years prior to this study to evaluate teacher candidates' demonstrations of various teaching methodologies in the on-ground graduate classes. To illustrate that teacher candidates' delivery of teaching methods using VC was equivalent to that of on-ground courses, we used the same rubric as in the past to compare their scores. We also transcribed the oral discourse of the selected demonstrations and then conducted a multimodal analysis, which included checking for the presence of the unique features of each method as well as coding multimodal (e.g., movements, body language, gestures) and linguistic data across on-campus and distant classrooms.

Our analysis focused on providing evidence for the Warrant for the domain definition inference (shown in Figure 6.1) that ESOL teacher candidates implemented specific language teaching methods within VC contexts across campuses, in order to provide backing in the form of performance data from classroom assignments. The results of this analysis, including teacher candidates' ability to accommodate their teaching demonstrations to the VC context and thus showcase their growing reliance on technology in language teaching, form the topic of the following sections.

Results

The results from our analysis of the teaching demonstrations showed that all the teacher candidates were able to adjust to a technology-rich environment. Table 6.1 reports the teacher candidates' scores on the teaching demonstrations across on-ground and distant pedagogical applications based on the assessment rubric in Appendix A. Through these scores as well as our observation of teacher candidates' performance, it became evident that ESOL teacher candidates were able to effectively integrate the new VC context into their teaching.

The equivalency of scores across teacher candidates' demonstrations from both on-ground and VC sections indicates that all teacher candidates were able to modify their teaching for the VC. However, a detailed qualitative analysis of the performance data during the VC teaching demonstrations shows that not all language teaching methodologies tended to lend

Table 6.1. Descriptive statistics of teacher candidate scores in on-ground and distant sections of the TESOL methods course

	Mean scores on teaching method demonstrations	Median	Standard deviation
f2f section (n = 12)	19.41	19.5	0.59
VC section (n = 12)	19.42	19.6	0.58

themselves to the VC modality. We will now turn to the results of three different types of videorecorded telecollaborative language teaching demonstrations carried out by teacher candidates in the VC section.

A Student-Centered VC Experience Using TBLT

In task-based language teaching (TBLT), the focus is on purposeful use of the target language (Nunan, 2004; Willis & Willis, 2007). In the demonstration of TBLT using VC technology, the teacher candidate (a student in the VC course) leading the demonstration provided his peers, who acted as middle school students for the purposes of the demonstration, with the task of developing a plan for a road trip. Sub-tasks included individual and group brainstorming, activation of vocabulary needed to complete the task, pair-share information gap activities, final development of the trip plan by small groups of students, and sharing of their itineraries from which the teacher candidate would choose the best in order to complete his own family's travel plans. Each of the sub-tasks was designed with supporting illustrations and handouts. Importantly, to accommodate the VC environment the "teacher" uploaded these documents to the course management system ahead of time for easy access by both local and distant cohorts.

During the task, "students" worked in small groups located on either side of the video bridge, as shown in the photograph in Figure 6.3. To complete the task, all students had opportunities to produce language as well as receive input in the form of language produced by others, both on and across campuses. The teacher played a minimal overt role in the development of

Figure 6.3. Students working in small groups on either side of the video bridge, on campus (left) and off campus (upper right)

classroom discourse with the exception of managing turn-taking during students' sharing of different sub-tasks. On-campus ESOL teacher candidates produced 10 utterances each while working in groups on their sub-tasks. Teacher candidates from the distant location produced seven utterances each as they engaged in extensive group conversations.

As shown in Text 1 below, in the final portion of the sub-task, the teacher candidate nominated his fellow students on each campus in turn to share their travel itineraries with the entire group. Neither group was unfairly advantaged or disadvantaged by the activity due to distance, as indicated by the equivalent opportunities for language output provided by the teacher.

Text 1. An excerpt of the final sub-task sharing of travel itineraries

Student 1 (on campus):	…We were saying on your first day you were going to do a bit of driving, and you're going to go to Ohio, and you're going to visit the Football Hall of Fame encampment, and then you're going to go to a Cavs game that night. Then, we thought you'd want to go to Nashville, which will take a little bit from Ohio, and listen to some country music and maybe go to a rodeo, and then you're going to work your way towards Colorado and go skiing in Durango.

Despite the apparently successful TBLT demonstration evidenced by a high score on the assessment rubric, the teacher candidate himself noted several inconveniences of using videoconferencing as a modality for this type of language instruction. For example, he was unable to record the results of student brainstorming due to the lack of a whiteboard in the classroom. He comments: "All right. If I had a whiteboard or anything, I'd put all your words up here."

A Teacher-Centered VC Experience Using ALM

The focus of this analysis is the demonstration of the Audiolingual Method (ALM). The ALM is known for its teacher-led, dialogue-centered, repetition-driven, and drill-focused, explicit teaching of language (Brooks, 1964; Richards & Rodgers, 2014). The teacher candidate who demonstrated ALM in this study relied on VC to exemplify most elements of this method for the participants on both ends of the video bridge. The teacher candidates who were acting as elementary students on both campuses were equally engaged in the repetition of the dialogue, drilling of the grammatical forms,

Figure 6.4. A teacher candidate (left, with sitcom image in the background) on campus leading students on both sides of the video bridge both on and off campus (right) using the ALM

including past tense verbs and contractions, and communicative drills – where students had to use specific expressions and phrases from the original dialogue to create their own conversation.

In the first phase of the lesson, the "teacher" orally introduced the dialogue to the "students" in class, illustrating it with an image from a popular sitcom as shown in Figure 6.4. Meanwhile, her peers acting as elementary students took turns repeating the lines from the dialogue. The "teacher" took seven turns and all "students" took the same seven turns in choral repetition. An excerpt of this task is shown in Text 2.

> *Text 2.* An excerpt of the first phase of the lesson using the ALM showcasing dialogue repetition and drilling of grammatical forms

Teacher:	What did you do last night?
Students:	What did you do last night?
Teacher:	What did you do last night?
Students:	What did you do last night?
Teacher:	I watched TV, and I went online to talk to friends.
Students:	I watched TV, and I went online to talk to friends.
Teacher:	I went online to talk to friends.
Students:	I went online to talk to friends.
Teacher:	I went online to talk to friends.
Students:	I went online to talk to friends.

In the second phase of the lesson, the "teacher" assigned one role to an interlocutor in the distant cohort and another role to a second interlocutor in the on-campus cohort. "Students" on both campuses had an equal number of turns while practicing the dialogue.

In the third phase of the lesson, the "teacher" reversed this practice, asking one "student" from the distant end and another from the on-campus classroom to recreate the dialogue. Finally, the "teacher" drilled "students" across campuses on past tense forms and contractions via a substitution drill where she provided a verb form in the present tense and students chorally repeated that verb in the past tense. The same type of drill was used with contractions; however, at the end of the contractions drill, the teacher candidate asked individual "students" specific questions about what they did or did not do. When the "teacher" did not hear clear responses from either the local or distant cohorts, she called on "students" individually or campus-wide to respond. This is shown in Text 3.

Text 3. An excerpt of the final phase of the lesson using the ALM showcasing the "teacher" leading "students" across campuses in the contractions drill

Teacher: Okay, [students on campus] now. I watched TV, and I went online to talk to friends.

Students on I watched TV, and I went online to talk to friends.
campus:

Based on this analysis, it was evident that VC did not impede the teaching demonstration using ALM for local and distant language learning. We observed equivalent participation from students on both ends and we found that the VC technology afforded the teacher opportunities to directly address any issues that occurred during the lesson. Moreover, the equivalent results on the aforementioned assessment rubric (Appendix A) across on-ground and VC sections indicated that the teacher candidate met all the requirements of the teaching demonstration.

A VC Experiential Content Lesson Using TPR

The final teaching demonstration chosen for analysis followed the Total Physical Response (TPR) method via VC in a simulated experiential science lesson. The TPR method is known for its integration of physical and linguistic processing of language (Asher, 1982). Traditional TPR involves students by engaging them in physical demonstrations of actions, repetitions of words associated with those actions, and pantomiming of propositions under study. The teacher candidate who demonstrated delivery of a lesson using TPR in this study had to rely on telecollaboration in order to get his peers, who played the role of middle school students, on both sides of the video bridge, physically and linguistically engaged. Figure 6.5 shows this setup.

Figure 6.5. A teacher candidate (left) on the distant campus leading students on both sides of the video bridge both on and off (right) campus using TPR in an experiential lesson

Right at the beginning of the presentation, it became evident that performing physical actions within a telecollaborative modality was not easily accomplished, particularly given the context of an experiential science lab.

The TPR experiential lesson consisted of three parts. First, participants were asked to point to images of laboratory-related objects that the distance-campus "teacher" named and projected for "students" on both campuses using a web-based presentation tool to control the slides. The projected images included artifacts from a science lesson, such as a beaker, a roll of paper towels, a microscope, an eye-washing station, a ruler, etc. In the second part of the lesson, participants had to take a virtual tour of the lab by physically moving their fingers clockwise and counterclockwise and "selecting" color-coded objects on the common screen. In the final part of the lesson, "student" participants verbally eliminated some of the objects from the screen while the teacher candidate predicted which objects they would keep. Text 4 below shows discourse from the first part of this lesson.

Text 4. An excerpt of the first phase of the experiential science lesson using TPR

Off-campus teacher candidate: All right, boys and girls, uh, today we're going to be reviewing some of our laboratory equipment that we talked about last time. So, the first thing we're going to do is review some of the words that we looked at. So, we're gonna use our pointer fingers, and we're gonna point at the objects on our screens. Ready? So, we're gonna point to the beaker. [students on both campuses point to the beaker on their individual computer screens] Point at the beaker. Excellent.

While the overall lesson was carried out successfully as evidenced by the scores on the evaluation rubric, there were clear issues with "student" participants' physical involvement in the demonstrated experiential content lesson using TPR. Instead of touching, pouring, filling up, and trying on various pieces of lab equipment, participants were limited to pointing at and touching images on their screens or pretending to complete the required actions. This limited physical activity appeared to undermine the premise of TPR, which involves the creation of physical memory traces through word association and achieves this through relating students' physical actions to word meanings. In order to overcome inability to physically touch, pour, try on, etc.; participants had to attempt to remember the names of lab artifacts by linking words to their images. It became apparent that the VC modality during this lesson presented limitations due to the absence of tangible objects that could be manipulated by participants. These limitations were two-fold: first, it was difficult if not impossible to ensure that the classrooms on both ends of the video bridge had the same equipment; and second, as the equipment was not available, this resulted in "students'" physical manipulations being reduced to virtual pointing, which deprived them of the typical experiential involvement of TPR and other types of instruction involving embodied participation. Moreover, the virtual pointing by the distant cohort "students" was difficult for the "teacher" to evaluate.

Discussion

In order to guide our discussion of the above findings, we would like to reiterate that this study has shown how teacher educators implemented specific language teaching methods within VC contexts in ways that aimed to be equivalent across VC and on-ground sections of a graduate TESOL methods course. Our study thus provides backing for the domain definition and evaluation inferences of an argument-based approach (Bachman & Palmer, 2010; Chapelle et al., 2008). Performance-based data from classroom assignments involving VC teaching demonstrations of different language teaching methodologies were used to support the warrant that teacher-educators in an MS TESOL program altered their traditional face-to-face teaching to sophisticated use of technology in synchronous online environments in ways that were equivalent to those of their on-ground peers (Gleason, 2013). This change was evidenced by equivalent scores on the assessment rubric (Appendix A) across sections and a detailed qualitative analysis of three videorecorded teaching demonstrations in the VC section as previously discussed.

As argued by Chapelle (2011), an argument-based approach to validity is simple and requires two basic phases. The first phase involves an interpretive argument that lays out the conceptual tools needed to express the multifaceted meanings of pedagogical task scores (Kane, 2006). In the present context, we chose to focus on the first two steps of the first phase, providing backing for the domain definition and evaluation inferences, as shown in Figure 6.2. Evaluating teacher candidates' performance by first describing the domain and then comparing the teacher candidates' scores across distant and on-ground sections not only allows us to avoid "the need to define the construct, which has proven to be so difficult" (Chapelle, 2011: 20), but also allows us to evaluate teachers' tech literacies in our specific context without an overt focus on the tools themselves. As tools change, we need flexible and adaptable ways of assessing teachers' tech literacies without depending on the ever-evolving technology and without having to rely on a static construct definition for teacher tech literacy.

As it is important to ensure that VC classes offer equivalent opportunities for teachers to develop their tech literacies, we took an approach similar to that of Gleason, who applied an interpretive argument to formative language tasks in technology-embedded contexts, arguing that the interpretive argument can provide guidance for design and implementation of blended instruction to ensure that students have "equivalent access to content and experiences in both online and face-to-face settings" (Gleason 2013: 607). By utilizing the same assessment rubric across VC and on-ground sections of the TESOL methods courses, and by comparing teacher candidates' scores on this rubric, we ensure equivalent learning opportunities to build teacher candidates' knowledge and skills.

At the start of the project, we hypothesized that student-centered methods would be more difficult to adapt to the VC modality than teacher-directed methods due to their implicit need for f2f negotiation of meaning, collaboration across campuses, and a more flexible nature of learning. Although all methods were effectively demonstrated in the VC environment as evidenced by equivalent scores on the rubric used to evaluate teacher candidate demonstrations, appropriate adaptations for VC classes were needed. For example, through our observation and analysis, it became evident that certain activities (including collaboration and meaning negotiation) experienced through VC learning closely mirrored f2f tasks of the same nature. For instance, as shown in Schmitt, Gleason, & Verplaetse (2016), a popular discussion-focused activity of a Progressive Brainstorm (Gibbons, 2015), where students walk in groups around the room to orally discuss and then write down their responses to a variety of posted questions, can be successfully simulated in a VC-class by using Padlet™, a virtual whiteboard that can be organized for different groups to engage in discussion and writing in a synchronous mode.

On the other hand, a lack of experience and practice with technological applications can result in teaching challenges ranging from a lack of preparation with tech tools for specific classroom tasks to diminished learning experiences by students in the distant settings. Recall that in the recorded teaching demonstration using task-based instruction, the teacher candidate failed to record a list of vocabulary proposed by the "students" in his lesson, lamenting the lack of a whiteboard and later acknowledging that he had not thought of using the virtual whiteboard or the interactive screen for writing down his "students'" contributions. Apprenticeship into online pedagogical practices – actual experience simulating this task in a VC mode – helped this teacher candidate rethink the available tools and develop his teacher tech literacies (Walqui & van Lier, 2010).

Other traditional f2f classroom activities may be more difficult to substitute in online contexts. In sheltered content instruction (Echevarria & Graves, 2015), for example, student and teacher experiential involvement (e.g., body movements, gestures, physical artifacts to mediate learning) in the lesson is essential. However, the teacher candidate who demonstrated an experiential science lesson using TPR discovered that providing equivalent objects/artifacts used in the on-ground classroom to the participants in the distant classroom was problematic. In a traditional experiential science lesson using TPR, the actual lab equipment would be available to demonstrate the actions of touching, pouring, filling, and mixing. The lack of availability of these tangible artifacts across VC campuses presented a limitation to experiential science instruction using TPR within a VC modality. Indeed, anything that involves the manipulation of physical objects and experiences may be challenging to approximate with comparable virtual experiences. Nonetheless, as Gleason (2013) argued, it is essential that learners in distance and blended environments have equivalent learning opportunities as their traditional classroom counterparts, insofar as such equivalent learning opportunities ensure that online/blended courses will have a positive washback, positively impacting factors such as student retention.

From this discussion, it is evident that certain methods illustrated in the teaching demonstrations did tend to yield themselves more naturally to VC whereas others proved more challenging. For example, the results of the experiential TPR science lesson were comparable to other teaching methods demonstrated over the semester, such as Community Language Learning (CLL) and Suggestopedia (Richards & Rodgers, 2014), all of which require special adaptations to a typical classroom environment. In the case of TPR, students often have to manipulate realia in order to achieve a total physical response, whereas in the case of CLL and Suggestopedia, comfortable and cozy environments that are conducive to relaxed conversation are needed (Richards & Rodgers, 2014). This also has implications for teaching younger learners in a VC environment which is limited by the potential to touch, experience, and manipulate physical realia.

Overall, our study has revealed that it is not the nature of the teaching method (i.e., teacher-centered, learner-centered, or learning-centered) (Kumaravadivelu, 2006) that determines the quality of online teacher preparation in a VC context. In fact, all 13 demonstrated language teaching methods were successfully presented and experienced by the participants as evidenced by the equivalent scores on the teaching demonstration rubric. This lends credence to the fact that students in both traditional and VC sections of this TESOL methods class had access to equivalent learning experiences.

The comparison of the results provided by the assessment rubric and the detailed analysis of the teaching demonstrations indicates that the rubric on its own may not provide a complete picture of teaching success. The rubric as it currently stands was unable to capture the deficit of the advanced preparation for physical presence of realia and availability of the virtual whiteboard in a VC classroom. Therefore, we propose an enhanced rubric, shown in Appendix B, which specifies the importance of making provisions for VC contextualization of teaching. Such an enhanced rubric could better help teacher candidates consider the demands of online teaching a priori, resulting in the development of their tech literacies for teaching in VC modalities.

Conclusion

Our study has relied on an argument-based approach to validity to make the claim that teacher-educators in an MS TESOL program were able to transform their teaching using traditional f2f pedagogies to sophisticated uses of technologies in VC environments. Furthermore, by comparing teacher candidates' scores across VC and on-ground courses, we were able to show how these teacher candidates gained equivalent access to content, knowledge, and skills. Although our study draws on limited data, we believe that it has broader implications for assessing the development of teacher tech literacies as well as for VC language education more generally. Moreover, the inclusion of an enhanced rubric, such as that suggested in Appendix B, which encompasses the affordances and limitations of teaching and learning in a VC mode, would help teachers develop their tech literacies in this situated context.

To provide further backing for our claim that the teacher candidates in our graduate TESOL program were able to transform their teaching from traditional face-to-face pedagogical practices into sophisticated technology-based pedagogical practices, the remaining steps of an interpretive argument would need to be taken (e.g., generalization, extrapolation, and utilization). A complete interpretive argument would help construct an eventual comprehensive validity argument for teacher tech literacies. Such an argument would necessarily show that teacher candidates can successfully employ their developed tech literacies in a VC environment with their own students.

The affordances and limitations of technology for language learning must always be carefully weighed. In our context, there is a desperate need for language teacher preparation in CALL. Furthermore, already teaching full-time, many teachers would not be able to take advantage of such opportunities without access to distance educational programs which apprentice them into hands-on pedagogical uses of technology, such as those showcased in this study. Having a fully online language educator preparation degree is not an excuse to sacrifice superior educational preparation; on the contrary, teacher candidates must be well prepared in their content areas as well as have valuable, hands-on tech literacies that can be readily applied for real life teaching domains (Darling-Hammond et al., 2005). As we know, these real-life educational domains are swiftly changing and thus, teachers must have access to graduate teaching experiences that afford them authentic uses of technology for teaching and not just training with technological tools in the abstract.

Future research in this area will further explore additional inferences of the interpretive argument in order to ensure not only that language teachers are afforded opportunities to develop their tech literacies while in their graduate programs, but also that they are able to effectively implement such knowledge and skills in their own classrooms and with their own students. Further investigation will shed light on how the development of teacher tech literacies presents opportunities for students in distant locations to simultaneously learn language, learn content through language, and learn teaching methodologies that focus on domain-specific uses of technology.

About the Authors

Jesse Gleason, PhD, is an Assistant Professor of Applied Linguistics and Spanish at Southern Connecticut State University. Her teaching and research interests include bilingualism/biliteracy development and technology-mediated instruction.

Elena Schmitt, PhD, is a Professor of Applied Linguistics in the TESOL/ Bilingual Education Program at Southern Connecticut State University. Her teaching and research focus on linguistic theory and its application to classroom teaching.

References

Asher, J. (1982). *Learning Another Language through Actions: The Complete Teacher's Guidebook* (2nd ed.). Los Gatos, CA: Sky Oak Productions.

Borthwick, K., & Gallagher-Brett, A. (2014). "Inspiration, ideas, encouragement": Teacher development and improved use of technology in language teaching through open educational practice. *Computer Assisted Language Learning*, 27(2), 163–183. http://dx.doi.org/10.1080/09588221.2013.818560

Bachman, L. F., & Palmer, A. S. (2010). Language assessment in practice. Oxford: Oxford University Press.

Brooks, N. (1964). *Language and Language Learning: Theory and Practice* (2nd ed.). New York, NY: Harcourt Brace.

Chapelle, C. A. (2008). The TOEFL validity argument. In C. A. Chapelle, M. K. Enright, & J. M. Jamieson (eds.), *Building a Validity Argument for the Test of English as a Foreign Language* (pp. 319–351). New York, NY: Routledge.

Chapelle, C. A. (2011). Validity argument for language assessment: The framework is simple. *Language Testing*, 29(1), 19–27.

Chapelle, C. A., Enright, M. K., & Jamieson, J. M. (2008). Test score interpretation and use. In C. A. Chapelle, M. K. Enright, & J. M. Jamieson (eds.), *Building a Validity Argument for the Test of English as a Foreign Language* (pp. 1–25). New York, NY: Routledge.

Cope, W., & Kalantzis, M. (2015). The things you do to know: An introduction to the pedagogy of multiliteracies. In B. Cope & M. Kalantzis (eds.), *A Pedagogy of Multiliteracies: Learning by Design* (pp. 1–36). London: Palgrave.

Darling-Hammond, L., Banks, J., Zumwalt, K., Gomez, L., Sherin, M. G., Griesdorn, J., & Finn, L.-E. (2005). Educational goals and purposes: Developing a curricular vision for teaching. In L. Darling-Hammond & J. Bransford (eds.), *Preparing Teachers for a Changing World* (pp. 169–200). San Francisco, CA: John Wiley & Sons, Inc.

Echevarria, J., & Graves, A. (2015). *Sheltered Content Instruction: Teaching English Learners with Diverse Abilities.* New York, NY: Pearson.

Gibbons, P. (2015). *Scaffolding Language Scaffolding Learning: Teaching English Language Learners in the Mainstream Classroom.* Portsmouth, NH: Heinemann.

Gleason, J. (2013). An interpretive argument for blended Spanish tasks. *Foreign Language Annals*, 46(4), 588–609. https://doi.org/10.1111/flan.12050

Godsey, M. (2015, March 25). The deconstruction of the K-12 teacher. *The Atlantic.* http://www.theatlantic.com/education/archive/2015/03/the-deconstruction-of-the-k-12-teacher/388631/.

International Technology Education Association (ITEA) (2003). *Advancing Excellence in Technological Literacy: Student Assessment, Professional Development and Program Standards*. Reston, VA: ITEA.

Jamieson, J. M., Eignor, D., Grabe, W., & Kunnan, A. J. (2008). Frameworks for a new TOEFL. In C. A. Chapelle, M. K. Enright, & J. M. Jamieson (eds.), *Building a Validity Argument for the Test of English as a Foreign Language* (pp. 55–96). New York, NY: Routledge.

Kane, M. T. (2006). Validation. In R. Brennan (ed.), *Educational Measurement* (4th ed.) (pp. 17–64), Westport, CT: American Council on Education and Praeger.

Kumaravadivelu, B. (2006). TESOL methods: Changing tracks, challenging trends. *TESOL Quarterly*, 40(1), 59–81. https://doi.org/10.2307/40264511

Lynch, M. P. (2016, April 24). Teaching in the time of Google. *The Chronicle of Higher Ed.* http://chronicle.com/article/Teaching-in-the-Time-of-Google/236180

Messick, S. (1989). Validity. In R. L. Linn (ed.), *Educational Measurement* (pp. 13–103). New York, NY: Macmillan.

Nami, F., Marandi, S. S., & Sotoudehnama, E. (2016). CALL teacher professional growth through lesson study practice: An investigation into EFL teachers' perceptions. *Computer Assisted Language Learning*, 29(4), 658–682. https://doi.org/10.1080/09588221.2015.1016439

New London Group (1996). A pedagogy of multiliteracies: Designing social futures. *Harvard Educational Review*, 66(1), 60–92.

Nunan, D. (2004). *Task-Based Language Teaching*. Cambridge: Cambridge University Press.

Richards, J. C., & Rodgers, T. S. (2014). *Approaches and Methods in Language Teaching* (3rd ed.). Cambridge: Cambridge University Press.

Schmitt, E., Gleason, J., & Verplaetse, L. (2016, April 11). Screen to screen: Use of telecollaboration for instruction in a MS TESOL program. Paper presented at the American Association of Applied Linguistics (AAAL) Conference, Orlando, FL.

Sehlaoui, A., & Albrecht, N. (2009). Online professional development for TESOL teachers in rural and suburban Kansas: An innovative model. *International Journal of Technology, Knowledge and Society*, 5(6), 65–82. https://doi.org/10.18848/1832-3669/cgp/v05i06/56049

Toulmin, S. E. (2003). *The Uses of Argument*. Cambridge: Cambridge University Press.

Walqui, A., & van Lier, L. (2010). *Scaffolding the Academic Success of Adolescent English Language Learners: A Pedagogy of Promise*. San Francisco, CA: West Ed.

Willis, J., & Willis, D. (2007). *Doing Task-Based Teaching*. Oxford: Oxford University Press.

Appendix A

Original Assessment Rubric / Checklist for ESOL Teacher Candidates'
Teaching Demonstrations Involving Various Language Teaching
Methodologies

Checklist	Yes	Some	No
1. Did the lesson illustrate some of the key principles discussed in the readings?	2	1	0
2. Were the objectives measurable or observable?	2	1	0
3. Did the objectives describe skills appropriate for ELLs?	2	1	0
4. Were the activities congruent with the objectives?	2	1	0
5. Were the language and presentation of materials adapted for the specific needs of ELLs?	2	1	0
6. Were socio-cultural considerations included if appropriate?	2	1	0
7. Was the focus on meaning, with form attended to in function of the meaning?	2	1	0
8. Were content (topic) and form (language) integrated?	2	1	0
9. Was the reflection thoughtful and reference theoretical underpinnings to the pedagogical choices made?	2	1	0
10. Did the teacher explain any changes made in the plan?	2	1	0
Total /20			

Appendix B

Revised Assessment Rubric / Checklist for ESOL Teacher Candidates' Teaching Demonstrations Involving Various Language Teaching Methodologies

Checklist	Yes	Some	No
1. Did the lesson illustrate some of the key principles discussed in the readings?	2	1	0
2. Were the objectives measurable or observable?	2	1	0
3. Did the objectives describe skills appropriate for ELLs?	2	1	0
4. Were the activities congruent with the objectives?	2	1	0
5. Were the language and presentation of materials adapted for the specific needs of ELLs?	2	1	0
6. Were socio-cultural considerations included if appropriate?	2	1	0
7. Was the focus on meaning, with form attended to in function of the meaning?	2	1	0
8. Were content (topic) and form (language) integrated?	2	1	0
9. Was the reflection thoughtful and reference theoretical underpinnings to the pedagogical choices made?	2	1	0
10. Did the teacher explain any changes made in the plan?	2	1	0
Total /20			
For VC teaching			
1. Were all the materials equally available to the participants in on-ground and distant settings?	2	1	0
2. Did the teacher make provisions for providing equivalent feedback to the participants in on-ground and distant settings?	2	1	0
3. Were all the online tools uploaded and ready for use in both settings?	2	1	0
Total /26			

7 Face-to-Face Teacher to Online Course Developer

David Donnarumma* and Sarah Hamilton**

Introduction

As universities expand and deliver many of their programs online, English language teachers need to be ready to support students both through teaching and appropriate course development. In addition, they need to understand how best to support the English language learning process at a distance. This study explores the attributes, practices, and skills English language teachers need to design and develop online English language courses and the challenges those teachers face in transitioning from face-to-face to online course design. By understanding these particular attributes, practices and skills, we are able to highlight some implications for assessing English language teachers' readiness for online course development.

Even though many teacher development programs now include online learning, the question of whether these teachers are ready for online course development still remains. It has been well documented that language teachers need a working knowledge of information and communications technology because computers are now normal use, and students can access a wide range of technologies (Gilbert, 2013; Stickler & Emke, 2015). This leads to the challenge of how best to prepare teachers for online course design. Most studies have focused on what the teacher does during the online course with much emphasis to date being placed on technological competence. This small-scale study seeks to go beyond the obvious requirement for technical competence to show that readiness for online is as much about the values and beliefs of the teacher as it is about their digital literacy skills (technological competence). This study therefore seeks to progress the issue of readiness beyond just how to use software and what to use it for, but looks at

*	BPP University, UK; DavidDonnarumma@bpp.com
**	BPP University, UK; SarahHamilton@bpp.com

the softer skills such as attitudes towards online teaching and willingness to participate in peer review of learning materials, and the implications these have for assessing a teacher's readiness for online course development.

Literature Review

Moving from face-to-face to online teaching can be challenging for an English language teacher. Redmond (2011) argues that the transition can be confrontational as it challenges established patterns of teaching, instructor behavior, and the effectiveness of teaching approaches. It is often assumed that a teacher who is good at teaching face-to-face will also be good at teaching online (Davis & Rose, 2007), but this has been proven to be false (Redmond, 2011). Looking at some of the key differences experienced by face-to-face teachers in their move to online that evidenced the difference in skills and mindset required, Redmond (2011) found that face-to-face teachers often view the online space as a repository for their learning materials rather than embracing the dynamic nature of the online environment. The online environment provides more opportunities for engagement and interaction through the use of technology and should be perceived as a teaching and learning space rather than a file-sharing space. The role of the teacher is also significantly different; the face-to-face teacher is traditionally a content provider, a disseminator of knowledge, or the sage on the stage; whereas the online teacher's role expands to a more facilitative role providing opportunities for learners to create and discover new knowledge. Finally, to design, develop, and deliver online learning requires much more time and thinking. Face-to-face teachers as experts in their subject area can walk into a face-to-face class at the last minute as cover for a colleague and deliver a session on their topic with minimal preparation. This spontaneous teaching is not as feasible online where teaching requires more detailed planning and organization in order to accommodate for the limited facetime.

In order to determine how we might assess readiness for online course development, we need to understand what skills, attributes, and behaviors someone who is skilled in online course development has. It is reasonable to assume that the basic principles and knowledge of how people learn are part of the required skill set, but what skills beyond general learning and teaching practice are relevant to online course development? If we know what these specific skills are, then teachers who possess some or all of these skills might be assumed to be ready for online course development. Therefore, the identification of specific skills required for online course development provides a starting point for *what to assess to determine readiness for online* before deciding *how to assess readiness for online.*

The literature regarding online skills for English language teachers identifies some commonalities around skills needed for online teachers (see Table 7.1). The literature does not differentiate between the skills needed for online delivery and online design; instead, it leans towards a generic concept of the online teacher. The online teacher can therefore be seen as someone who is not only responsible for delivering the learning through discussion forums and live webinars, but someone who is also responsible for designing the online student journey and developing and producing online learning materials, whether it is through using online quiz software or designing online assessment and instructional videos. Agreement seems to exist between the various studies regarding the significance of technical skills needed. The focus appears to be primarily on digital literacy and technical competence in addition to online pedagogical knowledge.

Whilst many of the specific skills identified in Table 7.1 can be developed through training, what these researchers only start to imply, but do not elaborate on, are teachers' specific attitudes and behaviors that determine readiness for online course development. For example, Bennett and Marsh (2002) refer to concern for the learner rather than concern for yourself as the teacher. This fits in with Kugel's (1993) stages of teacher development, which move from Phase I where new teachers focus on themselves with an emphasis on teaching to Phase II where the emphasis is on the students' learning. In Phase I, the new teacher focuses on how much knowledge they personally have, and they feel an overwhelming need to impart all

Table 7.1. Skills needed for online language teachers

(Bennett & Marsh, 2002)	(Hampel & Stickler, 2005)	(Compton, 2009)
• Sufficient technical skills • Ability to identify significant differences and similarities between face-to-face and online teaching • Concern for the learner rather than the self • Strategies and techniques to facilitate online learning	• Basic computer/use of digital technology skills • Specific technical competence related to e-learning tools • Ability to deal with constraints and possibilities of the medium • Online socialization • Ability to facilitate communicative competence • Own teaching style	• Technological competence • Ability to make decisions around the right e-learning tools to use and creativity in using them • Pedagogical knowledge, application, and innovation • Response to evaluation of learning

their knowledge to their students. The teacher adopts a tutor-led approach of knowledge delivery, telling the students what to think rather than allowing the students to think for themselves. Meanwhile, the students struggle to cope with an overload of content and knowledge. This suggests that new teachers are potentially less ready for online teaching if they are still in Phase I of Kugel's stages of development. In Kugel's Phase II of teacher development, the teacher moves away from focusing on telling the students what to think and develops ways of helping the students learn how to think for themselves. The focus is not so much on *what* the student needs to learn but *how* they can learn. However, it should be acknowledged that whilst Kugel refers to "new teachers" it is possible that older teachers may remain in Phase I and not move on to Phase II. Therefore, rather than being specific to new teachers, any teacher still in Phase I of Kugel's stages of development is less likely to be ready for online course development as they will focus on content rather than learning. This is what Bennett and Marsh (2002) refer to when they talk about concern for yourself as the teacher compared to concern for the learner. This in turn leads on to Hampel & Stickler's (2005) research that identifies the need for flexibility and adaptability. They identify the relevance of a teacher's ability to develop and adapt their own style of teaching (and therefore how they approach course development) as an appropriate response to the tools and the capabilities of the learners. This confidence of flexibility and adaptability will usually only come once a teacher has moved out of Kugel's Phase I.

One framework that starts to identify the significance of attitudes and behaviors including the values and the belief systems belonging to the teacher is Bennett's (2014) Digital Practitioner Framework (DPF). Bennett (2014) uses a four-part model to explore what makes a competent online teacher. The four parts of the model are Attributes, Practice, Skills, and Access (see Table 7.2).

Table 7.2. The four parts of Bennett's (2014) Digital Practitioner Framework

Attributes	The stable aspects of lecturers' personalities which allows them to use their skills and practice to design and deliver learning activities which make use of technology
Practice	Practical expertise and pedagogical knowledge around designing, developing, and delivering online learning experiences
Skills	Technical knowledge and competence and use of online/e-learning tools.
Access	The availability of technology to use and the opportunity to use it in the learning environment

Although not specifically aimed at English language teachers, this framework identifies the importance of attributes, in particular lecturers' own orientation towards technology. Attributes in this context are best explained as behavioral competences or common characteristics evidenced by those that are competent Digital Practitioners. For example, a significant attribute would be a commitment and feeling of connection to online learning and the use of digital tools. Other attributes include a confidence in the use of technology, being proactive in learning about new technologies, and believing that online learning can be beneficial in developing language skills as much as face-to-face learning. Teachers who lack positive attributes towards online learning are unlikely to be ready for online course development. Bennett's (2014) work evidences a need to recognize that motivation, values, and beliefs are as much of an indication of teacher readiness for online as some of the more practical skills such as those identified in Table 7.1.

In addition to attributes, Bennett's (2014) framework looks at the concept of access as a factor of online competence. This includes not just physical access, i.e., availability of software licences, but also includes the concept of time as access, i.e., the time to experiment and play with online tools. The literature acknowledges that opportunities to play with online tools for the English language teacher are constrained primarily by time (Bennett, 2014; Germain-Rutherford & Ernest, 2015). This lack of time means there is a lack of opportunities to practice the use of technology for learning and therefore the lack of opportunities to build confidence in their use. Access is the foundation that drives technical competence that leads to improved practice and ultimately positive attributes and increased confidence towards online course development. This suggests that teachers will be more ready for online course development if they have attributes that support the issue of access, such as the willingness and ability to find a way to make time to explore and experiment with new technologies in their free time.

Having access to technology and making the time to play is not sufficient without the skills to develop and use that technology effectively. Skills, therefore, apply to a range of activities from generic workplace skills to those more specific to an educator, such as time management, organizing and arranging files on a network, the ability to write effective online learning materials, and the ability to understand and apply pedagogical principles to online learning. Therefore, those already in possession of a teaching qualification with basic digital literacy skills are more likely to be ready for online than those without these foundations. Finally, those teachers who evidence adherence to good practice in teaching and learning such as being a critically reflective practitioner (Redmond, 2011), trialling and learning from new practices (Bennett, 2014), and seeking feedback and designing learning to meet the needs of the learner (Bennett & Marsh, 2002) are likely to be more ready for online teaching than those who do not have these attributes or values.

Technical skills and the ability to use particular tools and understand their limitations are more easily taught than some of the more behavioral attributes and practices that evidence a particular mindset and orientation towards online. Therefore, a balance of those skills identified in Table 7.1 from the wider literature and the attributes and behaviors evidenced in Bennett's (2014) work provide an appropriate starting point for assessing readiness for online.

The purpose of this study is to assess a teacher's readiness for online course development. The research questions whether a teacher's readiness is as much about their own values and beliefs as a teacher, as it is about their digital literacy skills (technological competence). In addition, the study investigates the implications for assessing teachers' readiness for online materials development.

Methodology

In this small-scale study, we report on how we assessed the readiness for online teaching of a group of English language teachers who designed and developed an online English language support program. The study design was mixed methods based on what Creswell and Plano Clark (2011) refer to as a Triangulation Design, which brings together the differing strengths and weaknesses of quantitative methods (such as generalization) with those of qualitative methods (such as in-depth study). In this study the quantitative data are collected using two questionnaires, one at the beginning and one at the end of the development. The second questionnaire was used to assess the accuracy of the first. You would normally expect to see an increase in confidence and skills as they develop through practice. Therefore the evidence of any reduction in confidence and skills at the end would demonstrate the initial assessment of readiness may not have been so accurate. The qualitative data are collected using a focus group, which is used to expand on the findings from the questionnaires.

Context

The English language support program is a series of 70 hours of stand-alone online asynchronous English language learning materials, which are designed specifically for the worldwide student members studying for the ACCA qualification. The qualification is made up of nine fundamental (F) exams (F1–F9) and seven professional (P) exams (P1–P7). Each exam focuses on a different accountancy topic, for example, the F2 exam focuses on Management Accounting.

The 70 hours of language support are distributed across the exams according to the needs of each exam, so some exams have more hours of language support than others (see www.englishforacca.bppuniversity. ac.uk). The 70 one-hour learning units focus on reading, writing, listening, and language development. Due to the written nature of these accountancy exams, speaking is not a skill that is required by students in order to succeed in their exams. Students can select the learning units they wish to study according to their own schedules and language abilities, but may find particular units relevant and more helpful to certain exams. The online program was launched in June 2016, with the final units going live in January 2017. There are a total of 12,500 registered users with many students regularly revisiting the materials as they progress through the ACCA qualification.

This approach to online education provides a very different learning journey from more established online courses. There was no teacher support or student community, and no requirement for contact between students built into the learning. Such an approach with no teacher contact meant that the teaching presence needed to be embedded in the learning material and not delivered through asynchronous and synchronous communication.

Participants

A total of five English for Academic Purposes (EAP) module leaders participated in the study (Table 7.3). The participants had all taught EAP in a higher education context and had experience in designing materials for face-to-face programs. All had postgraduate qualifications in English language teaching, which included modules on designing materials, and were involved in developing courses for high-stakes language testing. However, Participants 1, 2, and 3 had received little to no training in designing materials for an online environment or their previous experience in online course development was limited to a maximum of one year. Such online development experience is similar to many language instructors outside of this study. Also, although the whole group included expert speakers of English, two of the teachers had learnt it as a second language, thus representing the vast majority of English language teachers (Graddol, 2006).

Table 7.3. Description of English for Academic Purposes (EAP) module leaders

ID	Gender	Primary first language	Degree	Years of English teaching experience	Description of experience with online design/ development
1	Female	French	MA in ELT with a focus on teaching online	More than 15 years in schools, colleges and universities	Approximately six months of experience in online materials development and teaching online
2	Male	English	MA in Applied Linguistics	Over 25 years in schools and university	Little to no experience in online or materials writing
3	Female	English	MA in ELT with a focus on online learning	Seven years in schools and university	One year experience in online materials development
4	Female	English	MA in Applied Linguistics	Over 15 years in schools and university	Designed and developed materials for over three years; one year of online materials development
5	Female	French	MA in ELT	Over 15 years at both university and college level	Designed materials for both and print and online purposes

Course Development

This study focuses on the readiness of the English language teacher for the development of online materials, rather than their readiness for asynchronous and synchronous delivery. The five English language module leaders were tasked with writing different learning units. The work was distributed equally between two of the teachers who were dedicated to the project full-time. The three other teachers were given associate roles, writing and developing fewer online learning units. There were also two internal English language reviewers, as well as an external reviewer who ensured the accountancy content was accurate. We also had the support of a full-time instructional designer. Each learning unit followed the process outlined in Figure 7.1.

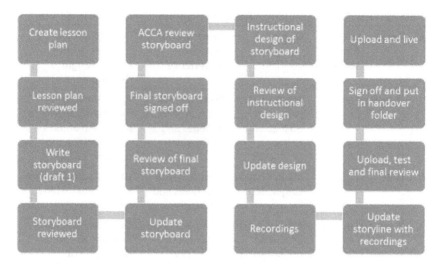

Figure 7.1. The English language learning unit development process

All the materials were first produced in a Word document (the storyboard) derived from the original lesson plan; once they had been signed off both internally and externally (ACCA), they were given to the instructional designer who used Articulate Storyline (e-learning software) to create the materials ready for the online environment. As part of the storyboard process video and audio scripts were written. These were then recorded in a studio and then inserted into the Articulate Storyline unit. As seen from Figure 7.1, there were a significant number of review stages as part of the quality assurance process. The quality of this product reflected not only on BPP University but on the ACCA qualification as well. It was only once the learning units had been signed off that they were uploaded and made live for students to access on the virtual learning environment. This lengthy quality assurance process was a change from what our teachers are used to.

Once we had a significant number of storyboards written, the two lead authors took on the role of instructional designer using the software package to create the materials, with the dedicated instructional designer finalizing the learning units.

Data Collection and Analysis

Pre- and post-material development questionnaires were administered. The first, Questionnaire A (see Appendix A), was identical to the second, Questionnaire B, apart from the change in wording to reflect the latter

Table 7.4. The purpose of different questions used in the questionnaire

Questions	Purpose	Link to Bennett's (2014) framework
1–2	To determine descriptive data about each participant – sex and age	n/a
3–8	To determine the participants' experience and qualifications in teaching face-to-face	n/a
7–8	To determine participants' experience in teaching and designing online	Attributes
9–10	A set of statements on a Likert scale to determine participants' level of confidence in designing and developing online learning materials	Attributes
11–12	A set of agree or disagree statements which focus on the participants' practice in the design of (online) learning materials	Practice
13–14	A set of agree or disagree statements which focus on the participants' skills (including time management) for developing online learning materials	Skills
15–16	A set of agree or disagree statements which focus on the participants' access to online learning networks, training and software	Access

coming after the development period. Table 7.4 shows the purpose of each question. The questions were based around Bennett's (2014) framework.

Questionnaire A aimed to assess the teacher's existing attributes, practices, skills, and perception of access in line with Bennett's (2014) framework for developing online materials. This was to enable us to determine how the teachers were positioned within Bennett's (2014) framework of requirements for the Digital Practitioner. Questionnaire B was distributed at the end of the development of online units to both compare whether the initial questionnaire was a good indicator of readiness and the extent to which Bennett's framework was appropriate. The responses to the questionnaires also helped us to understand the challenges that the group either identified or at least perceived as an issue in online development. The questionnaires helped to highlight teachers' values and beliefs about teaching English, and how digitally literate this group of teachers were. The questionnaire data were categorized into descriptive categories such as gender, age, years of experience, and analytical categories related to Bennett's (2014) Digital Practitioner Framework – attributes, practice, skills, and access. The data were then collated and transferred into an Excel spreadsheet using the categories to organize the data. The data from the two questionnaires was then compared using tables and graphs. We then narrowed the focus down to attributes, practice, and access as we were looking beyond skills (which really refers to technical competence) and were interested to see what was of significance under the other categories.

Focus Group

The focus group was conducted with all five participants after Questionnaire B and lasted for 90 minutes. The questions used in the focus group were selected from items 9 to 16 in the questionnaires and focused on four areas: participants' confidence in developing online learning materials, their own practice in materials design and development, their skills in developing online learning materials, and the access they have received to training or software (see Appendix B for the list of questions). The focus group was run by the two authors; one took written notes while the other asked questions. In addition the focus group was recorded and the notes were compared with the recording to eliminate any differences.

The focus group was an opportunity for teachers to reflect on the development of the online materials and explore the issues which had been identified in the questionnaires in more depth. Although there were some guided questions, there was also free-flowing discussion in order to allow any further points to emerge. The object of the focus group was to have an organized discussion with a group of individuals for them to comment on specific points that the researchers had selected (Powell, Single, & Lloyd 1996).The participants could either expand on thoughts so far expressed or add in new thoughts on their experience having been through the cycle of writing and designing an online course. Creswell and Plano Clark (2011) emphasize the importance of establishing rationales for each decision made around the dataset and how the information is processed. In keeping with this thinking and the very nature of a pilot study, the qualitative data in the questionnaires and from the focus group were prioritized as critical data in terms of informing our conclusions. Hence, once the data from the questionnaires had been collected and analyzed, the data were then expanded on through the focus group questions in order to explore some of the qualitative issues in more depth.

The focus group data were recorded and transcribed and then checked by a different person to ensure that what was transcribed was what was recorded. The data were then coded by one author thematically by reading through the contributions from the participants in the focus group and identifying patterns across the transcription. Both authors were then able to discuss the themes and agree on any differences.

Results and Discussion

The aim of this small-scale study was to report on the findings from assessing a group of language teachers who have developed an online program of English language support material. The research focused on investigating the key areas within Bennett's (2014) DPF to identify teachers' confidence and skills levels in relation to attributes, skills, practice, and access in their readiness for developing materials online. Three key themes emerged from the focus groups and the questionnaires that mapped to key findings in each of the three areas of Attributes, Practice and Access. One overriding theme that mapped across all three concepts was Communication and Collaboration, which suggests this is one of the most significant elements of readiness for online (see Table 7.5). Each of the three themes will be discussed in the following subsections.

Table 7.5. Specific themes within Bennett's Digital Practitioner Framework

Key themes	Attributes	Practice	Access
Communication and Collaboration	• Willingness to collaborate to build and engage in professional networks across different disciplines • Willingness to engage in peer review and critical reflection	• The use of images to convey meaning • Embedding of language learning within a discipline • Creation of authentic learning materials within the discipline	• Access to a peer network
Knowing your audience	• Willingness to engage in and experience online as a student • Committed and connected to ways of working and using digital tools in order to understand the students' perspective		
Time	• Time management		• Time to explore the discipline within which the language learning is situated

Communication and Collaboration

From both the questionnaires and the focus group, one of the key themes emerging was the need for the online material developers to communicate and collaborate with each other. Prior to any online development, the teachers showed that they were reflective practitioners by all agreeing or partially agreeing that they sought feedback, evaluated their practice through feedback and reflection, and reflected on innovations in their practice (Figure 7.2). During and after development, the participants continued to actively seek feedback and were given opportunities to engage with feedback from peers, including feedback from the professional accountancy teachers who taught the students and other English language experts face-to-face. This tendency to communicate and collaborate through feedback opportunities was reinforced by the focus group participants, who were keen to co-write and communicate as much as possible. *"Not a good idea to write on your own, need to talk to a lot of people regularly"* (focus group participant 2), and *"might be better to communicate too much"* (focus group participant 3). Furthermore, when asked about advice they would give other online writers, one commented – *"collaboration: – between you and a proof reader, you and an editor, you and other writers. [Online material development] needs more of a team than you would normally use in face-to-face"* (focus group participant 4), and another commented – *"[Online teachers] need feedback, loads of feedback at different stages"* (focus group participant 3).

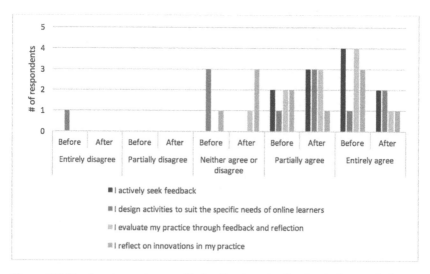

Figure 7.2. Teachers' experience with feedback and reflection before and after course development

Although all the participants in this study were already reflective practitioners and either partially or fully engaged with peer feedback, during the focus group, the teachers demonstrated and reinforced the need for what Bennett (2014) identifies as attributes of the Digital Practitioner – the willingness to engage with peer feedback. Therefore, teachers that actively engage with peer feedback in their face-to-face practice may be more ready for developing online materials. According to Covington, Petherbridge, & Warren (2005), peer support is a significant factor in assisting faculty in the transition from face-to-face teaching to developing online materials. Potentially, participants sought less feedback after the development as they were more confident in developing materials, and had less need for formal reflective feedback, but their journey began with communication and collaboration at the forefront.

The response to Questionnaire B shows that they gained confidence in their understanding the requirements of writing for online and their understanding of the difference between online and face-to-face learners (Figure 7.3). In addition, participants improved their confidence in designing online materials, as all the respondents stated that they were confident or very confident in transferring their teaching from face-to-face to online design. This confidence has come about through increased engagement in seeking feedback from peers and through the process of evaluating their practice through feedback. Confidence has thus come from feedback from others and from the self. The ongoing process of peer and quality review provided continuous confirmation of what they were doing well but also enabled them to

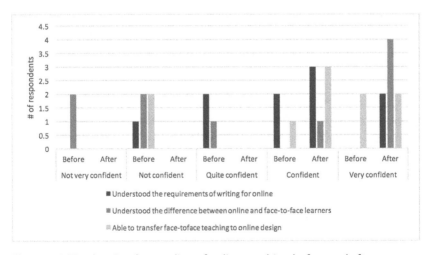

Figure 7.3. Teachers' understanding of online teaching before and after course development

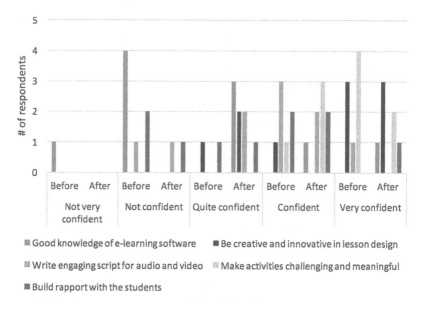

Figure 7.4. Teachers' confidence with developing online materials before and after course design

compare their work to others to see that they were not alone, which helped motivate and engage them in the material development process.

Figure 7.4 shows that all the participants seemed to improve in their knowledge of e-learning software and there was little or no change in their creative and innovative lesson design; this may be due to the difficulty in building rapport or social presence (COI, 2017) with the students. As one participant commented – "*I still don't know if students are struggling or not… need to know if the students think this [the material] is too difficult*" (focus group participant 1). It is also the case that "*in the classroom you can go backwards and use different examples, rephrase, adapt, see when students are confused*" (focus group participant 5).

In addition, teachers still found it challenging to write engaging scripts and make activities stimulating and meaningful. When creating online materials, the "*most challenging thing, [was] to be able to identify what needs extra explanation*" (focus group participant 4). Developing this online writing expertise can take time, and perhaps more time than the project allowed. The importance of teacher presence has been identified by a number of authors (COI, 2017; Shea, Li, & Pickett, 2006) and has been achieved in part through narrative – "*if loads of text on a slide, I wouldn't read it; I would skip it*" (focus group participant 1). However, finding the balance between text and images on a screen is challenging for online materials developers. Online developers may benefit from understanding more about the use of images to make meaning and use of images rather than text where appropriate.

Kress (2003) identified the use of images for spatial information and writing for more logical reasoning. For example, a teacher can use a diagram to explain the use of the prepositions in the noun phrases *in a house* or *sitting on a wall*. Or in terms of logic, a diagram can be used to explain a process far more easily than using speech or writing. When assessing whether a teacher is ready for online development, the practice of using images rather than text where appropriate would fit within Bennett's (2014) practice level in her DPF. Although this particular practice was not specifically investigated through the initial questionnaire, it did, however, raise more general questions around online practices. Two of the teachers were confident they could transfer their knowledge from face-to-face to online, but no one considered the specific practice of the use of images to convey meaning instead of words.

In the focus group, the issue of image use and the need to reduce the reliance on text did emerge as an important but challenging practice. Therefore, those teachers who incorporate the use of images, pictures, and diagrams in their practice are more likely to be ready for online, and this is something that should be assessed when trying to determine a teacher's readiness for designing online learning materials.

Knowing Your Audience and Their Needs

Prior to any face-to-face course development, a needs analysis is usually completed and this often results in the need for specific materials development. Often in the face-to-face context, it is not until the students are in the classroom and they have been there for a period of time that the teacher is able to adapt the teaching and materials to the context of the student. In face-to-face materials development, different student contexts are catered for through other support materials or detailed teachers' notes, rather than adapting existing materials in response to the students throughout the course of the program. In the online context, for materials which are accessible globally, needs analysis and developmental testing are far more challenging, and knowing the end user is more complex. Hence, participants expressed difficulty with sourcing materials – "*if sourcing materials for a general English course it would be a lot quicker, but when sourcing materials that are within a specific subject discipline it is a lot harder*" (focus group participant 5). This difficulty may have been because of the specific nature of the English program for accountants, with individual papers relating to specific areas of accountancy, which the English language teachers were not as familiar with. This is also evidenced in the questionnaire feedback (see Figure 7.5), in which participants found understanding the subject content and adapting the learning material within a subject-specific context challenging. Allowing that the English language teachers had the time to explore the specific subject area and online context, what Bennett (2014) calls accessibility, is key here to increasing confidence in online learning. In addition, the language teachers who make the time to build the networks across subject areas by engaging with colleagues in other disciplines and schools on a regular basis (accountancy and online learning) are more ready to develop online learning materials. The ability to engage with and build collegiate networks across subject disciplines is therefore essential for the online English language teacher to ensure they can situate the language accurately within the context of the discipline and produce authentic materials for engaging the online learner.

Another challenge was not knowing the audience, both in terms of the stakeholders (the professional accountancy body, professional accountancy students and senior management) and the students. This is very different from a face-to-face course that you are teaching, as you are able to adapt the materials to your class instantaneously – *"Know the audience face-to-face and how the students will respond"* (focus group participant 3). In addition, in the questionnaire participants expressed that writing storyboards

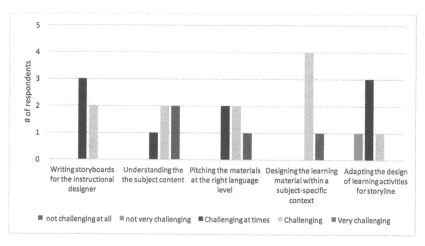

Figure 7.5. Participants' understanding of designing subject-specific materials for an online environment after development

and pitching the materials at the right level was challenging for them. Although before and during the material development the team had worked closely with professional accounting teachers, there had been little contact with actual online students. As Bennett (2014) identified, it is important for online developers to experience online learning themselves and be committed and connected to ways of working and using digital tools in order to understand the students' perspective. For any future assessment of teachers' online experience, participating in or attending an online course in the role of a student would be relevant experience. This is what Bennett (2014) identifies as accessibility and attributes – not only having the time and access, but also the attribute to be proactive to learn new things.

If only we had more time!

In line with the findings of previous authors (Bennett, 2014; Germain-Rutherford & Ernest, 2015), the participants in our study struggled with time. This may have been due to a lack of confidence in writing materials, as they commented it was "*difficult to know how long things would take*" (focus group participant 3). The development process of materials has included a significant amount of peer review, and student and client feedback. Although time was built into the project plan for feedback and review, the tight schedules and turnaround times meant that there was little time available for self-reflection and to play or experiment with the software.

Both questionnaires asked the teachers to express their confidence in their ability to manage their time (see Figure 7.6). It was interesting to note

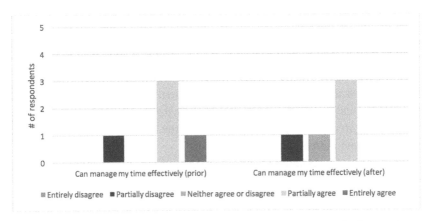

Figure 7.6. How confident teachers were in managing their time before and after the development

that in the initial questionnaire, four participants were able to express confidence in their time management skills whilst in the final questionnaire this dropped. This evidences that self-assessment of one's time management capabilities is not always particularly accurate. If teachers haven't previously been put under the level of pressure required for development of online projects, they are unlikely to be able to realistically assess how well they manage time under pressure.

In assessing a teacher's readiness for online development, there is an element of ensuring they understand that there are limits to the amount of time available and, as with any project, time for reflection and review can be allocated at particular points. Assessing not only access but also the skills (Bennett, 2014), meaning the time management skills required by the teacher as a member of the project team, is very important.

Conclusion

In this study, we identified that although Bennett's (2014) Digital Practitioner Framework is relevant to online course development, there were specific themes that were significant when assessing a teacher's readiness. The three themes were: communication and collaboration, knowing your audience, and time.

Throughout this study, we trialled the use of self-assessment questionnaires. Whilst the questionnaires proved helpful in identifying some of the challenges and skills required for online development, they were not as successful in assessing readiness. If tutors have a limited experience in online course development, then completing a self-assessment on the topic proved difficult to do.

Although a basic level of information and communications technology skills and digital literacy are required for online course development, overall technical skills have been proven to be more effectively developed through use. The more the teachers used the specific software the more confident they became. However, the software (Articulate Storyline) had some limitations, and it was through trial and error that most of those limitations were discovered. Some prior knowledge of the limitations of the software would indicate more readiness for online.

One of the strongest indicators of readiness for online that has come out of this study is within Bennett's (2014) concept of attributes. This study has shown that the key attributes that indicate a readiness for online are a willingness to engage in and experience online as a student; a willingness to collaborate to build and engage in professional networks across different disciplines; effective time management; and a willingness to engage in peer review and critical reflection. It is therefore not possible to assess readiness on the basis of skills alone, but these attributes must be taken into consideration.

About the Authors

David Donnarumma is Head of English for BPP University. He has been involved in the field of English Language Teaching for 15 years as a manager, academic, teacher educator, test developer, and materials developer both online and in print. He is also an author of a Communication Skills textbook. He has presented at several international conferences and written in the areas of ELF communication, assessment, and online learning. In his current role he is responsible for English language development and delivery at the University. He also holds external examining positions at the Universities of Wolverhampton and Exeter.

Sarah Hamilton is the Online Programme Leader for the BPP University School of English Language and Foundation Studies. Prior to joining the school Sarah worked both as a tutor in the Business School and as a member of the Universities Central Learning and Teaching team focusing on Assessment Enhancement activities. She is also an online author of Business Communication Skills and Human Resources e-Learning materials for accountancy students. In her current role she is responsible for online curriculum design and supporting the teaching team in their move from face-to-face to online.

References

Bennett, L. (2014). Learning from the early adopters: Developing the Digital Practitioner. *Research in Learning Technology*, 22 (July). https://doi.org/10.3402/rlt.v22.21453

Bennett, S., & Marsh, D. (2002). Are we expecting tutors to run before they can walk? *Innovations in Education and Teaching International*, 39(1), 14–20.

Community of Inquiry (COI). (2017). Retrieved from https://coi.athabascau.ca/

Compton, L. K. L. (2009). Preparing language teachers to teach language online: A look at skills, roles and responsibilities. *Computer Assisted Language Learning*, 22(1), 73–99. https://doi.org/10.1080/09588220802613831

Covington, D., Petherbridge, D., & Warren, S. E. (2005). Best practices: A triangulated support approach in transitioning faculty to online teaching. *Online*

Journal of Distance Learning Administration, VIII, I. Retrieved from http://www.westga.edu/~distance/ojdla/spring81/covington81.htm

Creswell, J. W., & Plano Clark, V. L. (2011). *Designing and Conducting Mixed Methods Research*. California: Sage.

Davis, N., & Rose, R. (2007). *Research Committee Issues Brief: Professional Development for Virtual Schooling and Online Learning*. Vienna, VA: North American Council for Online Learning.

Germain-Rutherford, A., & Ernest, P. (2015). European language teachers and ICT: Experiences, expectations and training needs. In U. Stickler and R. Hampel (eds.), *Developing Online Language Teaching: Research Based Pedagogies and Reflective Practices* (pp. 12–27). Basingstoke: Palgrave Macmillan UK.

Gilbert, J. (2013). English for Academic Purposes. In G. Motteram (ed.), *Innovations in Learning Technologies for English Language Teaching* (pp. 117–144). British Council.

Graddol, D. (2006). *English Next: Why Global English May Mean the End of "English as a Foreign Language."* British Council.

Hampel, R., & Stickler, U. (2005). New skills for new classrooms: Training teachers to teach languages online. *Computer Assisted Language Learning*, 18(4), 311–326. https://doi.org/10.1080/0958822050033545

Kress, G. (2003). *Literacy in the New Media Age*. London: Routledge. https://doi.org/10.4324/9780203164754

Kugel, P. (1993). How professors develop as teachers. *Studies in Higher Education*, 18(3), 315–328. https://doi.org/10.1080/03075079312331382241

Powell, R. A., Single, H. M., & Lloyd, K. R. (1996). Focus groups in mental health research: Enhancing the validity of user and provider questionnaires. *International Journal of Social Psychology*, 42(3), 193–206. https://doi.org/10.1177/002076409604200303

Redmond, P. (2011). Changing demands, changing directions. In G. Williams, P. Statham, N. Brown, and B. Cleland (eds.), *Proceedings ASCILITE Hobart 2011* (pp. 1050–1060). Retreived from http://www.ascilite.org.au/conferences/hobart11/procs/Redmond.pdf

Shea, P., Li, C. S., & Pickett, A. (2006). A study of teaching presence and student sense of learning community in fully online and web-enhanced college courses. *The Internet and Higher Education*, 9(3), 175–190. https://doi.org/10.1016/j.iheduc.2006.06.005

Stickler, U., & Emke, M. (2015). Part-time and freelance language teachers and their ICT Training needs. In U. Stickler and R. Hampel (eds.), *Developing Online Language Teaching: Research Based Pedagogies and Reflective Practices* (pp. 28–44). New York: Palgrave Macmillan Publishers. https://doi.org/10.1057/9781137412263_3

Appendix A

Questionnaire A

Before you begin the survey we would be grateful if you could answer a few basic questions

1. Are you male or female?
2. What is your age?
   17 or younger
   18–20
   21–29
   30–39
   40–49
   50–59
   60 or older
3. How many years of experience do you have teaching face-to-face?
   0–1 year
   2–5 years
   6–10 years
   10+ years
4. Do you have a teaching qualification?
   Yes / No / Currently studying towards one
5. Please specify what teaching qualification/s you hold and dates you completed them.
6. Are you a member of the Higher Education Academy?
   Yes / No / In application
7. **Prior** to teaching online for BPP how many years experience did you have of online teaching elsewhere?
   0–1 year
   2–5 years
   6–10 years
   10+ years
8. **Prior** to writing online materials for BPP how many years experience did you have of writing online materials elsewhere?
   0–1 year
   2–5 years
   6–10 years
   10+ years

Confidence/Self-Efficacy

9.   **Prior** to undertaking any design or development of online materials for BPP how confident were you that you

	Not confident				Confident
	1	2	3	4	5
understood the requirements for writing online materials					
understood the difference between the needs of online learners compared to those of face-to-face learners					
were able to transfer your face-to-face teaching skills to online development and course design					
had a good knowledge of e-learning software and tools					
could manage your time to meet the online deadlines					
could be creative and innovative in your online lesson design					
could write engaging scripts for both audio and video					
could make online activities challenging and meaningful to the student					
would be able to build rapport with students					

10.   Do you have any further comments regarding the above or anything you would like to expand upon?

Practice

11. **Prior** to undertaking any online course development work for BPP
to what extent would you have agreed/disagreed with each of the
statements below:

	Don't agree		Neither agree or disagree		Agree
	1	2	3	4	5
I actively seek peer feedback on my work					
I design online learning activities to suit the specific needs of online learners					
I explore the capabilities of technology for teaching and learning					
I evaluate my practices through regular feedback and reflection					
I reflect on innovations in my practice					
I experiment with e-learning tools in my practice					
Technology has the potential to enhance and transform learning					

12. Do you have any further comments regarding the above or anything you would like to expand upon?

Skills

13. **<u>Prior</u>** to undertaking any online development work for BPP to what extent would you have agreed or disagreed with the following statements

	Don't agree		Neither agree or disagree		Agree
	1	2	3	4	5
I can manage my time effectively					
I can install and update software and plug ins					
I can manage, organize and arrange files on the network					
I have excellent proof reading skills and attention to detail					
I can write effective online materials (using Word or Powerpoint)					
I understand and can apply the basic principles of effective online learning design					
I understand the functionality and can use the e-learning tools that are available to me					

14. Do you have any further comments regarding the above or anything you would like to expand upon?

Access

15. **Prior** to undertaking any online development work to what extent would you have agreed or disagreed that you had access to the following:

	Don't agree		Neither agree nor disagree		Agree
	1	2	3	4	5
People who can support me in using technology					
A network of people with ideas for using technology					
E-learning software / tools					
Networked devices, applications and materials					

16. Do you have any further comments regarding the above or anything you would like to expand upon?

Is there anything else you'd like to mention concerning how you felt about developing online materials and teaching online for BPP prior to doing so?

Please provide your email address.

Thank you for taking the time to complete our survey

Appendix B

Focus group questions

General questions
    a.   What are the key skills you need for developing online materials? Talking generally.
    b.   What do you think are some of the key challenges?

Project-specific questions
    c.   Do you think the skills are still the same? What skills have you used in face-to-face context? Are there new skills?
    d.   What difficulties did you face? How did you overcome these?
    e.   What do you think you pass on to other developers? What "nuggets of wisdom" would you pass on?

PART THREE

ASSESSMENT TOOLS FOR ONLINE ENVIRONMENTS

8   Innovative Implementation of a Web-Based Rating System for Individualizing Online English Speaking Instruction

Hyejin Yang* and Elena Cotos**†

Introduction

The primary goal of computer-assisted language learning (CALL) in general, and of online language instruction in particular, is to create and evaluate language learning opportunities. To be effective, online language courses need to be guided by an integrated set of theoretical perspectives to second language acquisition (SLA), as well as by specific curricular goals, learning objectives and outcomes, appropriate tasks and necessary materials, and learners' characteristics and abilities – to name a few factors that are essential in both online and face-to-face teaching (Xu & Morris, 2007). Doughty and Long (2003) articulate pedagogical principles for computer-assisted language teaching, which highlight the importance of exercising task-based activities, elaborating the linguistic input, enhancing the learning processes with negative feedback, and individualizing learning. Chapelle (2009) further puts forth a framework of evaluation principles that define the characteristics of tasks and materials drawing on SLA theories. Notably, she remarks that "[t]he groundwork for such evaluation projects is an iterative process of stating ideals for the materials based on the theoretical framework and providing a judgmental analysis of the degree to which the desired features actually appear in the materials" (Chapelle, 2009: 749). In other words, she calls for a judgmental analysis as pre-evaluation. With

*   Sookmyung Women's University and Yonsei University, Korea;
        hjyang1112@gmail.com
**   Iowa State University, USA; ecotos@iastate.edu
†   Both authors contributed equally to this chapter.

regard to online language instruction, pre-evaluation is rather challenging when it comes to individualizing learning in view of learners' characteristics and abilities, which are different in every iteration of the course.

Individualization is part of learner fit (Hubbard, 1988), a critical concept from cognitive and psycholinguistic SLA perspectives (Chapelle, 2009) as well as from the perspective of CALL evaluation (Chapelle, 2001, Hubbard, 2006). In essence, learner fit refers to the language level and the opportunities for engagement with language under appropriate conditions accounting for learner characteristics (Jamieson, Chapelle, & Preiss, 2005). When considering learner fit, Hubbard (2006) recommends determining if the skills and the level of language difficulty (i.e., the level of grammatical, lexical, phonetic challenge) are compatible with learner variables (e.g., native language, proficiency level, learner needs) and the course objectives in the syllabus, accentuating that learner variables are individual by nature and not evident to the teacher. In that case, how can language teachers and online course designers be informed about learner variables thorough a pre-evaluation judgmental analysis? How can they make informed decisions regarding whether or not the linguistic forms targeted in their courses are at an appropriate level of difficulty for individual learners? These questions pose a considerable practical challenge for online speaking courses.

Concerned with this challenge, we turn to curriculum-related assessment (Carr, 2011) in an attempt to leverage its underexplored capacity to strengthen the learner fit of online language teaching. Our work focuses on the need to inform language instruction in the context of oral language proficiency courses for international teaching assistants (ITAs) at a large university in the Midwest United States, which are to undergo a transition from the face-to-face to the online mode. The purpose of our mixed-methods study is to examine the potential of R-PLAT (Rater Platform), a computer-based tool for speaking assessment, to generate diagnostic evidence of the language ability of prospective individual students. We follow the theoretically-grounded argument-based validation approach (Kane, 2016), highlighted in Chapter 6 and further discussed in Chapter 12, by empirically investigating a judgmental assumption about the intended use of assessment results from R-PLAT. The results obtained from qualitative and quantitative data support the intended use of R-PLAT as a diagnostic informant for the design of online course materials and tasks that would tailor the level of language difficulty to individual needs and speaking ability. On a broader scale, this work sets the scene for assessment-enhanced development of sound pedagogical principles necessary for curriculum design of online language courses.

Curriculum-Related Assessment

Carr (2011: 6) distinguishes assessments that "are closely related to teaching or learning curriculum, and those that are not," defining the former as curriculum-related because teachers and administrators draw on specific curricula when planning and developing them. Such assessments include placement, diagnostic, progress, and achievement tests. Of these, placement and diagnostic assessments are especially suitable for individualizing curriculum planning at the pre-evaluation stage. Among the types of assessment that Carr places outside the curriculum-related domain are proficiency tests, for they are used to determine learners' level of language ability "without respect to a particular curriculum" (Carr, 2011: 8). In practice, though, proficiency tests are often used for placement into certain levels of language courses. Sometimes diagnostic information can be derived from placement tests (Fox, 2009). Therefore, despite their distinct purposes, placement, diagnostic, and proficiency tests can complementarily serve to obtain evidence to inform curriculum design with descriptive details about the language ability of individual students.

Although leveraging the potential of these assessment types is appealing and equally justifiable, a problem surfaces with regard to individual performance descriptors. It is a common assumption that scaled proficiency descriptors of different performance tests (e.g., TOEFL, IELTS, CEFR, ACTFL) have evident diagnostic potential (Jang, 2012). In other words, performance-level descriptors provide a depiction of language ability within given performance levels that can help teachers form diagnostic judgments about learners' mastery of language based on an external standard of performance. However, those descriptors are "absolute" in nature (Carr, 2011: 10). For example, ACTFL characterizes a novice's speaking ability to use language functionally as "[c]an ask highly predictable and formulaic questions and respond to such questions by listing, naming, and identifying" and "[m]ay show emerging evidence of the ability to engage in simple conversation" (ACTFL, 2012: 14). Such descriptors are not sufficiently informative to make specific diagnostic inferences about individual learners' strengths and weaknesses in the skills assessed. That is not to say that obtaining such information is not possible, as technological advancements in computer-assisted language testing (CALT) have increasingly enabled the integration of assessment in teaching and learning (Chapelle, Chung, & Xu, 2008). In this chapter, we provide an example of how technology can interlace the connection between assessment and teaching with diagnostic information, and how systematic evidence can be gathered and evaluated under the validity argument framework.

Argument-Based Validation and Speaking Assessments for Online Teaching

In language assessment, validation is the most essential process for justifying the use and interpretations of test outcomes. The argument-based approach to validation (Kane, 2016) consists of an interpretive argument and a validity argument. The interpretive argument specifies "the proposed interpretations and use of test results by laying out the network of inferences and assumptions leading from the observed performances to the conclusions and decisions based on the performances" (Kane, 2006: 23). The inferences include: domain description, evaluation, generalization, explanation, extrapolation, and utilization (Chapelle, Enright, & Jamieson, 2008). Each inference is authorized by an explicit warrant; each warrant, in turn, has underlying pre-evaluation assumptions that need to be investigated empirically. The validity argument, in essence, is a process for evaluating the "coherence, completeness, and plausibility" of the proposed assumptions in the interpretative argument (Kane, 2016: 202). The final chapter in this book provides an extended description of the approach.

CALT studies employing the argument-based approach have proliferated in the past few years. With regards to ITA contexts, a number of studies provide evidence supporting the validity of the interpretation and use of the TOEFL iBT® Speaking scores for ITA certification (Farnsworth, 2013; Lim et al., 2012; Wylie & Tannenbam, 2006; Xi, 2007). Another test with a speaking component, the Pearson Test of English Academic, was similarly evaluated in university contexts on the basis of an assessment use argument (Bachman & Palmer, 2010; Wang et al., 2012). The rigor and depth of these works are exemplary; however, no such studies have been conducted for the purpose of examining diagnostic evidence with an emphasis on learner fit for online language teaching.

Online language courses focused on speaking have successfully integrated technologies for various assessment purposes. Most commonly, teachers adapt to the affordances of commercial and open-source applications to enable e-assessment of students' progress and achievement. For example, Volle (2005) used voiced audio emails and MSN Messenger in an online Spanish class to measure improvement in learners' pronunciation, stress, and intonation, as well as accuracy and overall oral proficiency. Blake et al. (2008) reported on the use of Versant, a phone-delivered automated speaking test, to assess students' oral language proficiency in the final weeks of distance learning, hybrid, and face-to-face Spanish courses. Levy & Kennedy (2004) utilized audio-video conferencing tools for enhancing Italian language learners' focus on language form and for ongoing formative assessment, which is conceptually close to diagnostic assessment in that both aim to inform differentiated instruction (Nichols, Meyers, & Burling, 2009). However, to our knowledge, no computer-based assessment of speaking has been used as a pre-evaluation diagnostic measure that would identify error patterns and discrepancies from expected performance to tailor online teaching to individual learner needs. Moreover, interpretive arguments for curriculum-related assessments in the context of ITA language instruction have not been articulated.

The Study

Assumption and Research Questions

This study centers on the *evaluation* inference in the interpretive argument for using R-PLAT in order to inform the transition from face-to-face to ability-tailored online ITA speaking courses. Because test scores are to be interpreted in relation to this domain, we conform to the definition of evaluation for lower stakes testing contexts by Chapelle & Voss (2016) – that summaries of test-taker performance are accurate and relevant. Our warrant presumes that R-PLAT captures appropriate diagnostic descriptors of individual speaking ability needed for a strong learner fit quality of online language instruction. The pre-evaluation assumption underlying this warrant is that these diagnostic descriptors are indicative of target speaking ability levels used for placement into the respective levels of the course. Considering this assumption, we aim to answer the following research questions:

(1) Can raters' markings of diagnostic descriptors in R-PLAT serve as indicators of individual speaking ability?
(2) Can raters' descriptive comments in R-PLAT serve as indicators of individual speaking ability?

R-PLAT and the ITA Assessment Context

R-PLAT is a web-based assessment system that enables the delivery of the face-to-face institutional Oral English Certification Test (OECT), which is used for ITA certification and placement into level-based sections of the speaking course. It consists of two sections: an Oral Proficiency Interview (OPI) and a teaching simulation (TEACH). Following the ACTFL protocol, the OPI begins with an unrated "warm-up" introduction, which is followed by three impromptu questions and a role-play situation. The TEACH is intended to assess ITA candidates' ability to use English for teaching a topic in their field of study. Examinees present a mini-lecture on a topic in their discipline based on textbook materials they are provided. This mini-lecture is followed by a question-answer session, during which the raters ask questions about the presented content.

R-PLAT is designed as a rating platform for both OECT sections. It also integrates the scoring rubric and the OPI test items, which are provided as prompt sets developed based on ACTFL guidelines for eliciting a ratable sample. Each set contains proficiency-level-based impromptu questions on three different topics and different language functions (e.g., narrate, describe, compare, contrast, persuade, etc.), and a role-play task for four intended difficulty levels: advanced (230–300), intermediate-high (210–220), intermediate-mid (170–200), and intermediate-low (120–160). Individual students' performance is evaluated by two or three raters simultaneously; one of the raters acts as the interviewer in the OPI. All the raters use R-PLAT as follows:

(1) to assign a score for each response to each of the three OPI questions
(2) to assign a score for the performance on the OPI role-play
(3) to assign a total OPI score by averaging the four scores for each OPI prompt
(4) to assign a score for the TEACH performance
(5) to write descriptive comments about various aspects of language use in both OPI and TEACH.

Figure 8.1. The OPI rating page in R-PLAT

Figure 8.1 demonstrates these affordances on the OPI page of R-PLAT. Additionally, R-PLAT enables raters to mark up to 30 descriptors divided into seven diagnostic categories that are based on the OECT scoring criteria:

(1) Comprehensibility (ease of understanding, accent, and volume)
(2) Pronunciation (vowels, consonants, insertion, enunciation, reduction, intonation, rhythm, and word stress)
(3) Fluency (phrasing, choppiness, halting, false starts, pauses, incomplete utterances, and pace)
(4) Vocabulary (breadth of vocabulary, word choices, and expression)
(5) Grammar (grammatical complexity, word order, verbs, word form, singular or plural, pronouns, and articles)
(6) Pragmatics (interaction and compensation strategies)
(7) Listening.

As shown in Figure 8.2, each diagnostic descriptor within each category can be marked on a five-point scale.

With these affordances, R-PLAT facilitates language sample elicitation and evaluation processes. It also adds complementary functionality. For instance, the raters can access R-PLAT to verify their rating schedules. Test administrators can access the Administrator Portal in R-PLAT to adjudicate and finalize scores, then report the test results to students, departments, and the instructors of ITA speaking courses into which students are placed. The system's database also contains demographic information including first language, graduate program, gender, etc. The speaking courses for ITAs have been offered face-to-face, but there is a pressing need for larger-scale and more learner-tailored online instruction. R-PLAT's affordances have thus been designed to capture multiple types of evidence indicative of prospective students' English-speaking ability.

Figure 8.2. Diagnostic descriptors for Comprehensibility

Participants

Eight OECT raters participated in this study. The raters had at least one-year rating experience and had participated in the assessment of ITAs prior to the implementation of R-PLAT. As is required before each test administration, the raters completed the so-called "brush-up" rater-training session. The rater-training included a review of test items and a tutorial for how to use R-PLAT. During the training sessions, raters practiced using R-PLAT for mock rating sessions with four video recordings and live testing of two ITAs. OECT data were collected from 53 prospective ITAs. These were graduate students in a wide variety of disciplines who were admitted to the university and considered for a teaching assistantship based on the following cut-off scores: TOEFL iBT 79, TOEFL PBT 550, IELTS 6.5, Pearson Test of English (PTE) 53.

Data and Data Analysis

A total of 146 OECT diagnostic ratings of the ITA participants were recorded during the administration of the test using R-PLAT. Of these, 50 ratings pertained to the advanced level, 39 to intermediate-high, and 57 to intermediate-mid. Intermediate-low is generally extremely rare, which is why this dataset did not contain this level. To examine the extent to which the diagnostic descriptors marked by the raters in R-PLAT indicated students' different speaking ability levels, the frequencies of 30 diagnostic descriptors marked on a five-point scale were collected from each rating. Henceforth, these will be referred to as diagnostic descriptor markings. In total, 2,524 markings for each proficiency level were analyzed. To compare the frequencies of these markings at each scale point (dependent variables) across the three proficiency levels (independent variables), we ran Chi-Square tests, which are generally used to establish whether there is a relationship between two categorical variables (Larson-Hall, 2010). Next, seven Chi-Square tests were run separately to compare the markings across the three proficiency levels for each of the seven diagnostic indicators of speaking ability – comprehensibility, pronunciation, fluency, vocabulary, grammar, pragmatics, and listening.

In a similar vein, we examined whether the raters' descriptive comments can serve as diagnostic indicators of prospective ITA's speaking ability. The raters provided specific examples of patterns of language errors and/or appropriate language use as well as general impression comments about the test-takers' language performance on the OECT. The analysis of rater comments unfolded as follows. First, in the tradition of grounded theory (Glaser

& Strauss, 1967), we identified themes in each rater's comments about individual test-takers' performance. The themes that emerged contained positive and negative assessments of language ability. The positive comments indicated strengths in language use with expressions such as "excellent," "strong," "good," etc. Negative comments highlighted weaknesses and examples of erroneous language use. The comments were further quantified using the metric of evaluative unit, defined as a segment (word, phrase, or clause) that expresses a rater's positive or negative assessment. For instance, the positive comment "*No effort to understand. Excellent enunciation and vocabulary.*" contains three evaluative units. In the negative comment, "*Some word stress issues. Lots of pausing and halting when nervous. Some sounds deleted. ([w] in wooden),*" four evaluative units are underlined. In total, 1,900 evaluative units were coded. Our reliability of coding rater comments into positive and negative evaluative units, measured by Cohen's kappa, was high ($k = 0.900$, $p = 0.000$).

To further establish if the diagnostic descriptors discriminate among the target speaking ability levels, the evaluative units were grouped by proficiency level: advanced (475 units), intermediate-high (523 units), and intermediate-mid (902 units). Additionally, the evaluative units were mapped onto each of the six criteria in the scoring rubric: functional competency (348 units), comprehensibility (150 units), pronunciation (526 units), fluency (424 units), vocabulary (167 units), and grammar (285 units). Cohen's kappa for coding into these evaluation criteria was also high ($k = 0.823$, $p = 0.000$). Descriptive statistics and Chi-Square tests were used to analyze differences in the frequencies of positive and negative evaluative units across the three proficiency levels, and for each of the six scoring criteria across the three proficiency levels. The dependency of the proficiency levels on the frequencies of positive and negative evaluative units was established by a Chi-Square test with a critical p-value of less than 0.05.

Results

Diagnostic Descriptor Markings

The first research question centered on raters' markings of the diagnostic descriptors enabled by R-PLAT. The analysis of raters' markings was conducted at two levels: first, 30 distinct descriptors were analyzed separately, and then the descriptors were grouped into seven higher-up diagnostic categories for analysis. Overall, the analysis provided evidence supporting our assumption that the diagnostic descriptors are indicative of target speaking

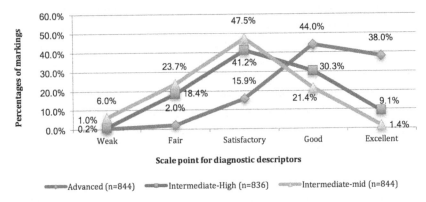

Figure 8.3. Distribution of the diagnostic descriptor markings on each scale across three proficiency levels

ability levels. This can be inferred from the association between the markings of all diagnostic descriptors and the three proficiency levels depicted in Figure 8.3. The markings on the higher end of the scale (Good and Excellent) were more frequent for the advanced level, whereas the markings on the lower end (Weak and Fair) were greater for intermediate-high and intermediate-mid.

The Chi-Square test yielded significant differences in the frequencies of the markings at each scale point grouped by the three proficiency levels, X^2 (8, n markings = 2,524) = 830.92, $p < 0.01$. The more proficient students were given more markings higher on the scale compared to the less proficient students. These results suggest that the diagnostic descriptor markings support the proficiency ratings, especially distinguishing between the advanced and the two intermediate levels.

The results based on the markings grouped into diagnostic categories were similar. Those pertaining to five of the seven categories – Comprehensibility, Pronunciation, Fluency, Vocabulary, and Grammar – were consistently higher for the advanced level and lower for intermediate-mid and intermediate-high. The Chi-Square tests on these categories showed significant differences in the frequencies of the constituent descriptor markings at each scale point grouped by the three proficiency level ratings: Comprehensibility, X^2 (8, n = 340) = 83.99, $p < 0.01$; Pronunciation, X^2 (8, n = 707) = 185.95, $p < 0.01$; Fluency, X^2 (8, n = 610) = 232.02, $p < 0.01$; Vocabulary, X^2 (8, n = 178) = 116.53, $p < 0.01$; and Grammar, X^2 (8, n = 531) = 289.83, $p < 0.01$. The markings related to the other two categories – Pragmatics and Listening – exhibited somewhat different patterns. While the higher proficiency levels had more diagnostic descriptors marked as Excellent and Satisfactory and the vice versa, the percentages of descriptors marked as Good did not distinguish among the proficiency levels (Figures 8.4a and b). For Pragmatics, for instance, the percentages of the descriptors evaluated as Good clustered close together (advanced 42.6%, intermediate-high 42.6%, and intermediate-mid 40.0%). Nonetheless, these results are not surprising because pragmatic and listening abilities are not sub-traits of speaking proficiency. It is worth mentioning that the Chi-Square tests for the seven categories, including Pragmatics (X^2 (8, n = 158) = 43.26, $p < 0.01$) and Listening (X^2 (8, n = 73) = 34.41, $p < 0.01$), showed statistically significant differences. Thus, it can be inferred that the diagnostic descriptor markings for the seven categories were distributed at each scale point reflective of different proficiency levels.

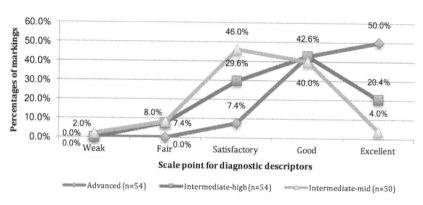

Figure 8.4a. Distribution of diagnostic descriptor markings for Pragmatics on each scale across three proficiency levels

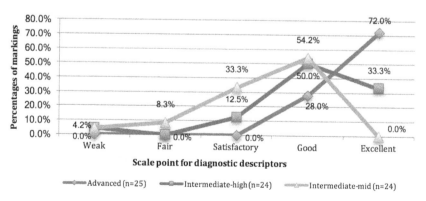

Figure 8.4b. Distribution of diagnostic descriptor markings for Listening on each scale across three proficiency levels

Descriptive Comments

To answer the second research question, we analyzed the diagnostic information provided by raters in the form of open-ended comments enabled by
R-PLAT. Here, too, our assumption appeared to be supported. The analysis
of positive and negative evaluative units exhibited clear associative patterns
between the type of evaluative units and the three proficiency levels. The
percentage of positive evaluative units was higher for the advanced level
(61.0%) and much lower for intermediate-high (18.5%) and intermediate-
mid (13.4%); the negative evaluative units indicated the opposite (Figure
8.5). Chi-Square results showed significant differences in the frequencies
of positive and negative evaluative units across the three proficiency levels,
X^2 (2, n = 1,900) = 386.50, $p < 0.01$. Overall, the comments were reflective
of students' different proficiency levels and can thus be considered as diagnostic indicators of speaking ability.

In a parallel strand of analysis, the positive and negative evaluative units
were grouped based on the OECT scoring criteria: functional competency,
comprehensibility, fluency, vocabulary, pronunciation, and grammar; and
then compared across proficiency levels. Descriptive comments related to
the first four criteria exhibited patterns similar to the one in Figure 8.5.
For grammar and pronunciation, the number of negative evaluative units
exceeded that of positive units regardless of proficiency level. The percentages for negative units were much greater than those for positive evaluative
units (e.g., pronunciation in Figure 8.6). This is likely due to the fact that
the raters pay a lot of attention to language errors, recording which helps
them determine if those appear to be error patterns or mistakes. It is also
possible that the prompt in R-PLAT's comment box ("Please write specific
comments and error examples") encourages them to focus on errors. All
Chi-Square tests for each scoring criterion showed significant differences in
the frequencies of positive and negative evaluative units across levels, con-
firming the association of the two types of evaluative units with the three
proficiency levels.

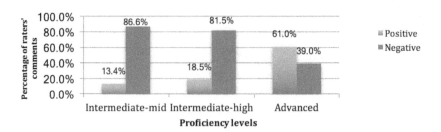

Figure 8.5. Overall distribution of positive and negative evaluative units across
proficiency levels

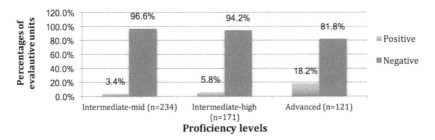

Figure 8.6. Distribution of positive and negative evaluative units across proficiency levels for pronunciation

Discussion

The results of this first effort towards supporting assumptions about the intended use of R-PLAT will be used to develop a principled approach to designing online ITA instruction with a learner fit quality substantiated by reliable diagnostic information. In the face-to-face course, individualizing teaching from the very beginning has been beyond the bounds of possibility. R-PLAT's affordances, however, will greatly facilitate transition to the online mode and will allow for a fuller integration of proficiency assessment in online course design.

ITA program administration will use R-PLAT-recorded data to develop a formalized, multifaceted spec model of diagnostic descriptors, containing clearly defined characteristics and representative of both proficiency level and first language. The diagnostic spec model will enable tailoring the curriculum to more specific needs. Most importantly, a judgmental analysis will be conducted to determine whether the desired linguistic features detected through R-PLAT would appear in the course materials. Once level-based diagnostics-to-materials mapping is accomplished, multiple types of enhancement will be applied to the desired features. The model will also become an essential resource for teacher and rater training. Additionally, the OECT performance-level descriptors will be revised in view of the new spec model to improve the level of detail often sought not only by teachers and students, but also by raters, course and test coordinators, and students' graduate programs.

Instructors, successively, will be provided with diagnostic information derived from R-PLAT about the students placed in the section of the course they will be teaching, which they will use to develop learning and practice plans for individual students given their proficiency level and language background. To capacitate teachers to tailor the syllabus to group-specific needs, diagnostic group-level reports will also be supplied. This will help teachers determine the appropriateness of the level of linguistic difficulty and adapt the materials and tasks in order to focus on the desired linguistic forms. For this purpose, the 30 diagnostic descriptors for both segmental (e.g., vowels, consonants) and suprasegmental (e.g., intonation, stress) features will be particularly useful. In the future, R-PLAT could be customized further to enable diagnostically-driven formative feedback by the teacher as well as by peers.

The implications of this study extend to curriculum-based assessment in online language education as well. Language tests are generally categorized based on the type of decisions they are used to inform. OECT serves the dual purpose of assessing ITAs' level of speaking ability and to decide which section of the course they should be placed in. While facilitating the former, the value of R-PLAT is in its unique capability to catalog diagnostic evidence in order to inform curriculum design and the learner fit quality of online teaching. This purpose overlaps with diagnostic assessment where the goal is to exert positive change in student learning; yet, it is slightly different in that the focus is on curriculum and course design. Considering this primary focus on pedagogy, it seems to us that a new form of curriculum-based assessment could emerge – assessment for language instruction (ALI). Despite its focus on learning tasks, ALI would be distinct from learning-oriented language assessment. The latter "is inherently interactive" and entails learner-involved assessment (i.e., self and peer evaluation) and learning-focused feedback (i.e., interlocutor scaffolding, immediate feedback, and focus on feed-forward), which are essential during teaching and learning but immaterial for learner diagnostics-based pre-evaluation of instruction.

On a broader scale, such an innovation in assessment practices seems to be particularly called for, given the proliferation of web-based instructional environments. As Chapelle and Voss (2016: 120, 121) argue, "[a]n innovative agenda for language assessment extends beyond the goal of making more efficient tests to expanding the uses of assessment and their usefulness"; and technology is "ideally suited to play a role in this vision because of their capacity for individual treatment of test takers as learners," who "should actually be given opportunities to learn from both the process and the results of test taking." Apart from instantiating positive changes in learning, ALI would impact teachers, who would no longer be pressed to adapt haphazardly to their subjective interpretations based on the results of diagnostic tests, which may or may not be developed. Instead, they would be guided by reliable diagnostics, perhaps from several raters, as is the case with R-PLAT.

Conclusion

This study investigated the potential of R-PLAT to capture diagnostic evidence from a speaking test. The data consisted of diagnostic descriptor markings and descriptive comments about individual students' oral proficiency provided by raters via R-PLAT. Our judgmental assumption that these types of diagnostic evidence are indicative of speaking ability was substantiated by the associations between the diagnostic descriptors and the target proficiency levels, which are used for placement into respective levels of the speaking course for ITAs. Continuing this research agenda, each aspect of online course development informed by this study will be investigated as warrants and assumptions for a range of inferences in the validity argument for R-PLAT. Although there is much yet to do, we have molded the first building block for leveraging technology to collect multiple types of diagnostic evidence for assessment for online language instruction.

About the Authors

Hyejin Yang is a Lecturer at Sookmyung Women's University and Yonsei University, Korea. Her research interests include language assessment, computer-assisted language learning, and L2 speaking and writing.

Elena Cotos is an Assistant Professor in the Applied Linguistics Program at Iowa State University. She is also the Director of the Center for Communication Excellence of the Graduate College at Iowa State University. She investigates computer-assisted language learning and assessment, written and spoken genres, and automated writing evaluation.

References

ACTFL (American Council on the Teaching of Foreign Languages), (2012). *ACTFL Oral Proficiency Interview Familiarization Manual*. Retrieved December 12, 2016 from http://www.languagetesting.com/wp-content/uploads/2013/05/ACTFL-OPI-Familiarization-Manual1.pdf.

Bachman, L. F., & Palmer, A. S. (2010). *Language Assessment in Practice: Developing Language Assessments and Justifying Their Use in the Real World*. Oxford: Oxford University Press.

Blake, R., Wilson, N., Cetto, M., & Pardo Ballester, C. (2008). Measuring oral proficiency in distance, face-to-face, and blended classrooms. *Language Learning & Technology*, 12(3), 114–127. Retrieved from http://llt.msu.edu/issues/june2016/blake.pdf

Carr, N. T. (2011). *Designing and Analyzing Language Tests*. New York, NY: Oxford University Press. http://dx.doi.org/10.1017/s0272263112000800

Chapelle, C. (2001). *Computer Applications in Second Language Acquisition: Foundations for Teaching, Testing, and Research*. Cambridge: Cambridge University Press.

Chapelle, C. (2009). The relationship between second language acquisition theory and computer-assisted language learning. *Modern Language Journal*, 93(S1), 741–753. http://dx.doi.org/10.1111/j.1540-4781.2009.00970.x

Chapelle, C. A., Chung, Y-R., & Xu, J. (eds.). (2008). *Towards Adaptive CALL: Natural Language Processing for Diagnostic Language Assessment*. Ames, IA: Iowa State University.

Chapelle, C. A., Enright, M. K., & Jamieson, J. (eds.). (2008). *Building a Validity Argument for the Test of English as a Foreign Language*^{TM}. New York: Routledge. http://dx.doi.org/10.4324/9780203937891

Chapelle, C. A., & Voss, E. (2016). 20 years of technology and language assessment in language learning & technology. *Language Learning & Technology*, 20(2), 116–128. Retrieved from http://llt.msu.edu/issues/june2016/chapellevoss.pdf

Doughty, C. J., & Long, M. H. (2003). Optimal psycholinguistic environments for distance foreign language learning. *Language Learning & Technology*, 7(3), 50–80. Retrieved from http://llt.msu.edu/vol7num3/pdf/doughty.pdf

Farnsworth, T. L. (2013). An investigation into the validity of the TOEFL iBT speaking test for international teaching assistant certification. *Language Assessment Quarterly*, 10, 274–291. http://dx.doi.org/10.1080/15434303.2013.769548

Fox, J. (2009). Moderating top-down policy impact and supporting EAP curricular renewal: Exploring the potential of diagnostic assessment. *Journal of English for Academic Purposes*, 8, 26–42. http://dx.doi.org/10.1016/j.jeap.2008.12.004

Glaser, B. G., & Strauss, A. L. (1967). *The Discovery of Grounded Theory*. New York: Aldine.

Hubbard, P. (1988). An integrated framework for CALL courseware evaluation. *CALICO Journal*, 6(2), 51–72. http://dx.doi.org/10.1558/cj.v6i2.51-72

Hubbard, P. (2006). Evaluating CALL software. In L. Ducate & N. Arnolds (eds.), *Calling on Call: From Theory and Research to New Directions in Foreign Language Teaching* (pp. 313–334). San Marcos, TX: CALICO.

Jamieson, J., Chapelle, C., & Preiss, S. (2005). CALL Evaluation by developers, a teacher, and students. *CALICO Journal*, 23(1), 93–138. http://dx.doi.org/10.1558/cj.v23i1.93-138

Jang, E. (2012). Diagnostic assessment in language classrooms. In G. Fulcher & F. Davidson (eds.), *The Routledge Handbook of Language Testing* (pp. 120–133). New York: Routledge. http://dx.doi.org/10.4324/9780203181287

Kane, M. T. (2006). Validation. In R. L. Brennan (ed.), *Educational Measurement* (4th ed.) (pp. 17–64). Westport, CT: American Council on Education.

Kane, M. T. (2016). Explicating validity. *Assessment in Education: Principles, Policy & Practice*, 23(2), 198–211. http://dx.doi.org/10.1080/0969594x.2015.1060192

Larson-Hall, J. (2010). *A Guide to Doing Statistics in Second Language Research Using SPSS*. New York: Routledge.

Levy, M. & Kennedy, C. (2004). A task-cycling pedagogy using stimulated reflection and audio-conferencing in foreign language learning. *Language Learning & Technology*, 8(2), 50–69. Retrieved from http://llt.msu.edu/vol8num2/pdf/levy.pdf

Lim, H., Kim, H., Behney, J., Reed, D., Ohlrogge, A., & Lee, J. E. (2012, March). Validating the use of iBT Speaking scores for ITA screening. Paper presented at the TESOL Annual Convention and Exhibit, Philadelphia, PA.

Nichols, P. D., Meyers, J. L. & Burling, K. S. (2009). A framework for evaluating and planning assessments intended to improve student achievement. *Educational Measurement: Issues and Practice*, 28(3), 14–23. http://dx.doi.org/10.1111/j.1745-3992.2009.00150.x

Volle, L. M. (2005). Analyzing oral skills in voice e-mail and online interviews. *Language Learning & Technology*, 9(3), 146–163. Retrieved from http://llt.msu.edu/vol9num3/pdf/volle.pdf

Wang, H., Choi, I., Schmidgall, J., & Bachman, L. F. (2012). Review of Pearson test of English academic: Building an assessment use argument. *Language Testing*, 29(4), 603–619. http://dx.doi.org/10.1177/0265532212448619

Wylie, E. C., & Tannenbam, R. J. (2006). *TOEFL® Academic Speaking Test: Setting a Cut Score for International Teaching Assistants*. Research Memorandum (RM-06-01). Princeton, NJ: Educational Testing Service. Retrieved from https://www.ets.org/Media/Tests/TOEFL/pdf/ngt_itastandards.pdf

Xi, X. (2007). Validating TOEFL® iBT Speaking and setting score requirements for ITA screening. *Language Assessment Quarterly*, 4(3), 318–351. http://dx.doi.org/10.1080/15434300701462796

Xu, H. & Morris, L. V. (2007). Collaborative course development for online courses. *Innovative Higher Education*, 32, 35–47. http://dx.doi.org/10.1007/s10755-006-9033-5

9 A Systematic Approach to Vetting Reading Comprehension Items for Inclusion in Cloud-Based Assessments

Fabiana MacMillan[*]

Introduction

Effective assessments are an essential component of online language instruction. Because in this environment learners often have more freedom to choose their individual path of learning, assessments are particularly important, as they provide valuable information to help guide those choices. For example, assessments can help customize the learning experience by determining learners' baseline proficiency level, identifying specific skills learners need to develop, and monitoring progress.

In order to develop an effective online assessment, especially in a computer adaptive environment, a very large item pool must be created and maintained. Unfortunately, the item development process is time-consuming and costly. It is not uncommon for a significant number of items to be discarded or require revisions after they are field tested due to redundant difficulty ranges or poor performance. Alderson, Clapham, & Wall (1995: 74) stated, "It is surprising how often items, however thoughtfully designed, fail to distinguish between students" at different levels. For that reason, "for standardized tests, test developers often create six times as many items as those used on the actual test" (Balogh, 2016: 50).

Prior to field testing, new items typically go through several rounds of review intended to ensure that, among other things, each question has only one correct answer and that incorrect options are attractive but not acceptable or defensible answers. However, this review process can be quite

* Rosetta Stone, Inc.; fmacmillan@rosettastone.com

subjective and have variable results. The present study investigated a possible way to address these limitations through a systematic process for vetting reading comprehension test items before field testing. The goal was to produce more high-functioning items (i.e., items that successfully discriminate between high and low ability learners) that could be used in online reading assessments. Specifically, this chapter describes the Systematic Approach to Item Vetting (SAIV) method, which is largely based on Hoey's (1991) written discourse analysis model applied to test development and Jamieson et al.'s (2000) qualitative analysis of variables affecting item difficulty. SAIV is a two-step process in which items are coded for a variety of discourse and item characteristic features and then flagged if certain criteria are not met. SAIV might also help predict item difficulty so that the desired dispersion of ability levels is represented in an item pool.

In the current study, the effectiveness of SAIV was evaluated by using empirical data collected on 96 multiple-choice, EFL reading comprehension items developed for inclusion in placement and achievement tests in the cloud-based language-learning solutions offered by Rosetta Stone®. The results of these assessments are used to automatically direct learners to content at the appropriate level and measure their achievement as they approach the end of the assigned language learning program. First, each test item was coded regarding features of the SAIV model. Then, an analysis was conducted that flagged weak items a priori. The same items were inspected after the field test to identify which were found to have poor discrimination values. Finally, to investigate which, if any, discourse and item characteristic features of SAIV were most predictive of item difficulty, the features were analyzed using a multiple regression model.

The chapter will begin with an outline of the SAIV system used to perform a qualitative analysis of all items in the dataset prior to field testing. Next will be a brief general description of the dataset and the tests for which the items were developed. This will be followed by a description of the quantitative analysis of learner response data using the Rasch model (Rasch, 1980) to obtain difficulty parameter estimates and discrimination indices for each item. The penultimate section will discuss results of the analyses and the extent to which qualitative data correlate with field test outcomes. Finally, the concluding section will comment on the limitations and implications of this study for the assessment and instruction of reading comprehension skills in online programs.

A Theory-Based System for Vetting Reading Comprehension Items

The Systematic Approach to Item Vetting (SAIV) offers a method for vetting items in a consistent way such that more items can be retained in an item pool for an online assessment. The SAIV process is derived from two main bodies of work. The first is Hoey's (1991) written discourse analysis model. This work along with extensions by MacMillan (2007) forms the basis for coding items according to discourse links. Items that violate certain assumptions can be flagged and then revised or replaced with more suitable items before field testing. The second line of research is based on Jamieson et al. (2000), which highlights features that might be related to empirical item difficulty. These features, combined with Hoey's (1991) and MacMillan's (2007) work, can presumably help item developers predict item difficulty before field testing to ensure that enough items are being represented at all ability levels, which is important for online testing, especially in adaptive environments. The theoretical underpinnings of Hoey's (1991) and Jamieson et al.'s (2000) models are described below.

Text Analysis Model

In his widely acclaimed book, *Patterns of Lexis in Text* (1991), Michael Hoey demonstrated that different forms of lexical repetition combine to organize text by establishing semantic connections, referred to as links, between sentences. Sentences that share an above-average number of lexical links are described as bonded. Hoey (1991) has identified five main categories of repetition that form connections between sentences in a text. The five categories are: lexical repetition, paraphrase, superordinate/hyponymic repetition, co-reference, and substitution, with this last category being the only one involving non-lexical cohesive devices. MacMillan (2007) later proposed modifications to the paraphrase category and the addition of a final category, labeling. Both modifications are discussed in more detail below.

The first category of repetition, lexical repetition, may be classified as simple or complex. Simple lexical repetition, as the name implies, refers to the repetition of the same exact content word or an inflected form of the same word (e.g., the plural form of the same noun, a different tense of the same verb) in more than one sentence. Complex lexical repetition refers to cases where derivatives of the same word (e.g., "quick" vs. "quickly") occur in more than one sentence. This category also includes instances where the repeated words share the same form but not the same part of speech (e.g., "to sprint" [v.] vs. "a sprint" [n.]).

Hoey's (1991) second category of repetition, paraphrase, may also be classified as simple or complex. Simple paraphrase encompasses repetition by means of synonyms that are part of the same word class (e.g., "vast" [adj.] vs. "extensive" [adj.]). Complex paraphrase, on the other hand, involves antonyms that don't share the same root (e.g., "hot" vs. "cold"). Note that in this taxonomy, antonyms formed by adding an affix to a common root (e.g., "happy" vs. "unhappy") are categorized as complex lexical repetition, not complex paraphrase. MacMillan (2007) later proposed making the different instances of paraphrase more clear-cut by classifying them instead as synonymy and antonymy. Further, in order to account for instances that a strict application of the original model would disregard, MacMillan (2007) included synonyms and antonyms that are not the same part of speech under complex synonym (e.g., "vastly" [adv.] vs. "extensive" [adj.]), and complex antonym (e.g., "heat" [n.] vs. "cold" [adj.]), respectively. Simple and complex antonyms are used to repeat or reiterate ideas by means of sentence reformulation. For example, the sentence "Penguins huddle together to keep warm" may be reformulated later in the same text as "This behavior helps them endure the frigid cold of Antarctic winter," where a complex antonym link connects the words "warm" [adj.] and "cold" [n.].

The third category of repetition, superordinate/hyponymic repetition, accounts for cases in which words are related by class membership, where a more general term (e.g., "animals") may be said to contain a more specific term (e.g., "birds"). If a general term is used to repeat a more specific term in a previous sentence, this is an instance of superordinate repetition. By contrast, if a more specific term is used to repeat a more general term in a previous sentence, then it represents an instance of hyponymic repetition.

Hoey's (1991) fourth category of repetition, co-reference, refers to instances where words or phrases in different sentences share the same referent, but do not hold a lexical relation. Rather, the link between these words or phrases is context-dependent or tied to background knowledge (e.g., "Michael Jackson" vs. "the King of Pop").

The fifth category of repetition, substitution, differs from the previous ones in that it involves function words rather than content words alone. This category accounts for instances of pronouns (e.g., "this," "it") or phrases (e.g., "the former," "another one") substituting for, or referring back to, specific lexical items or chunks of language appearing earlier in the text. It should be noted that ellipsis is also included in this category, where an earlier term in the text is replaced by zero, as in "Students were not obligated to attend the event. Many chose not to." Here, "Students" and "attend the event" in the first sentence are replaced with zero in the second sentence, thus forming substitution links with that sentence.

The final category, labeling, which was not present in Hoey's (1991) original model, is based on Francis's (1994) description of retrospective labels. Labeling accounts for instances in which phrases formed by a deictic (e.g., this, that, such) and a head noun that is metalinguistic in nature are used to refer back to earlier stretches of text. An example of labeling is the phrase "this hypothesis" in reference to an earlier statement such as "It is possible that …."

Hoey's (1991) written discourse analysis model was originally designed to identify lexical links between adjacent and non-adjacent sentences in prose texts. MacMillan (2007) applied a revised version of this model to the analysis of links in multiple-choice reading comprehension tests. Her hypothesis was that, as sentences that are central to the development of a theme "have an unusually high level of bonding" with other sentences in the text (Hoey, 1991: 113), similarly, item keys (or statements formed by combining the question stem and the correct option) and target sentences in the passage have an above-average number of lexical links with one another.

Results of MacMillan's (2007) study involving 608 reading comprehension questions from the TOEFL® (Test of English as a Foreign Language) showed that, for the majority of the items in her corpus, keys bonded with target sentences in the passages in question by means of multiple lexical links. Exceptions included, for example, items that called for the identification of the one option that is untrue according to the passage, where bonds were observed connecting each of the distractors (rather than the correct option) to the target sentences in the reading passage.

Features from Hoey's (1991) model were integrated into the SAIV process. As a first step, bonds between an item's answer options and the target sentences in the related reading passage are tallied. Only options having a minimum of three links with a target sentence in the passage were considered to form a bond. Then, for each bond observed, the category of the dominant links connecting the item's answer choices and the target sentences in the passage are recorded. Dominant links are defined as the category of repetition carrying the most weight in the establishment of each bond (MacMillan, 2010) because it is the category featuring the largest number of links between item options and passage and/or because it involves a link found exclusively in the key and not any of the distractors. Consider the following excerpt from a sample reading comprehension set from one of the achievement tests in the dataset. Sentence numbers have been added for ease of reference.

[3] I am currently employed as a sales representative for an IT company. [4] My main task is to develop and manage a client list, a role which I both enjoy and feel suited for. [5] I am responsible for establishing contacts with potential new customers both at home and abroad, and I also conduct market research for new projects.

Which of the following is NOT one of this person's responsibilities?
A Technical support
B Finding new clients
C Sales
D Market research

This item tests learners' ability to identify the untrue statement based on information in the passage and, as such, the key (option A) is the one option that does not form a semantic bond with the passage, while bonds are observed connecting all distractors (B, C, and D) with the passage. For example, the statement formed by connecting the question and option B ("One of this person's responsibilities is finding new clients.") bonds with sentence 5 in the passage by means of one complex repetition link ("responsibilities" – "responsible") and a string of simple synonymy links ("finding new clients" – "establishing contacts with potential new customers"). In this case, simple synonymy would be recorded as the dominant link between this item option and the target sentence in the passage.

This portion of the SAIV process is concerned with the quality of test items. The focus is on ensuring that the key is unambiguously the only correct option. Therefore, items with distractors that connect with the same sentence as the key by means of an equivalent or higher number of links are flagged. Additionally, items whose keys do not hold clear semantic links with the passage are also flagged.

The next part of the SAIV process is to evaluate whether items are likely to yield the desired level of difficulty. The method draws from work by Jamieson et al. (2000), as described below.

Qualitative Analysis of Variables Affecting Item Difficulty

The previous sub-section described the first step of the SAIV process, which draws from Hoey's (1991) text analysis model and aims to predict which items are likely to be weak or yield poor discrimination values. In this sub-section, the second part of the SAIV process is discussed. This second step aims to predict item difficulty by means of the qualitative analysis of item content according to Jamieson et al.'s (2000) framework. To determine the effectiveness of SAIV, results of these analyses were subsequently compared with field test outcomes.

Jamieson et al. (2000) argue that the relationships between test items and text features may be described in terms of several variables, two of which were considered to be the most closely related to the purposes of this research: *type of match* (with several features) and *plausibility of distractors*. These variables concern the processes used by examinees to relate information in the test item to the necessary information in the passage in order to identify the correct answer and disambiguate it from distracting information.

According to Jamieson et al. (2000) the scoring of *type of match* in prose processing tasks involves the assessment of five features: (1) strategy type, (2) number of phrases to search on (i.e., number and complexity of the clauses in the question stem), (3) number of responses required (i.e., number of correct answers examinees must identify), (4) type of match for given information (i.e., degree to which examinees have to make inferences to match the language in the question with corresponding information in the passage), and (5) requirements to identify requested information (i.e., degree to which examinees have to make inferences to match the correct answer with corresponding information in the passage). In this study, only strategy type (1) and requirements to identify requested information (5) were considered. This decision was made because the questions in the dataset do not show enough variability in the number of phrases to search on (all questions are close in length and complexity) or number of items in response (all questions have a single correct answer). Additionally, because the written discourse analysis model used involves identifying lexical connections between the passage and statements formed by connecting the question stem and each of the options, it was felt that the fourth feature (type of match for given information) was subsumed under the fifth (requirements to identify requested information). Therefore, only the latter one was scored.

The first *type-of-match* feature considered in this study, strategy type, consists of a range of four strategies on a rising scale of difficulty: locating, cycling, integrating, and generating. Locating tasks (scored 1) require test takers to match one or more pieces of information within the test item to either identical or synonymous information in the passage in question. Cycling tasks (scored 2) require that respondents engage in a series of locating actions in order to satisfy the conditions entailed in the test item. Integrating tasks (scored 3) involve the use of one or more cycling strategies to identify pieces of information within the passage, followed by the relation of the different pieces of information (e.g., cause – effect; hypothesis – evidence) according to requirements in the question. Finally, generating tasks (scored 5) require that test takers use an integrating strategy to relate pieces of information based on categories or connections they have inferred from the passage.

The other *type-of-match* feature of interest, requiring test takers to identify requested information, concerns the processes involved in the identification of points in the passage yielding the correct answer to the question. In multiple-choice questions, it specifically concerns the processes involved in matching relevant points in the passage to correct options, or keys. Four requirements are taken into account, namely: (a) identification of a paradigmatic relation (i.e., recognizing synonyms that appear as the same part of speech, in the same syntactic relation, and in the context of one or more identical words) (scored 0); (b) low-level text-based inference (e.g., matching a pronoun with its referent) (scored 2); (c) some prior knowledge or identification of a syntagmatic relation (i.e., recognizing synonyms that occur in a context that does not meet all three conditions in a paradigmatic relation) (scored 3); and (d) high-level text-based inference (e.g., using background knowledge to draw a logical conclusion) (scored 4).

Finally, the *plausibility-of-distractors* variable is concerned with how attractive incorrect answers are, based on whether they contain information found in the text and, if so, where that information is located relative to the key. In this study, this variable was operationalized by identifying which, if any, distractors bonded with sentences in the passage. Items where no distractors formed bonds with the passage were scored 1, and those where only one distractor held such bonds were scored 2. Items where two or more distractors bonded with the passage were scored 3 if bonds were distant from the correct answer, and 5 if those were adjacent to the key.

The SAIV process allows for each item to be coded for four features, the first one of which is from Hoey (1991) and the last three, from Jamieson et al. (2000). These four features are: (1) the type of dominant links observed, (2) the type of match for strategy type, (3) the type of match for requirements to identify required information/key, and (4) plausibility of distractors.

In this trial of SAIV, items were coded for all four features and then field tested to obtain difficulty parameter estimates and discrimination indices. Results of the first step of the SAIV process were checked against field test outcomes to investigate whether flagged items correlated with poor discrimination. Finally, a multiple regression analysis including the four coded features (from the first and second steps of SAIV) was performed in order to determine if they predict empirical item difficulty, and if so, which features contribute most to accounting for the variability.

The Dataset

The dataset in this study consists of a total of 96 reading comprehension questions developed for inclusion in an achievement test and a placement test available in two different cloud-based language-learning solutions offered by Rosetta Stone®.

Approximately 75% of the questions were sampled from the item pool developed for the achievement test offered to learners enrolled in Rosetta Stone® Advantage (RSA) American English, an e-learning program for all proficiency levels. Learners are encouraged to take the RSA achievement test (RSA AT) toward the end of their program to determine their level of mastery in listening and reading with scaled scores that are aligned to the corresponding proficiency levels on the Common European Framework of Reference for Languages (CEFR) (Council of Europe, 2001) based on a standard-setting study involving 15 expert judges in 2015.

The RSA AT is a linear test with 180 questions, including vocabulary, grammar, and listening and reading comprehension. The reading comprehension section, for which the items in this dataset were developed, consists of 10 passages, each of approximately 150 words and followed by three questions. All questions are multiple-choice with four options and only one key.

The remaining 25% of the questions in this dataset were taken from the item pool developed for the placement test learners take before starting the Rosetta Stone® Advanced English for Business program (AEB). The AEB is an e-learning program designed for intermediate to advanced English learners. This program is available in American or British English and focuses on improving business-specific communication skills for the workplace. The AEB curriculum is aligned to the Common European Framework of Reference for Languages (CEFR) with learning paths ranging from levels B1 to C1. Prospective learners' performance on the AEB placement test (AEB PT), which is also aligned to the CEFR, is used to indicate whether the AEB program is right for them and to recommend the appropriate-level AEB content where applicable.

The AEB PT has 60 items, including grammar, vocabulary, and listening and reading comprehension questions. A total of four reading comprehension sets with passages of approximately 200 words followed by three questions each are included in each AEB PT test form. As in the RSA AT, all questions are multiple-choice with four options and only one key.

Psychometric Analysis of Item Performance

Participants

A total of 835 participants contributed data to new items for the RSA AT (n = 358 learners) and the AEB PT (n = 477 learners). Of the participants for which demographic data were available (n = 477), approximately 34% were female, 65% were male, and 1% did not report gender. Ages ranged from 21 to 59, with a mean of 34. Participants reported 47 different native languages, of which the most largely represented were Hindi (25%), Spanish (21%), and Albanian (10%).

Methodology

Learner response data were analyzed using the Rasch measurement software Winsteps (Linacre, 2016) to obtain difficulty parameter estimates and point-measure correlations (i.e., discrimination values) for each item.

First, participants with erratic response patterns were screened out of the analysis to avoid distorting item measures. Following Linacre's (2016) recommended cutoff values, all participants with a point-measure correlation below 0 and/or an outfit mean square above 2.00, indicating that the participants' responses were contradicting the expected model, were removed from the analysis.

Subsequently, the items' ability to discriminate between high- and low-ability test takers was considered. The statistic of interest for this purpose was the point-measure correlation of responses and Rasch measures. A conservative threshold of 0.30 was adopted to ensure that the items had a strong ability to discriminate. Approximately 9% (n = 9) of the items in the dataset yielded discrimination values under 0.30 and were, therefore, deemed unsuccessful. Finally, the unsuccessful items were removed from the analysis to generate a clean model for estimating item difficulties.

Results and Discussion

The purpose of the first analysis was to see what percentage of the items could be identified as weak a priori using the SAIV model. Approximately

10% of the items developed for the AEB PT and the RSA AT were flagged due to ambiguity between the key and one or more distractors or due to a lack of clear semantic links connecting the key and the passage. Out of these flagged items, approximately 56% yielded poor discrimination values (i.e., below 0.30) after field testing, as expected. Out of the items that passed this first analysis (i.e., unflagged items), the vast majority (about 96%) indeed yielded acceptable statistics.

It is worth noting that two of the unsuccessful AEB PT items (with –0.07 and –0.19 discrimination values) were subsequently revised using the discourse analysis model outlined in this study. In each of these items ambiguity was caused because one of the distractors had an equivalent number of links with the target sentence as did the correct answer. Revisions to items aimed at ensuring that the key held the strongest bond with the passage compared to the distractors. The revised items were then field tested and yielded very good discrimination values (0.37 and 0.41, respectively).

The goal of the second analysis was to determine which features of the SAIV model, if any, have the most predictive power in determining item difficulty. Two multiple regressions were run, one for each dataset with items from different tests (RSA AT and AEB PT). In all, four features were considered:

- dominant links connecting item options and target sentences (DL)
- type-of-match score for strategy type (TOM_Type)
- type-of-match score for requirements to identify requested information (TOM_Req)
- plausibility-of-distractor score (POD).

For the RSA AT items, the SAIV model significantly predicted item difficulty, $F(4, 60) = 3.07$, $p < 0.05$, $R^2 = 0.17$. The feature with the most predictive power was TOM_Req, which added statistically significantly to the prediction, $p < 0.05$. The equation for predicted item difficulty is: $(0.005 \times DL) + (-0.333 \times TOMType) + (0.210 \times TOMReq) + (0.009 \times POD) - 0.362$.

For the AEB items, the finding was replicated. The SAIV model again significantly predicted difficulty, $F(4, 15) = 3.78$, $p < 0.05$, $R^2 = 0.50$. Likewise, TOM_Req added statistically significantly to the prediction, $p < 0.05$ as did POD, $p < 0.05$. The equation for predicted item difficulty is: $(0.005 \times DL) + (0.134 \times TOMType) + (0.254 \times TOMReq) + (0.459 \times POD) - 1.525$.

Although in isolation, the DL feature was not found to significantly predict difficulty, a strong connection was observed between that variable and the most predictive feature, TOM_Req. Specifically, in over 60% of the items requiring the identification of a paradigmatic relation (the lowest difficulty score for TOM_Req), the dominant link connecting passage and key was simple paraphrase, and in over 70% of the items requiring the identification of a syntagmatic relation (the second highest difficulty score for TOM_Req), the dominant link was complex paraphrase.

Overall, findings showed that the SAIV model identified over half of the items that field test data determined were ineffective with regard to discriminating high-performing learners from low-performing learners. Additionally, the features used in the SAIV system appeared to also significantly account for empirical item difficulty.

These results suggest that, by introducing a measure of objectivity to the evaluation of the quality of reading test items, this systematic vetting process at least in part addresses the unpredictability of traditional methods that rely exclusively on the intuition of experienced test writers. Furthermore, these results shed light into the types of lexico-semantic connections that learners at different ability levels are able to process, and the conditions necessary to effectively tap these skills.

Conclusion

This chapter reported the trial of a systematic process for vetting reading comprehension items for inclusion in online placement and achievement assessments. The high percentage (approximately 86%) of unflagged items yielding acceptable statistics (i.e., 0.30 discrimination values or higher) provides some indication that the SAIV vetting process may help predict which items will be successful after field testing. Further, the results suggest that the model also has promise in predicting item difficulty.

There are several limitations to be noted regarding this study. First, only one variable in the proposed vetting system (type-of-match score for requirement to identify requested information) accounts for most of the variance in determining item difficulty of both tests in the dataset. Therefore, it would be beneficial to explore additional features that might contribute to the SAIV model, such as "type of information requested" (Jamieson et al., 2000: 21), and subsequently simplify it to include only the most predictable variables. Finally, in this experimental application of the vetting system, while each item was reviewed by a minimum of two assessment specialists, only one trained analyst was available to record scores for the different variables under consideration. This is admittedly not ideal, and should be addressed in a replication study by involving multiple raters and evaluating inter-rater reliability in order to ensure the accuracy of the results.

The results of this study have implications for the interface of assessment and language instruction in online programs. The possibilities extend to automating the SAIV system and potentially creating a more targeted review process. Item developers can be provided with a tool that automatically highlights bonds between target sentences and item options, which can help inform the content review process. The SAIV data for items deemed ready for field testing would be stored and subsequently compared with obtained difficulty and discrimination values. As new patterns emerge, this information can be used to continually refine the SAIV system. The improved ability to generate high-functioning items at desired difficulty levels will benefit computer-assisted language instruction programs by providing ever more specific information to learners about which skills need improvement (allowing for customized instruction), and, most importantly, showing that an online program is working by demonstrating a learner's gains in language ability over time.

About the Author

Fabiana MacMillan, PhD, serves as Head of Assessment at Rosetta Stone, Inc. She has focused her research on the interface of language assessment, particularly reading assessment, and written discourse analysis. She has taught English as a second or foreign language in Brazil and Canada and has been involved in language test development in several languages for over 15 years.

References

Alderson, C., Clapham, C., & Wall, D. (1995). *Language Test Construction and Evaluation.* Cambridge: Cambridge University Press.

Balogh, J. (2016). *A Practical Guide to Creating Quality Exams.* Menlo Park, CA: Intelliphonics.

Council of Europe. (2001). *Common European Framework of Reference for Languages: Learning, Teaching, Assessment.* Cambridge: Cambridge University Press.

Francis, G. (1994). Labelling discourse: An aspect of nominal-group lexical cohesion. In M. Coulthard (ed.), *Advances in Written Text Analysis* (pp. 83–101). New York: Routledge.

Hoey, M. (1991). *Patterns of Lexis in Text.* Oxford: Oxford University Press.

Jamieson, J., Jones, S., Kirsch, I., Mosenthal, P., & Taylor, C. (2000). TOEFL 2000 framework: A working paper. TOEFL-MS-16. Princeton, NJ: Educational Testing Service.

Linacre, J. M. (2016). Winsteps® Rasch Measurement [computer software]. Beaverton, OR: Winsteps.com.

MacMillan, F. (2007). The role of lexical cohesion in the assessment of EFL reading proficiency. *Arizona Working Papers in Second Language Acquisition and Teaching*, 14, 75–93.

MacMillan, F. (2010, September). *The Role of Lexical Cohesion in Multiple-Choice Reading Item Difficulty.* Paper presented at the Midwest Association of Language Testers Conference, Wright State University, OH.

Rasch, G. (1980). *Probabilistic Models for Some Intelligence and Attainment Tests.* Chicago: University of Chicago Press.

Rosetta Stone Ltd. (2015). Rosetta Stone® Advantage. American English Achievement Test.

10 The Lingo of Language Learning Startups: Congruency between Claims, Affordances, and SLA Theory

Gabriel Guillén,[*] Thor Sawin,[**] and Sarah Springer[***]

Introduction

Five-hundred and forty-one language learning startups, attracting 2,660 investors (as of June 1, 2017) and valued at an average $3.7m per company, appear on the venture capital crowd funding site AngelList (AngelList, n.d.), proving the industry's momentum. Perusing these startups' slogans, a selection of which are presented in Table 10.1, reveals pitches aimed at disrupting the language learning industry by making it more effective and affordable, just as companies like Uber and Airbnb have famously disrupted the transportation and hospitality industries. Leveraging vast amounts of data, Uber and Airbnb have implemented a sharing economy model, in which peers connected by the internet directly provide services to each other. As a result, consumers have more information, options, and overall power over their purchasing experience, whereas traditional transportation and hospitality companies lose profits and often struggle to remain in business. However, language learning is dependent on complexly interrelated skills and situated interactions with more capable users, and, thus, the language learning industry may prove more difficult to disrupt than hotel and travel bookings.

Language startups often explicitly connect themselves to Duolingo and Rosetta Stone, two language learning companies with strong recognition,

[*]   Middlebury Institute of International Studies, Monterey, USA;
        gaguillen@miis.edu
[**]   Middlebury Institute of International Studies, Monterey, USA;
        tsawin@miis.edu
[***]   Middlebury Institute of International Studies, Monterey, USA;
        sarah.springer@miis.edu

Table 10.1. A selection of language learning startups seeking "disruption"

Startup	Slogan	Website
Interlinguals	Airbnb for language learning	interlinguals.com
Colingo	Airbnb for English-teaching	colingo.com
Italki	Airbnb + community for language teachers and students	italki.com
Tutlo	Uber for languages	tutlo.com
Ediket	Uber for editing	ediket.com
Learned by me	oDesk + Uber for 1:1 language tutoring	odesk.com

as seen in Table 10.2. Yet, whether Duolingo and Rosetta Stone have themselves disrupted the language learning industry is debatable. While Rosetta Stone effectively complements traditional language learning (Bowles et al., 2015), users may not reach true communicative competence (Lord, 2015). Likewise, although Duolingo outperforms writing-based placement tests (Vesselinov & Grego, 2012), it has limited success in getting users to the intermediate level (Guillén, 2016).

Fortunately, some language startups make more specific and assessible claims than those in Tables 10.1 and 10.2. Analyzing the 72 most active startups, we discovered six areas of language focus (Figure 10.1): vocabulary building (27 companies), spontaneous speaking (26 companies), scaffolding input for receptive skills (12 companies), pronunciation training (12 companies), grammatical accuracy (9 companies), and writing enhancement (6 companies). While these startups provide learners a range of options, the authors hypothesized that their claims, made to lure investors and users, might not reflect the findings of second language acquisition (SLA) research.

Table 10.2. A selection of startups seeking association with acclaimed language learning platforms

Startup	Slogan	Website
Click and Study	Duolingo for long-term education	clickandstudy.com
Language Zen	2.2x more effectively than Rosetta Stone	languagezen.com
Language Zen	1.4x more efficiently than Duolingo	languagezen.com
MonoLibre	Duolingo for accent training	monolibre.com
Pili Pop	Duolingo for kids	pilipop.com
TogoTown	Rosetta Stone meets FarmVille	togotown.com
Flashcard Tree	A Rosetta Stone that works	flashcardtree.com
The World Phone	Rosetta Stone + ChatRoulette	theworldphone.com

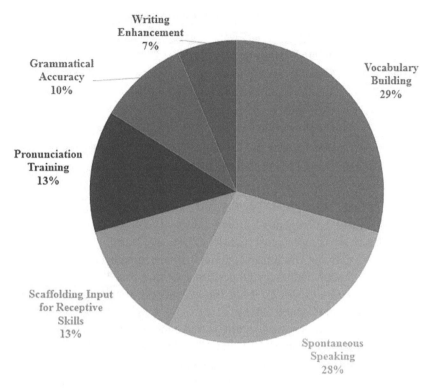

Figure 10.1. Language focus among 72 most active startups

Consequently, these startups may be unable to deliver on their bold claims. For instance, startups consistently minimize the effort required to learn a language: "the only way to disrupt the $56bn language learning market is to make language practice at home as easy as playing Cut the Rope or Fruit Ninja" (Pili Pop at AngelList, n.d.). Startups also attack a straw man of "bad" classroom pedagogy: "… the 3 reasons traditional language education fails to engage language students: (1) they are not motivating enough, (2) they teach the wrong material, and (3) they do not expose people to the real thing" (Jamtok at AngelList, n.d.). Interestingly, an analysis of founders' biographies on AngelList revealed a striking trend: only 5 of the 72 companies' founders indicated any prior experience or academic training in language education; most have either data science and technology (36 companies) or finance (24 companies) backgrounds.

This study builds on the work of Heil et al. (2016), who found little alignment between SLA research and the 50 most popular commercially-available mobile language learning applications. To determine the congruence between language startups' claims, the actual affordances of their

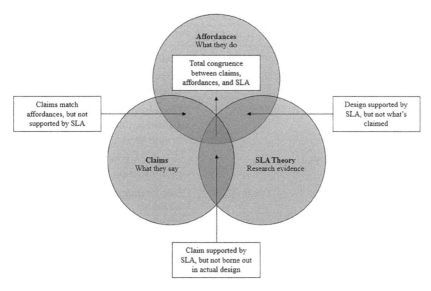

Figure 10.2. Congruence between the claims, affordances, and theoretical foundations of major language education startups

platforms, and recommendations from the field of instructed language acquisition, we analyze a selection of six representative startups. Ideally, as Figure 10.2 depicts, a startup's claims, affordances, and SLA research would be both aligned and made transparent in their marketing literature. Thus, for the six startups we seek to determine how congruent are the *claims* made by the startup, the *affordances* of their actual design, and the recommendations from instructed language acquisition *research*. The results will inform not only language professionals and the startup field but also learners who seek critical information about the different available platforms.

Methodology

To assess this three-way congruence, within each of the six main startup categories identified in Figure 10.1, the authors selected one with a high number of downloads, a high user rating, and bold claims about its effectiveness (Table 10.3).

Three reviewers with in-depth knowledge of SLA, extensive classroom teaching experience, and experience with apps for both formal and informal learning, identified claims found in the marketing discourse (i.e., in AngelList, the app website, and AppStore) that could be compared to user

Table 10.3. Representative startups for six different language foci

Language acquisition focus	Startup chosen	AngelList slogan
Vocabulary building	Memrise	Learning is entertainment
Spontaneous speaking	Verbling	Video chat with a fantastic language teacher
Scaffolding input for receptive skills	BliuBliu	Learn languages by reading articles and talking with people at your level
Pronunciation training	Elsa	Siri who teaches English pronunciation
Grammatical accuracy	Duolingo	Free language education for the world
Writing enhancement	ChattingCat	Instant English correction service by native-speakers

experience and SLA research findings. Reviewers used a rubric, containing these questions:

- What are the claims made by this language platform?
- Is the use of this language platform consistent with such claims?
- Does the use of this language platform align with instructed SLA?

The number of claims identified varied by reviewer and app, but those noted by at least two of three reviewers form the basis of the *claims* section of the analysis. Each of the reviewers then used each app and noted its *affordances*: how the app design delivers on its claims, what language knowledge is explicitly taught and implicitly learnable, and what range of learner actions (input, interaction, feedback, and output) are possible. The time spent on each app varied with the complexity of the app design, but reviewers spent from one to ten hours using each app. The reviewers' rubric notes for each app were cross-referenced and affordances that were identified by at least two of the reviewers were analyzed in the affordances section. Finally, the authors addressed SLA *research findings' alignment* relative to app design.

Findings

Vocabulary Building: Memrise

Memrise claims: Memrise aims to provide enjoyable entertainment – "We make learning languages and vocab so full of joy and life, you'll laugh out loud" (Memrise, n.d.). They also state, "more than 8 million people use our uniquely potent learning tech to cram vast amounts of information into their brains" (Memrise at AngelList, n.d.). Finally, they claim that cognitive research is a core value: "We're obsessed with using brain science to help you learn faster. This isn't a marketing ploy – we're really experts in this stuff" (Memrise, n.d.).

Figure 10.3. Memrise screen capture of a Japanese vocabulary word and meme, or "mem"

Memrise affordances: The claim of "being full of joy and life" is not borne out in the actual design. At best, a user might discover or create a funny meme (an affordance its competitor Quizlet lacks) which increases processing depth and lexical retention. Memrise exposes users to vocabulary, offering fast-paced interactions with de-contextualized lexical items across a range of four or five formats: initial exposure, selecting L1-target language (TL) translations, hearing and seeing the TL word, and eventually, typing the TL word when shown its L1 equivalent. Thus, learners merely acquire passive recognition of cognitive mappings between TL orthography, TL phonology, and a single L1 translation. Still, Memrise affords increased motivation by using spaced repetition and incremental indicators of "progress" – small actions with immediately perceptible rewards – such as increased recognition rates in the engaging word-association game.

Memrise alignment with SLA: Language input in Memrise seems to lack opportunities both for meaning-focused practice and fluency development, which are widely accepted as essential in vocabulary learning (Nation, 2001). Memrise has proven effective in lexical studies for Latin (Walker, 2016) and character recognition in Chinese (Wu, 2016). However, mere word recognition is necessary but insufficient for full lexical acquisition, which involves more than "cram[ming] vast amounts of information into our brain" (Memrise at AngelList, n.d.). Memrise lacks critical information about when, how often, and with what collocations words are *used*. If Memrise were used in combination with a course, groups could curate their own word lists and add multimedia content, which would aid retention of novel vocabulary by increasing the felt need, search intensity, and evaluation in the learning process, also known as the involvement load (Hulstijn & Laufer, 2001). In other words, being "obsessed with using brain science to help you learn faster" might be counterproductive for usable lexical acquisition.

Table 10.4. Summary of Memrise congruence between claims, affordances, and SLA theory

Claims	Affordances	SLA theory
Memrise is full of joy and life, allowing users to learn faster, cramming vast amounts of information	Somewhat engaging and effective but teaches only portion of passive knowledge needed to acquire lexicon	Few opportunities for meaningful practice and involvement load needed to retain deep lexical knowledge

Spontaneous Speaking: Verbling

Verbling claims: Verbling is the single most followed language learning startup in AngelList (693 followers, as of May 31, 2017) and claims to offer "video chat with a fantastic language teacher." Their teachers "are available 24/7/365, covering all time zones globally" and are all "vetted to meet rigorous standards. The average student rating of a teacher is 4.9/5" (Verbling at AngelList, n.d.).

Verbling affordances: The availability of thousands of instructors, together with the informative, minimalist, and very usable interface, facilitates easy and quick access to spontaneous speaking. Booking a lesson for a specific time with a specific teacher can be done in minutes. Yet, despite Verbling users getting not just numerical ratings of instructors but also user reviews, video and written introductions, credentials, prices, and links to their Verbling-developed courses, whether this "rigorous vetting" includes any external quality control is unclear. Finding a trained teacher remains challenging, since Verbling only sorts by popularity, price, and how active teachers are. While learners can specify the subject they want to practice (e.g., preparation for the French proficiency test DELF), some subjects such as accent reduction have few instructors, unbacked by actual credentials. Verbling is also unique within the narrow field of Language Learning Social Networks (LLSNs) in connecting learners with teachers rather than with other learners. While perhaps affording more than other language startups, Verbling is also less affordable (tutor rates range from $7 to $60/hour).

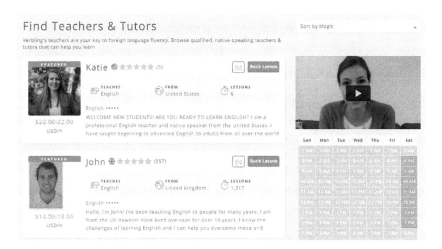

Figure 10.4. Verbling screen capture showing tutor selection and availability

Table 10.5. Summary of Verbling congruence between claims, affordances, and SLA theory

Claims	Affordances	SLA theory
Offers synchronous video lessons with fantastic, well-vetted native speakers (average rating of 4.9/5)	Teacher vetting dependent on user experience, not standards. Allows interaction and situated feedback	Facilitates oral interaction, critical to SLA, but perpetuates the native-speaker fallacy

Verbling alignment with SLA: Spontaneous speaking startups are essential in an industry still dominated by automated tutorials (Heil et al., 2016). Conversations provide not only input but pushed output (Swain, 2005), accuracy building via metalinguistic feedback and negotiation of meaning (Long, 1996), and sociocultural learning via assisted performance (Ohta, 2000). In this sense, Verbling's design is ideal with respect to SLA. However, as a matchmaking platform lacking external quality control, actual alignment with SLA will depend on teachers' individual practices. While learners can scan teachers' credentials and qualitative feedback from other users, the platform would benefit from a credential-based search (i.e. by degree in SLA or language education). On the other hand, by accommodating learners' preferences for teachers, Verbling may perpetuate the native-speaker fallacy (Holliday, 2006). Those teachers best trained in language pedagogy may not be native speakers, and vice versa. In the end, Verbling's effectiveness derives from its users' ability to find the right tutor for their needs, which probably requires more nuanced search capabilities. Learners need training to evaluate the pedagogical soundness of teaching practices.

Scaffolding Input for Receptive Skills: Bliu Bliu

Bliu Bliu claims: Bliu Bliu claims to "teach a new language without teaching grammar," since learners "do not need grammar." Bliu Bliu instead claims comprehensible input is sufficient for acquisition, and provides learners only "content that is interesting" (as judged by the staff), "authentic," and "matched to a learner's level" – all of which ensures "a habit of learning" (Bliu Bliu, n.d.).

Bliu Bliu affordances: To deliver such comprehensible input, Bliu Bliu users initially decide whether isolated words which appear are "easy" (deemed known) or "hard" (unknown). The resulting estimated vocabulary size is shown on a slider. Using that calculation, texts wherein 90% of the words are easy/known are retrieved from the internet for the user to read.

Figure 10.5. Bliu Bliu screen capture showing hover feature with easy and hard rating option

The algorithm predicts and highlights words in the text deemed unknown to learners, who click "easy" or "hard" for each. Hovering over "hard" words triggers an automatic L1 Google translation, the sole strategy for rendering them comprehensible. Learners are meant to use new words acquired through these translations to engage in extensive, unassessed reading of the delivered texts. Automatic translations have questionable accuracy, and dozens of examples were found which ignored key context. For example, Lithuanian "esi buvęs" is translated as "are former" when contextually the meaning is "have you been?" Google translations seem blind to rich morphology ("nuvažuoti" is translated simply "go," rather than "to set out by car").

Bliu Bliu's claim to retrieve "authentic" texts is also overblown. At lower levels, most texts are artificial pedagogical dialogues (although often synced with helpful audio recordings), rather than potentially level-appropriate authentic texts such as advertisements or social media posts. However, a subset of users voluntarily but actively post in discussion forums where learners and native-speaking staff interact asynchronously.

Bliu Bliu alignment with SLA: Bliu Bliu explicitly cites Krashen's (1984) controversial claim that immersion in comprehensible input is sufficient for acquiring language. Yet, SLA research shows that comprehensible input without explicit feedback and interaction (Mackey, 2013) is insufficient to develop morphosyntactic accuracy (Lyster & Ranta, 1997), functional morphology being the bottleneck of acquisition (Slabakova, 2013). Indeed,

Table 10.6. Summary of Bliu Bliu congruence between claims, affordances, and SLA theory

Claims	Affordances	SLA theory
Bliu Bliu allows you to learn a language without grammar, through interesting, authentic and personalized content	Assists passive recognition of words but ignores multiword expressions and inflections. Not all content is authentic	Comprehensible input and single-word learning is insufficient. Provides reading support, effective for SLA

input in Bliu Bliu consists merely of monomorphemic content words. Multiword expressions (Wray, 2002), unfamiliar functional morphemes within a word, and contextually-dependent interpretations often render input *incomprehensible* even if learners "know" every word. Besides the problem that a user marking a passively-read word as "easy" guarantees neither breadth nor especially depth of vocabulary knowledge (Read, 2004), this extensive reading app also offers no comprehension checking to assess whether users actually processed the read input. That being said, research does support extensive reading's role in language acquisition (Nakanishi, 2014), which this app facilitates well.

Pronunciation Training: Elsa

Elsa claims: Billing itself as a "Siri who teaches English pronunciation" and the "world's smartest A.I. assistant for pronunciation" (Elsa at AngelList, n.d.), Elsa aims to help English learners sound "native" and to "speak fluently." They also inscrutably assure that 10 minutes a week on the app can improve users' pronunciation score 40% over four weeks.

Elsa affordances: Elsa provides automated feedback on English pronunciation. Mispronunciations involving major deviations from native-like pronunciation (i.e. "intraduce" instead of "introduce") are highlighted on a transcript with red-colored letters. Marginal pronunciations are shown in yellow (i.e. "good tu see you" instead of "good tə see you"), native-like pronunciations in green. Elsa facilitates pronunciation awareness in offline, yet meaningful activities (as opposed to merely mimicking sounds), using International Phonetics Alphabet (IPA) transcriptions, general metalinguistic feedback, and simplified articulatory phonetics instructions. Most feedback and practice is at the segmental and word level, but in upper-level lessons segmentals and suprasegmentals are practiced in the context of larger sentences.

However, Elsa's claim to be "the world's smartest A.I. assistant" is dubious, as it provides only single-sound feedback. For instance, when testing the limits of the system's processing, we said "Goodbye ELSA, nice to see you" instead of "Hi ESLA, nice to meet you" and Elsa provided positive feedback since "to" was the only element being assessed. For intonation/suprasegmental exercises, users can mumble, and yet still receive

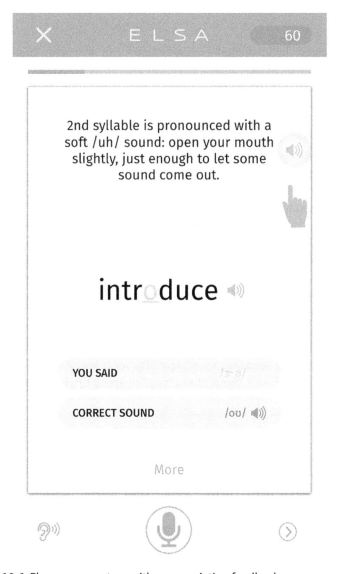

Figure 10.6. Elsa screen capture with pronunciation feedback

Table 10.7. Summary of Elsa congruence between claims, affordances, and SLA theory

Claims	Affordances	SLA theory
Elsa is the world's smartest AI assistant that helps you speak fluently with only 10 minutes of practice a day	Provides offline practice and automated feedback, which raises awareness yet may not carry over to spontaneous talk	Raises learners' awareness but lacks comprehension feedback and communicative practice

perfect scores. In segmental exercises, users can also score highly while using marked intonation and unexpected allophones (such as trills). Elsa nevertheless fulfills its promise to provide pronunciation feedback, which the raters judged to be mostly accurate at the single-sound level.

Elsa alignment with SLA: This app potentially raises users' awareness of their own pronunciation (sounds, word stress, and intonation), which aligns with the Noticing Hypothesis: input does not become intake unless it is consciously registered (Schmidt, 2010).

The ability to record your voice and then compare it to a slow, clearly enunciated model of the same word, phrase or sentence is particularly helpful for learners' ability to perceive and understand target language input (Meinardi, 2009). As an automatic speech recognition-based tool, Elsa crucially offers immediate and detailed feedback (van Doremalen et al., 2016). Finally, Elsa allows learners to focus on specific pronunciation needs, increasing learners' ownership over their learning (Deters et al., 2014).

While improving one's Elsa pronunciation score by 40% over four weeks may be possible, offline mimicking practice does not necessarily correlate with fluency in spontaneous online speaking, requiring comprehension. Learners still need communicative practice (Celce-Murcia, Brinton, & Goodwin, 1996). Elsa's claim of teaching "to speak English fluently" lacks validation.

Grammatical Accuracy: Duolingo

Duolingo claims: Duolingo claims to be "the world's most popular way to learn languages online" (Duolingo, n.d.). Only Verbling has more followers on AngelList (as of June 1, 2017). Their mission statement is both political and pedagogical: "Bring[ing] free language education to the world, we're building a future in which the highest-quality education is accessible to all

… language learning should be fun, personalized, and based on science." They claim that "Duolingo works," using a controversial study (Vesselinov & Grego, 2012) showing 34 hours of learning with Duolingo are more effective than one quarter of college Spanish college (11 weeks).

Duolingo affordances: Duolingo, as claimed, is entirely free and does not offer premium services in their mobile application. However, according to the founder of the app, Duolingo does not allow users to reach the intermediate level for interpersonal speaking (as quoted in Guillén, 2016). Unless Duolingo is integrated into a broader language course, language practice is restricted to sequenced written and oral syntax and vocabulary practice. Personalization is, therefore, limited. Duolingo's design is based on L1 contrasts and translations, spaced-repetition, immediate feedback, drawings and audio association, and affords learners explicit metalinguistic awareness. Users may enjoy the gamified experience and the variety of tasks (Munday, 2016). However, the raters in this study found new structures to be decontextualized, and the drawings and alerts may grow monotonous.

Duolingo alignment with SLA: Although Duolingo also claims to support "learning a language" in its entirety, it teaches only canonical word order, spelling-sound matches, and lexical semantics while ignoring frequency, collocational and pragmatic knowledge. In languages with rich inflection, many forms share a single L1 translation; disambiguating them and systematically constructing the needed paradigm is not well supported.

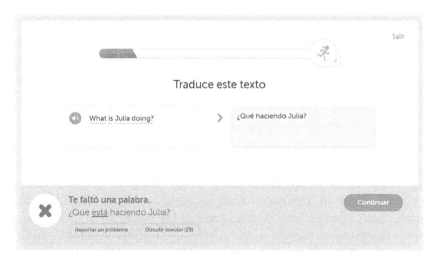

Figure 10.7. Duolingo screen capture with written translation task and immediate feedback

Table 10.8. Summary of Duolingo congruence between claims, affordances and SLA theory

Claims	Affordances	SLA theory
Duolingo brings free, fun, effective, high quality language education to the world	While engaging, does not allow users to reach the intermediate level, lacks personalization and context	Provides focus on forms but claims are not connected to SLA literature and learners' needs

Duolingo's belief in the primacy of contrastive analysis and explicit feedback is evident. This app exploits explicit language awareness (Schmidt, 2001, 2010) and potential roles for the L1 (Ellis, 2015) in second language acquisition. However, Duolingo affords little context for taught structures and no free meaning-focused production. Frequency of use is also not considered. Corpus mining, retrieving the structures most frequent in everyday discourse, would improve Duolingo's choices of target structures which raters found often awkward and rarely used.

Duolingo's claimed scientific basis seems to refer not to SLA literature but learners' behaviorist habit-formation while using the app. As a free, widely-used, well-funded startup with a social mission to provide "highest-quality education", Duolingo could better benefit society by providing spontaneous and meaningful practice among their 170 million users incorporating the full affordances of LLSNs (Lamy & Zourou, 2013), beyond asynchronous forums and gamified competitions.

Writing Enhancement: ChattingCat

ChattingCat claims: ChattingCat claims to "disrupt language education" by simultaneously improving texts via "instant corrections" from "native speakers" and benefitting L2 authors, who will "confidently write English" because of "chats" with "tutors" who "want to help them." (ChattingCat at AngelList, n.d.). This is pitched to users as a chance to improve language skills through graduated assistance by an expert, similar to Verbling.

ChattingCat affordances: While marketed as "disrupting language learning," ChattingCat in practice seems more an editing service for wealthier professionals or high-stakes academic assignments. An L2 author can submit texts at a rate of 560 characters per US dollar, up to 2,100 characters (subscription permits longer submissions). Users select their text's genre and register (e.g. social media, academic essay, business language, oral script) and pay to leave a note which guides the timely correction received from a tutor (actually a proof reader). Prospective tutors are vetted

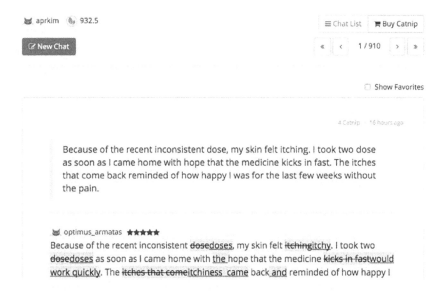

Figure 10.8. ChattingCat screen capture showing a sample text and feedback

by correctly identifying and revising grammar errors in sample texts, and subsequently by client ratings. The corrected texts include a color-coded visual record of deletions and additions. Any further chat with the tutor costs 25 cents/turn, which disincentives interaction, the main affordance of ChattingCat's design.

The app succeeds in improving the text more than improving the writer. A user wanting textual accuracy will receive timely edits, but the minimal and expensive feedback will disappoint a user wanting to become a better writer or learn to "confidently write English" as claimed. Neither are tutors necessarily incentivized to be correct; reviewers found many wording errors went unaddressed. Getting a second opinion is expensive, and while users can rate their tutor, the app does not allow users to choose a more highly-rated tutor instead of the one assigned.

ChattingCat alignment with SLA: In sociocultural approaches to SLA, whereby learners get help from a more qualified expert, interaction and negotiation is key (Ohta, 2000).Only a subset of motivated and metalinguistically savvy learners (Bitchener, 2017) "notice the gap" between their own and target-like production from feedback showing every error corrected. Qualitative formative feedback on the most salient error patterns (Ferris, 2010) is more helpful for improving writers. In ChattingCat, such formative feedback is expensive for the learner and more time-consuming (thereby revenue-decreasing) for the tutor; raters found editor-tutors either untrained

Table 10.9. Summary of ChattingCat congruence between claims, affordances and SLA theory

Claims	Affordances	SLA theory
ChattingCat disrupts language education via instant corrections from native speakers	No more than a fee-based editing for grammar errors, ignoring pragmatics and wording needs	Allows gap noticing but rarely provides formative feedback. Spreads native-speaker fallacy

or unwilling to provide such feedback. Correcting every error may overwhelm and demotivate writers (Lee, 2011) more than build "confidence" as claimed.

The ability of users to assign their submission a genre implies that editors will include feedback on genre appropriateness, not merely grammaticality. However, in the raters' experience, pragmatic errors were usually ignored. Instead, editors tended to focus on functional morphology errors (definiteness, number, countability) as well as orthographic and stylistic errors (i.e., comma placement) which even native speakers make. Native-speakerism (Holliday, 2006) is also present through highlighting the nativeness of their tutors, rather than their training in L2 writing. Overall, ChattingCat alters users' compositions to appear like better writers than they are. This may even disincentivize true language learning.

Implications

Startups represent a wide spectrum, from companies wanting to disrupt the market by reaching a billion language learners (the unicorn approach) to startups which target a specific skill (the niche solution). The niche startups seemingly use less hyperbolic language in marketing, yet they still deliver results and secure funding. Companies truly after measurable social impact should start by using more honest, transparent, and accurate language in their marketing literature.

Changing the language is critical. Otherwise, app users might come to believe claims about language learning which are not necessarily true or even, finding that apps do not deliver on their promises, give up on language learning altogether. The field of language education is negatively affected when popular startups reproduce commonly-held language fallacies to attract capital and users: the minimal effort myth, a preference for native speakers, or a focus on simplistic conceptions of language as isolated easily-translatable words.

It is not successful teachers that create companies but, rather, frustrated learners who want to hack the extremely complicated challenge of "acquiring" a second language. The fact that relatively few of the startups analyzed have a founder or team member with in-depth knowledge of SLA and language pedagogy is problematic. Perhaps the ideal language learning startup should represent a triangular core team of a curriculum designer conversant in current SLA, a seasoned entrepreneur willing to acknowledge the complexity of language learning, and a senior developer able to program and manage creative solutions for the complex challenges posed by acquisition. Perusing AngelList reveals the ongoing lack of social entrepreneurship in our field, filling the gap between startups, publishers, federally funded projects, and academic entrepreneurs.

Finally, startups should provide evidence for their claims. More longitudinal studies would benefit diverse stakeholders with shared interests: startups aiming to make a real difference in society, learners facing the overwhelming paradox of choice, and instructors recommending pedagogically sound apps.

About the Authors

Gabriel Guillén is an Assistant Professor in Spanish at the Middlebury Institute of International Studies (MIIS) in Monterey. At MIIS he teaches content-based language courses such as Social Entrepreneurship in the Hispanic World and Spanish in the Community, connecting his Spanish students with English learners in the county of Monterey. His dissertation focused on online intercultural exchanges and the use of language learning social networks in the context of hybrid language education.

Thor Sawin is an Assistant Professor of Applied Linguistics at the Middlebury Institute of International Studies (MIIS) in Monterey with a background in second language learning and linguistic anthropology. His research in language learning among cross-cultural workers on the front lines of globalization sparked his interest in mobile devices as a low-cost and low-barrier means of connecting autonomous learners with authentic language in diverse and superdiverse environments.

Sarah Springer works at the intersection of design, research, teaching, and technology as senior staff and adjunct faculty member at the Middlebury Institute of International Studies (MIIS) at Monterey. Based in the San Francisco Bay area, she leads workshops, creates materials, and facilitates experiences that integrate human-centered design practices within projects and organizations. Her increasing engagement with the world of entrepreneurship is driven by a recognition that, as with teaching, a deep understanding of human needs, motivations, and behaviors is at its core.

References

AngelList (n.d.). Retrieved from https://angel.co

Bitchener, J. (2017). Why some L2 learners fail to benefit from written corrective feedback. In H. Nassaji and E. Kartchava (eds.), *Corrective Feedback in Second Language Teaching and Learning*. Abingdon: Routledge.

Bliu Bliu (n.d.). Retrieved from https://bliubliu.com

Bowles, A. R., Frumkes, L. A., Harper, D., & Stone, L. (2015). Supporting language learning through technology: A response to Lord (2015). *The Modern Language Journal*, 99(3), 634–635. http://dx.doi.org/10.1111/modl.12270_2

Celce-Murcia, M., Brinton, D. M., & Goodwin, J. M. (1996). *Teaching Pronunciation: A Reference for Teachers of English to Speakers of Other Languages*. Cambridge: Cambridge University Press.

ChattingCat (n.d.). Retrieved from https://angel.co/chattingcat

Deters, P., Gao, X., Vitanova, G., & Miller, E. R. (eds.). (2014). *Theorizing and Analyzing Agency in Second Language Learning: Interdisciplinary Approaches* (Vol. 84). Bristol: Multilingual Matters.

Duolingo (n.d.). Retrieved from https://www.duolingo.com

Ellis, R. (2015). *Understanding Second Language Acquisition* (2nd ed). Oxford Applied Linguistics. Oxford: Oxford University Press.

Elsa (n.d.). Retrieved from https://angel.co/elsanow

Ferris, D. R. (2010). Second language writing research and written corrective feedback in SLA. *Studies in Second Language Acquisition*, 32(2), 181–201. http://dx.doi.org/10.1017/s0272263109990490

Guillén, G. (2016, October 18). ¿Revolución o Candy Crush? Una conversación con Duolingo. [Blog post] Retrieved from http://www.huffingtonpost.es/gabriel-guillen/language-crash-unaconver_b_12466542.html

Heil, C. R., Wu, J. S., Lee, J. J., & Schmidt, T. (2016). A review of mobile language learning applications: Trends, challenges, and opportunities. *The EuroCALL Review*, 24(2), 32–50. http://dx.doi.org/10.4995/eurocall.2016.6402

Holliday, A. (2006). Native-speakerism. *ELT Journal*, 60(4), 385–387. http://dx.doi.org/10.1093/elt/ccl030

Hulstijn, J. H., & Laufer, B. (2001). Some empirical evidence for the involvement load hypothesis in vocabulary acquisition. *Language Learning*, 51(3), 539–558. http://dx.doi.org/10.1111/0023-8333.00164

Jamtok. (n.d.). Retrieved from https://angel.co/jamtok-1

Krashen, S. D. (1984). Immersion: Why it works and what it has taught us. *Language and Society*, 12(1), 61–64.

Lamy, M., & Zourou, K. (eds.) (2013). *Social Networking for Language Education*. Basingstoke: Palgrave Macmillan.

Lee, I. (2011). Working smarter, not working harder: Revisiting teacher feedback in the L2 writing classroom. *Canadian Modern Language Review*, 67(3), 377–399. http://dx.doi.org/10.3138/cmlr.67.3.377

Long, M. (1996). The role of the linguistic environment in second language acquisition. *Handbook of Second Language Acquisition*, 2(2), 413–468. http://dx.doi.org/10.1016/b978-012589042-7/50015-3

Lord, G. (2015). "I don't know how to use words in Spanish": Rosetta Stone and learner proficiency outcomes. *The Modern Language Journal*, 99(2), 401–405. http://dx.doi.org/10.1111/modl.12234_3

Lyster, R., & Ranta, L. (1997). Corrective feedback and learner uptake. *Studies in Second Language Acquisition*, 19(1), 37–66. http://dx.doi.org/10.1017/s0272263197001034

Mackey, A. (2013). *Input, Interaction and Corrective Feedback in L2 Learning*. Oxford: Oxford University Press.

Meinardi, M. (2009). Speed bumps for authentic listening material. *ReCALL*, 21(3), 302–318. http://dx.doi.org/10.1017/S0958344009990048

Memrise (n.d.). Retrieved from https://www.memrise.com

Munday, P. (2016). The case for using DUOLINGO as part of the language classroom experience. *Revista Iberoamericana de Educación a Distancia*, 19(1), pp. 83–101. http://dx.doi.org/10.5944/ried.19.1.14581

Nakanishi, T. (2014). A meta-analysis of extensive reading research. *TESOL Quarterly*, 49(1), 6–37. http://dx.doi.org/10.1002/tesq.157

Nation, P. (2001). *Learning Vocabulary in Another Language*. Cambridge: Cambridge University Press.

Ohta, A. (2000). Rethinking interaction in SLA: Developmentally appropriate assistance in the zone of proximal development and the acquisition of L2 grammar. In J. Lantolf (ed.), *Sociocultural Theory and Language Learning*. Oxford: Oxford University Press.

Pili Pop. (n.d.). Retrieved from https://angel.co/pili-pop

Read, J. (2004). Plumbing the depths: How should the construct of vocabulary knowledge be defined. *Vocabulary in a Second Language: Selection, Acquisition, and Testing*, 10, 209–227. http://dx.doi.org/10.1075/lllt.10.15rea

Schmidt, R. (2001). Attention. In P. Robinson (ed.), *Cognition and Second Language Instruction* (pp. 3–32). Cambridge: Cambridge University Press.

Schmidt, R. (2010). Attention, awareness, and individual differences in language learning. In W. M. Chan, S. Chi, K. N. Cin, J. Istanto, M. Nagami, J. W. Sew, T. Suthiwan, & I. Walker, *Proceedings of CLaSIC 2010*, Singapore, December 2–4 (pp. 721–737). Singapore: National University of Singapore, Centre for Language Studies.

Slabakova, R. (2013). What is easy and what is hard in second language acquisition: A generative perspective In M. García Mayo., M. Gutierrez-Mangado, & M. Martínez Adrián, *Contemporary Approaches to Second Language Acquisition* (pp. 5–28). Amsterdam: John Benjamins (AILA Applied Linguistics Series, 9).

Swain, M. (2005). The output hypothesis: Theory and research. *Handbook of Research in Second Language Teaching and Learning*, 1, 471–483. http://dx.doi.org/10.4324/9781410612700

van Doremalen, J., Boves, L., Colpaert, J., Cucchiarini, C., & Strik, H. (2016). Evaluating automatic speech recognition-based language learning systems: A case study. *Computer Assisted Language Learning*, 29(4), 833–851. http://dx.doi.org/10.1080/09588221.2016.1167090

Verbling (n.d.). Retrieved from https://angel.co/verbling

Vesselinov, R., & Grego, J. (2012). *Duolingo Effectiveness Study* [White Paper]. Retrieved from https://s3.amazonaws.com/duolingo-papers/other/vesselinov-grego.duolingo12.pdf

Walker, L. (2016). The impact of using Memrise on student perceptions of learning Latin vocabulary and on long-term memory of words. *Journal of Classics Teaching*, 16(32), 14–20. http://dx.doi.org/10.1017/s2058631015000148

Wray, A. (2002). *Formulaic Language and the Lexicon.* Cambridge: Cambridge University Press.

Wu, J. (2016). A crowdsourcing approach to Chinese vocabulary learning. *IALLT Journal of Language Learning Technologies*, 44(2), 43–63. Retrieved from https://ialltjournal.org/index.php/ialltjournal/article/download/71/62

PART FOUR

FUTURE DIRECTIONS FOR ONLINE LANGUAGE ASSESSMENT

11 Toward Technology-Enhanced Alternative Assessment for Online Language Education

Zhi Li[*] and Stephanie Link[**†]

Introduction

Recent years have witnessed new trends in technologically rich environments (TREs) for language learning and teaching, such as massive open online courses (MOOCs), expanded classrooms with augmented reality (AR), virtual world-based simulation or gamification, and intelligent tutoring systems (ITS). With the advent of these technological advances comes the need for innovative assessments to understand and accurately measure the whole student learning experience (Bevitt, 2014; Shute et al., 2016). This experience includes a combination of social, cognitive, and affective dynamics as well as contextual factors such as the "quantity of exposure/ engagement and quality of the linguistic environment" that drive language development and shape individual trajectories (Thorne, Fisher, & Lu, 2012: 280). Traditional assessment practices (e.g., quiz, exam) focus largely on standardized, selected response test item formats because they are efficient and objective; however, they are not capable of measuring all the dynamics relevant to understanding a language learning experience and may not measure genuine language gains. A reform effort is needed to design, develop, and administer modern approaches to language assessment in TREs, such as technology-enhanced "alternative assessment."

Alternative assessment, unlike the traditional assessment practices, can be used to focus on learning beyond and in addition to the cognitive domain (Fox, 2008). In a face-to-face language learning experience, there

*   Paragon Testing Enterprises, BC, Canada; zlisu2010@gmail.com
**   Oklahoma State University, USA; steph.link@okstate.edu
†   Both authors contributed equally to this chapter.

is an assortment of alternative assessment options such as self- and peer-assessment, rubrics, and portfolio options. Technology has the potential to reconstruct and diversify these more conventional notions of alternative assessment by utilizing the ever abundant data points collected in TREs to inform assessment design. In this sense, technology-enhanced alternative assessments can maintain a stronger connection with cognitive and noncognitive domains, provide both formative and summative feedback, be "for learning, not just of learning," and become so ubiquitous as to one day produce "seamlessly integrated learning and assessment environments" (Cope et al., 2011: 81, 86). These assessments can attend to processes *of* learning (e.g., interaction with peers), activities *for* learning (e.g., engagement with learning tasks and materials), and affective states *while* learning (e.g., emotions and dispositions). The combination of assessment methods can affect how accurately the students' whole learning experience is assessed. Moreover, careful integration of new data sources and analytic techniques into the design of assessments can provide useful, actionable information to target language instruction and facilitate student success by enhancing our understanding of the learning occurring in TREs.

In this chapter, we argue that accountability practices for ensuring satisfactory learning outcomes in the new era of TREs necessitate a reformulated approach to assessment by utilizing multifaceted, technology-enhanced alternative assessments. We support our call by discussing the important roles that technology currently has in assessment practices, including the impact that new data sources can have in shaping these assessments. We then share special considerations for designing and evaluating technology-enhanced assessments in online language education. Here, we provide theoretical recommendations for supporting online language educators and evidence-based models for evaluating these innovative and unobtrusive assessment tools in TREs.

A Reformative Agenda for Assessment in TREs

From blended classrooms and language MOOCs to virtual worlds, AR technology, and ITS, formal and informal language learning opportunities in TREs are pervasive. The many language learning affordances that technology currently provides stimulate the need for new language assessments for today's technologically beset world. New assessments are needed because assessment is central to not only learning but also the learner experience, and in a traditional classroom, learner experience, in particular, is easier to gauge than in TREs because teachers can read students' nonverbal communication and check for understanding more readily. In face-to-face environments, daily, informal assessment of interaction and engagement with and among students can also supplement understanding of learning outcomes. In online contexts, the nature of how course content is delivered makes interaction, engagement, and proficiency development difficult to measure. Furthermore, while educational assessment as a whole has focused on expanding the scope of assessment (Reeves, 2000), online language education programs tend to generate course grades purely based on quizzes and exams and ignore other sources for evaluative purposes. These methods align with the so-called "standard assessment paradigm" where items are predefined, responses are discrete, and learning during assessment is negligible (Mislevy et al., 2012: 12). Accounting for learning and learner experience in TREs is thus important for broadening assessment practices, gathering richer data, and viewing learning and assessment as compatible.

Understanding the whole language learner experience induces a need to advance assessment methods by first recognizing that learning is not limited to cognitive activities. Cognitive activities would include learning processes that lead to language progress and development. These may include gains in producing and understanding language, knowledge retention, and problem-solving. However, considering the agency of learners also impacts language development, understanding factors that go beyond the cognitive domain is also important in efforts to diversify assessment practices. These include strategy-related factors such as self-regulated learning, affective factors such as motivation and identity, and contextual/environmental factors such as quantity of exposure/engagement and quality of the linguistic environment. The challenge is to formulate a considerately multifaceted assessment approach that can account for the many processes *of* learning, activities *for* learning, and affective states *while* learning. This is where we turn to alternative assessment. Alternative assessments are process-oriented in nature; they move beyond the standard paradigm by complementing rather than replacing traditional assessments. These assessments can also take advantage of technological advances.

The Role of Technology in Designing and Developing Alternative Assessments

Technology has dramatically changed the learning environment, the processes in which learners learn and interact, and the assessment landscape, propelling the shift towards technology-enhanced assessments that can coalesce disparate components of the student experience. Technology-enhanced assessments can take on four variations: (1) assessment with reference to tasks as seen in the widespread use of computer or internet-based language proficiency tests such as the TOEFL iBT, (2) assessment integrated in a task and context such as simulation-based assessment, (3) assessment using natural digital activity with assessment features such as stand-alone digital games, and (4) assessment with accumulation of information from a variety of natural digital activity such as multiple learning activities in an assessment ecosystem (DiCerbo & Behrens, 2012). Among other implications, this final variation features a seamless merger between assessment and technology in which technologies can be used to mediate natural or authentic tasks whilst collecting and analyzing response and process data.

We believe the collection of natural digital activity, therefore, bolsters three important roles that technologies can play in the design and development of alternative assessments: (1) create more authentic assessment tasks through simulating a target learning environment; (2) personalize assessment experiences with ongoing, adaptive support or scaffolding; and (3) collect and analyze fine-grained response processes in addition to final products for understanding the whole learning experience in TREs. We expand on each of these roles in the following discussion.

Creation of Authentic Assessment Tasks

The first role of technology in alternative assessment is to create authentic assessment tasks that simulate target learning environments. This role is particularly meaningful for validating score interpretations with regard to the assessment task's situational and interactional authenticity (Bachman, 1991). Situational authenticity "depends on the relationship between [the] test method characteristics and the features of a specific language use situation," and interactional authenticity pertains to "the degree to which [the task] invokes the test taker's language ability" (Bachman, 1991: 671). Examples may include oral performance assessment in virtual worlds for occupational English (Park, 2015), or multimodal writing assessment using augmented reality (Liu & Tsai, 2013), or again in virtual worlds (Tan, O'Halloran, & Wignell, 2016). Occupational English, for instance, is often highly contextualized and may involve high stakes because of the detrimental consequences of failing to accurately assessing English proficiency, such as in the field of aviation communication. To enhance both situational authenticity and interactional authenticity of an assessment of aviation English-speaking abilities for control tower personnel, Park (2015) simulated a control tower environment in Second Life, an online 3D virtual world (http://secondlife.com/), and presented the input materials through highly interactive tasks. Assessment in other virtual learning environments could also benefit from the affordances of alternative assessment in a similar way. Nevertheless, Tan et al., (2016) remind us that these environments will need to technically evolve in order to approximate conventional face-to-face settings and create a more authentic learning experience.

Likewise, augmented reality provides an interesting and engaging approach to enriching target learning environments and establishing novel assessment practices. AR is characterized by a fusion of the physical environment with electronic information presented on screens through built-in cameras on smartphones or other portable digital devices. Two main forms of AR are usually used, namely artifact-based and geolocation. Artifact-based AR utilizes on-site visual analysis to retrieve overlaying digital information about a scanned artifact (Vanoni, Seracini, & Kuester, 2013). One such free AR app is from Blippar (https://blippar.com) which provides a tool to view through hand-held devices Blippar-supported objects for pre-defined information or other normal objects for relevant information. Geolocation AR provides location-based services, which enable the users to see their surroundings annotated with computer-generated digital information (Delić, Domančić, & Vujević, 2014). Users can also create their own annotations of artifacts or locations as a form of alternative assessment; there are several apps for this, including Aurasma (https://www.aurasma.com/), which is also freely available.

Both forms of AR require users to explore a specified environment, similar to visiting a building on campus for example, and to activate overlaying digital information, such as to trigger an oral or even written narrative about the building. That is, language learners can use AR-enabled apps on their handheld devices to interact with the local environment and thus draw on multimodal information from their experiences to support their essay writing with more details. By conducting a quantitative analysis of words and sentences in students' essays and a reflective open-ended questionnaire, Liu and Tsai (2013) found that EFL learners, when completing an AR assessment task in an L2 writing course, constructed linguistics knowledge of English words and expressions, gained content knowledge related to composition subjects, and produced meaningful essays. The students also noted feelings of engagement in the learning scenario because of the comfortable environment, denoting a promising area for assessment in TREs as these technologies are capable of expanding the spatial limit of classrooms, paving the way for delivery of sophisticated assessment tasks, promoting situated learning, and testing with a gamification touch.

Adaptive Support of Learning

The second role of technology in the design and development of alternative assessments is for personalized assessment experiences with ongoing, adaptive support or scaffolding to assess learning and learning experiences. Computer-based adaptive tests have already achieved this flexibility in standardized tests by providing tailored items that are appropriate to test takers' proficiency levels (Chalhoub-Deville & Deville, 1999). New technologies also offer affordances for building adaptivity in alternative assessment platforms. For example, in response to a call for next-generation English language proficiency assessments, Wolf et al. (2016) developed three technology-supported scaffolding assessment tasks (scaffolded story retelling, optional prompting, and selected response multiple trials) to assess young English learners' language proficiency. Each format draws on Vygotsky's concept of the zone of proximal development (ZPD), which suggests that a learner when presented with a challenging task may not be able to solve the task independently due to limited proficiency; but when guided by adults or in collaboration with a skilled peer, the learner's zone of reflective capacity is developed and the learner's abilities increase (Vygotsky, 1978). Scaffolded story retelling, for instance, measures a learner's ability to retell a story. To administer this assessment, an avatar or a narrator can prompt the learner to retell the story first without assistance and the second time with assistive guiding questions that help break down the story into smaller segments. Wolf et al.'s (2016) preliminary findings suggest positive values of these formats as the new tasks elicited more informative responses from young learners and helped them perform to their best capabilities through the provision of adaptive support.

Additional adaptive assessment options include automated feedback systems. The development of automated writing evaluation (AWE) systems such as Criterion and MyAccess! enable adaptive support by guaranteeing timely and constant feedback and scoring to learners on their writing (Grimes & Warschauer, 2010; Shermis & Burstein, 2003). Students can import their writing or use the embedded text editor; they can then submit their work to obtain holistic evaluation and more analytical feedback on rhetorical conventions (e.g., organization) and linguistic features (e.g., grammar and usage). Although automated feedback may not be as accurate or individualized as an instructor, the immediacy of feedback results can suggest a more active role of the feedback in learners' writing processes (Li, Link, & Hegelheimer, 2015). An AWE system called CyWrite from a team at Iowa State University has been developed to specifically target the processes that occur while students write. Their system utilizes integrated keystroke logging and eye-tracking to visualize engagement in the writing process in the form of characters typed, cursor location, scrolling behavior, and eye fixation/movement (Ranalli, Feng, & Chukharev-Hudilainen, 2017). Writers can then self-assess using information from a post-session viewer and/or receive personalized strategy instruction based on the instructor's assessment of the students' activity.

Personalization in alternative assessments may be strengthened in intelligent tutoring systems (ITS), which can recommend learning materials to match learners' needs based on their learning processes. In language education, Writing-Pal (W-Pal) is one example of an intelligent tutoring system that provides personalization. According to Roscoe and McNamara (2013), W-Pal is designed to train English learners in writing strategies for the stages of pre-writing, drafting, and revising and to provide formative feedback that matches learners' writing proficiency level and their use of writing strategies. In other subject fields, systems like AutoTutor and its variants are gaining more attention for their use of animated conversational agents to interact with learners using human-like natural dialogue moves (Graesser, Li, & Forsyth, 2014). The conversational agents are more than a chatbot, in that in addition to chatting with learners, they are able to identify learners' misconceptions in a knowledge domain and offer assistance or guidance accordingly. Through monitoring learners' interaction with the intelligent tutor or agent, these systems are actually conducting a series of stealth assessments which are not visible to learners but capture important information about cognitive learning processes and learning outcomes. Although this information is valuable, large datasets need to be collected to uncover social, affective, and contextual dynamics that impact learning experiences.

Collection and Analysis of New Data Sources for Assessment

The third role of technology in alternative assessment is to collect and analyze fine-grained learning experience data in addition to final products. Learners' digital footprints in a computer-based learning environment are regarded as a "goldmine" to be explored for learners' affective status, learning behaviors, as well as interactive patterns with peers and instructors (Abdous, He, & Yen, 2012). One method of collecting these details is to utilize educational data mining techniques and learning analytics.

Educational data mining is a general term for specialized data mining techniques for identifying patterns of learning processes that may inform instructional practices (Mislevy et al., 2012). Patterns of interest may include learner characteristics, such as knowledge and skills, errors and misconceptions, learning styles and preferences, cognitive and metacognitive traits, and affective states. These data can help explain individual differences in language proficiency or achievement by connecting learners' affective dynamics and strategy use.

Learning analytics refers to the application side of educational data mining and focuses on "the measurement, collection, analysis and reporting of data about learners and their contexts, for purposes of understanding and optimizing learning and the environments in which it occurs" (Ferguson, 2012). Log files are the most common sources analyzed in learning analytics. Typical log data in TREs such as learning management systems (LMS) and ITS may contain learners' behavior data (e.g., access to instructional materials, time spent on learning activities, participation in team projects, sequence of learning activities), text-based data (e.g., textual contributions to forum discussions), and other types of data (e.g., survey responses, physiological data, and oral products for assignments). Analytics of various capabilities are already built into popular LMS such as Moodle and Blackboard Learn. From the dashboard in the LMS, one can conveniently observe learner progress and make sense of the assessment results. Teachers and researchers can collect assessment grades or scores and supplement their understanding of student performance with additional data about learning behaviors. These data points can also be used to truly evaluate both the process and product of learning experiences as learner behaviors can be linked to final product performance, completion rates for individuals or team-based tasks, and overall language development (Lowes, Lin, & Kinghorn, 2015). For example, poor performances can be traced to aberrant response time and/or uncommon progression patterns in a learning module or activity, which may suggest a low level of motivation or poor use of learning strategies.

While the implications of using data mining and learning analytics in language education are relatively unexplored, several general education studies have utilized a number of data sources for mapping learner experiences. Some of these sources include log data (Agudo-Peregrina et al., 2014; Kinnebrew, Loretz, & Biswas, 2013), text data (Abdous et al., 2012; Hsu, Chou, & Chang, 2011; Lin, Hsieh, & Chuang, 2009; Yoo & Kim, 2014), social network data (Rabbany et al., 2013), and other unique sources such as facial expressions and keystroke indices (Allen et al., 2016; Bouchet et al., 2013). For example, Agudo-Peregrina et al. (2014) showcased the use of students' log data to predict their success in two university learning environments in Spain, namely, online course and virtual learning environment (VLE)-supported face-to-face (f2f) course. They operationalized three types of interactions captured in the log data: agent-based interaction (initiating party and interactants), frequency-of-use-based interaction (frequency of occurrence of certain interactions), and participation mode-based interaction (active and passive participation). Their multiple regression models indicated that four interaction variables were significant predictors of students' course performance in the online courses while the patterns did not apply to the VLE-supported f2f courses. The four predictors included student-student interaction, student-teacher interaction, evaluating students or student assessment, and active participation. These results indicate that learners' interaction with instructional materials can help determine their learning strategies in relation to their learning outcomes, and can thus be useful for future developments of technology-enhanced alternative assessment.

Text data gathered from online discussion forums and asynchronous Q&A sessions are another source that can be integrated into assessment systems (Knight & Littleton, 2015). Traditionally, text data of this type are approached with content analysis which relies on manual coding and is labor-intensive. In this new era of technological advances, much of this work can be performed automatically using new techniques like text mining. Abdous et al. (2012) focused on the online question themes extracted from interactive data in a live video streaming delivery system. Through text mining techniques, they identified four typical themes: learning/comprehension, check-in, deadline/schedule, and evaluation/technical issues. Such a classification of interaction themes is very revealing of what learners were concerned about and how they contributed to the conversations; the types of question themes could also help predict students' final grades.

Text data have also been interpreted within the framework of Bloom's cognition in Hsu et al. (2011), who investigated the role of EduMiner, a learning analytic system, in a graduate-level course of human resource management in Taiwan. The researchers operationalized six levels of cognition, namely knowledge, comprehension, application, analysis, synthesis, and evaluation. Then, with textual characteristics captured in group project-based discussions, they used a machine-based classifier to label each posting with the cognition level system. The cognition levels embodied in the group discussions were then visualized for students as a form of formative feedback. It was found that the students receiving the visualized feedback became more motivated and engaged with higher-order thinking in their postings.

Embedded in the forum discussions and other group-based activities are the networking data about students and their peers or interaction patterns among students. This networking information may be even more valuable in online education in which students are less like to meet face-to-face frequently and such networking efforts will help build a sense of learning community. Social network analysis (SNA) is a data mining technique to reveal relationships or interaction patterns between students and their peers or teachers (Suraj & Roshni, 2015). Rabbany et al. (2013) reported on their use of Meerkat-ED, an interaction analyzing toolbox for asynchronous computer-mediated communication, in online courses at the University of Alberta. The researchers were able to track the change in the interaction patterns across the semesters as well as capture the hierarchical relationships among the discussion posts, in addition to visualizing participants' roles in the online discussions and the interaction patterns among the participants. By using SNA, they demonstrated how to identify effective group work and decide on intervention strategies, if needed. These interaction data are valuable for facilitating collaborative learning with insightful team-forming strategies and for evaluating learner performance at both individual and group levels.

There are other sources of interesting data reported in educational data mining studies that can be applicable to alternative assessment in TREs. For example, in addition to the readily available data from log files in an ITS and questionnaire responses, Bouchet et al. (2013) attempted to collect facial expressions, diagrams drawn on paper, notes handwritten on paper, and eye-tracking data to profile individual students' learning. These sources, however, are limited because they require access to software that can be expensive, and the techniques are more obtrusive to students than analyzing log, text, or social networking data. Nevertheless, this effort with the new sources of data may be worthwhile to better understand learner behaviors and their use of self-regulated learning strategies.

How to more efficiently supply data from these sources for assessment purposes could be a thriving area of future research. For collecting and analyzing facial expressions to understand emotions, in particular, a useful resource is Affectiva (https://www.affectiva.com/). This company uses computer vision, machine learning, and deep learning (i.e., studying the multiple layers of artificial neural networks and related machine learning algorithms) methodologies to train algorithms to classify emotions. Data can be obtained by using any major mobile or desktop platforms and a standard webcam. Research has begun exploring facial expressions in CALL (Price, 2016), but more efforts are needed.

Considerations for Technology-Enhanced Alternative Assessment

As discussed above, new technologies have shown the potential to enrich alternative assessment in TREs. Nevertheless, the excitement brought by the new technologies needs to be revisited and evaluated in light of theoretical considerations and comprehensive frameworks for designing and evaluating this next generation of assessments.

Theoretical Recommendations

Technology-enhanced alternative assessment may pose some challenges to language educational practitioners conceptually, compared with the traditional practices in and perspective of educational assessment. Rather than devoting themselves to the assessment of final products or learning outcomes, many of the aforementioned technologies and examples address learning processes and individual experiences. These process-centered technologies present an opportunity to align with the trend of promoting assessment *for*, *of* and *as* learning. Conceptually, this suggests a re-thinking of the scope of constructs to be assessed. If a construct is to be expanded to reflect expected performance in a particular target domain, we will need to think about how to better model the construct of interest with proper support of theories from relevant fields, such as theories about individual differences in language learning or acquisition, theories about cognitive processes in language learning, and complexity theories such as emergentism (Ellis, 1998, 2013) and dynamic systems theory (DST, see Larsen-Freeman & Cameron, 2008; Van Geert, 2008).

With all the internal and external factors that affect a learning experience and learning outcomes, a DST approach to language assessment seems rather fitting. DST views language development as a system because the elements of a system are ever-changing and continuously adapting in response to feedback. This system is dynamic because it is nonlinear, complex, adaptive, and open. A students' development, therefore, is nearly impossible to predict but valuable to understand. CALL researchers have been urged to acknowledge this ecological perspective because it helps account for the many networks of interactions between others and the environment that learners encounter and that impact language development (Marek & Wu, 2014). The complex systems perspective opens up consideration for individual differences and learners' unique "repertoires of input and interaction" (Sockett, 2013, p. 50). It also addresses the need for fully understanding the linguistic environments as in the online gaming world, where complex and distributed semiotic ecologies of linguistic influences abound, providing users with a context for online language socialization and engagement (Thorne et al., 2012). By taking on this ecological perspective, assessments can be designed to gather data on the whole learner, including the factors that extend beyond cognitive dynamics, so that language researchers and practitioners can become more accountable for achieving satisfactory learning outcomes.

A relevant concern about the construct is the nature of performance elicited in TREs. One direct implication of using more technology in assessment practices is that the construct tapped may be better operationalized through elevated levels of situational authenticity and interactional authenticity. It should be cautioned that new contextual variables may be introduced in technology-mediated alternative assessment which will, in turn, change the construct assessed in a face-to-face setting. Taking speaking as an example, interactional competence, which includes topic development organization, listener support strategies, and turn-taking management (Galaczi, 2014), has been regarded as an important component of the speaking construct. Group-based or pair-based performance tests would be optimal to assess this aspect of the speaking construct. Conversational agents in intelligent tutoring systems and human partners in the same virtual environment will be potential interlocutors to carry out a speaking task. However, it is not clear to what extent the online chat is impacted by variables like the turn-taking patterns in an online environment where floor management may be different from face-to-face communication.

Models for Designing and Evaluating Technology-Enhanced Assessment

Embracing theoretical foundations is one step towards appropriate integration of new alternative assessments in TREs, but theory can also be used to discover and develop new assessment models. In particular, earlier psychometric models may need to catch up with the development of technology-enhanced assessment; as Shute et al. (2016) point out, these models are particularly useful in dealing with unidimensional constructs measured with discrete items, but may fall short in taking care of performances elicited by sophisticated tasks. New measurement models are thus needed to accommodate technology-enhanced assessments.

Furthermore, recent work in assessment provides a suitable foundation for modified assessment models. One line of progress is evidence-centered design (ECD) for assessment design and development (Almond, Steinberg, & Mislevy, 2002; Mislevy et al., 2012); another is an argument-based framework for evaluating the validity of assessments (Kane, 1992, 2006), which is discussed in Chapters 6 and 8 in this book as well as in the final chapter where the framework is used to suggest future research assessment across online language education. We will briefly discuss ECD in this chapter, and suggest that the reader refer to the other chapters for an introduction to the argument-based framework.

ECD can be used to describe the conceptual, computational, and inferential elements of educational assessment (Almond et al., 2002; Mislevy et al., 2012). In this model, educational data mining can be used to establish student models that describe students' knowledge and behaviors, identify patterns derived from raw data, and connect these patterns with learners' proficiency or achievement. Designing technology-enhanced assessments can factor in the advantages of technologies as well as educational data mining in various design layers. These layers include domain analysis (to understand a targeted domain by documenting representative tasks, interactions, activities, etc.), domain modeling (to capture the relationships among the elements identified in the targeted domain), conceptual assessment framework (to identify the relationship between construct of interest and the representative elements in the targeted domain), implementation (to develop assessment tasks), and assessment delivery (to collect assessment performance data).

To illustrate the plausibility of this framework, Mislevy et al. (2012) explicate how each layer can benefit from educational data mining techniques and at the same time how ECD can guide the development of technology-enhanced assessment. They advocate that "good educational data mining in assessment contexts is best viewed in terms of evidentiary reasoning using the lens of evidence-centered design" (Mislevy et al., 2012: 40).

Concluding Remarks

As technologies advance, we will be presented with more opportunities to enhance assessment for online language education. Still, one reasonable consideration in technology-enhanced assessment is about the utility of learning analytics, which although only discussed briefly in this chapter is indeed a promising area for harvesting various educational data and identifying the relationships between learning patterns and academic achievements or language learning outcomes in TREs. However, this data-driven approach is not without problems and the utility of learning analytics is still to be confirmed as its approaches are highly exploratory in nature.

Dawson, Mirriahi, and Gasevic (2015: 3) summarized some critical questions regarding the relationship between learning theories and use of learning analytics, namely: "What counts as meaningful data? How can theory inform direct action? Are algorithms transportable across context?

Are often utilized educational theories still relevant in a changing learning paradigm?" Furthermore, Link and Li (2015: 379) provide a theory-based research agenda to further research in computer-assisted language learning and answer additional questions, for example, "What kinds of data should be collected and how should we interpret the data? Who would benefit from [learning analytics] and under what conditions? Are the educational data properly managed, stored, and protected in line with national laws?" For assessment purposes, some similar questions should be asked to raise concerns about what constructs are being measured and how theoretical foundations and models can best support a comprehensive, ecological view towards the whole learner experience.

Despite a variety of concerns, we will need to remain open and cautious in incorporating technologies in assessment practices. As Bennett (2002: 15) put it, "The question is no longer *whether* assessment must incorporate technology. It is how to do it responsibly, not only to preserve the validity, fairness, utility, and credibility of the measurement enterprise but, even more so, to enhance it. In this pursuit, we must be nothing less than inexorable." This review of technology-enhanced alternative assessment for TREs may facilitate a discussion of the implications for both language education practitioners and researchers. Language teachers are encouraged to pay more attention to the evidence of whole learning experiences; utilizing this support, they can explore and implement alternative assessment with existing technologies on commonly used learning platforms. Researchers in both language education and assessment may take advantage of the abundance of learning process data, using a proper theoretical lens to examine the connection between alternative assessment and other measures gathered from summative assessment and/or standardized tests.

About the Authors

Zhi Li is a Language Assessment Specialist at Paragon Testing Enterprises, BC, Canada. He holds a PhD degree in applied linguistics and technology from Iowa State University. His research interests include language assessment and computer-assisted language learning. His research papers have been published in *System* and *Language Learning & Technology*.

Stephanie Link is an Assistant Professor of TESL/Applied Linguistics and Director of International Composition at Oklahoma State University. She earned her PhD from Iowa State University and a dual Master's degree from Winona State University in Minnesota, USA and Tamkang University in Taiwan. She primarily teaches graduate-level courses in TESL, grammatical analysis, language and technology, and research methods. Her research interests include the study of emerging technologies for language learning and assessment, written genre analysis, and L2 pedagogy.

References

Abdous, M., He, W., & Yen, C.-J. (2012). Using data mining for predicting relationships between online question theme and final grade. *Educational Technology & Society*, 15(3), 77–88.

Agudo-Peregrina, Á. F., Iglesias-Pradas, S., Conde-González, M. Á., & Hernández-García, Á. (2014). Can we predict success from log data in VLEs? Classification of interactions for learning analytics and their relation with performance in VLE-supported F2F and online learning. *Computers in Human Behavior*, 31, 542–550. http://doi.org/10.1016/j.chb.2013.05.031

Allen, L. K., Mills, C., Jacovina, M. E., Crossley, S., D'Mello, S., & McNamara, D. S. (2016). Investigating boredom and engagement during writing using multiple sources of information. *Proceedings of the Sixth International Conference on Learning Analytics & Knowledge – LAK '16.* http://doi.org/ 10.1145/2883851.2883939

Almond, R. G., Steinberg, L. S., & Mislevy, R. J. (2002). Enhancing the design and delivery of assessment systems: A four-process architecture. *Journal of Technology, Learning, and Assessment*, 1(5), 1–62.

Bachman, L. F. (1991). What does language testing have to offer? *TESOL Quarterly*, 25(4), 671. http://doi.org/10.2307/3587082

Bennett, R. E. (2002). Inexorable and inevitable: The continuing story of technology and assessment. *Journal of Technology, Learning, and Assessment*, 1(1), 2–24.

Bevitt, S. (2014). Assessment innovation and student experience: A new assessment challenge and call for a multi-perspective approach to assessment research. *Assessment & Evaluation in Higher Education*, 40(1), 103–119. http://doi.org/ 10.1080/02602938.2014.890170

Bouchet, F., Harley, J. M., Trevors, G. J., & Azevedo, R. (2013). Clustering and profiling students according to their interactions with an intelligent tutoring system fostering self-regulated learning. *JEDM – Journal of Educational Data Mining*, 5(1), 104–146.

Chalhoub-Deville, M., & Deville, C. (1999). Computer adaptive testing in second language contexts. *Annual Review of Applied Linguistics*, 19, 273–299. http://doi.org/10.1017/S0267190599190147

Cope, B., Kalantzis, M., McCarthey, S., Vojak, C., & Kline, S. (2011). Technology-mediated writing assessments: Principles and processes. *Computers and Composition*, 28(2), 79–96. http://doi.org/10.1016/j.compcom.2011.04.007

Dawson, S., Mirriahi, N., & Gasevic, D. (2015). Importance of theory in learning analytics in formal and workplace settings. *Journal of Learning Analytics*, 2(2), 1–4. http://doi.org/10.18608/jla.2015.22.1

Delić, A., Domančić, M., & Vujević, P. (2014). AuGeo: A geolocation-based augmented reality application for vocational geodesy education. *Proceedings ELMAR-2014*. http://doi.org/10.1109/elmar.2014.6923372

DiCerbo, K. E., & Behrens, J. T. (2012). Implications of the digital ocean on current and future assessment. In R. W. Lissitz & H. Jiao (eds.), *Computers and Their Impact on State Assessment: Recent History and Predictions for the Future* (pp. 273–306). Charlotte, NC: Information Age Publishing.

Ellis, N. C. (1998). Emergentism, connectionism and language learning. *Language Learning*, 48(4), 631–664. http://doi.org/10.1111/0023-8333.00063

Ellis, N. C. (2013). Emergentism. In C. A. Chapelle (ed.), *The Encyclopedia of Applied Linguistics*. Oxford: Blackwell Publishing Ltd. http://doi.org/10.1002/9781405198431.wbeal0364

Ferguson, R. (2012). Learning analytics: Drivers, developments and challenges. *International Journal of Technology Enhanced Learning*, 4(5/6), 304–317. doi:10.1504/ijtel.2012.051816

Fox, J. (2008). Alternative assessment. In N. Hornberger (ed.), *Encyclopedia of Language and Education* (pp. 2240–2250). Boston, MA: Springer US. http://doi.org/10.1007/978-0-387-30424-3_170

Galaczi, E. D. (2014). Interactional competence across proficiency levels: How do learners manage interaction in paired speaking tests? *Applied Linguistics*, 35(5), 553–572. http://doi.org/10.1093/applin/amt017

Graesser, A. C., Li, H., & Forsyth, C. (2014). Learning by communicating in natural language with conversational agents. *Current Directions in Psychological Science*, 23(5), 374–380. http://doi.org/10.1177/0963721414540680

Grimes, D., & Warschauer, M. (2010). Utility in a fallible tool: A multi-site case study of automated writing evaluation. *Journal of Technology, Learning, and Assessment*, 8, 4–43.

Hsu, J.-L., Chou, H.-W., & Chang, H.-H. (2011). EduMiner: Using text mining for automatic formative assessment. *Expert Systems with Applications*, 38(4), 3431–3439. http://doi.org/10.1016/j.eswa.2010.08.129

Kane, M. T. (1992). An argument-based approach to validation. *Psychological Bulletin*, 112, 527–535.

Kane, M. T. (2006). Validation. In R. L. Brennan (ed.), *Educational Measurement* (4th ed.) (pp. 17–64). Westport, CT: American Council on Education and Praeger Publishers.

Kinnebrew, J. S., Loretz, K. M., & Biswas, G. (2013). A contextualized, differential sequence mining method to derive students' learning behavior patterns. *JEDM – Journal of Educational Data Mining*, 5(1), 190–219.

Knight, S., & Littleton, K. (2015). Discourse-centric learning analytics: Mapping the terrain. *Journal of Learning Analytics*, 2(1), 185–209. doi:10.18608/jla.2015.21.9

Larsen-Freeman, D., & Cameron, L. (2008). Research methodology on language development from a complex systems perspective. *The Modern Language Journal*, 92(2), 200–213. http://doi.org/10.1111/j.1540-4781.2008.00714.x

Li, J., Link, S., & Hegelheimer, V. (2015). Rethinking the role of automated writing evaluation (AWE) feedback in ESL writing instruction. *Journal of Second Language Writing*, 27, 1–18. http://doi.org/10.1016/j.jslw.2014.10.004

Lin, F.-R., Hsieh, L.-S., & Chuang, F.-T. (2009). Discovering genres of online discussion threads via text mining. *Computers & Education*, 52(2), 481–495. http://doi.org/10.1016/j.compedu.2008.10.005

Link, S., & Li, Z. (2015). Understanding online interaction through learning analytics: Defining a theory-driven research agenda. In E. Dixon & M. Thomas (eds.), *Researching Language Learner Interactions Online: From Social Media to MOOCs* (Vol. 13, pp. 369–385). San Marcos, TX: CALICO.

Liu, P.-H. E., & Tsai, M.-K. (2013). Using augmented-reality-based mobile learning material in EFL English composition: An exploratory case study. *British Journal of Educational Technology*, 44(1), E1–E4. http://doi.org/10.1111/j.1467-8535.2012.01302.x

Lowes, S., Lin, P., & Kinghorn, B. (2015). Exploring the link between online behaviours and course performance in asynchronous online high school courses. *Journal of Learning Analytics*, 2(2), 169–194.

Marek, M. W., & Wu, W.-C. V. (2014). Environmental factors affecting computer assisted language learning success: A Complex Dynamic Systems conceptual model. *Computer Assisted Language Learning*, 27(6), 560–578. http://doi.org/10.1080/09588221.2013.776969

Mislevy, R. J., Behrens, J. T., Dicerbo, K. E., & Levy, R. (2012). Design and discovery in educational assessment: Evidence-centered design, psychometrics, and educational data Mining. *JEDM – Journal of Educational Data Mining*, 4(1), 11–48.

Park, M. (2015). Development and validation of virtual interactive tasks for an aviation English assessment. Unpublished doctoral dissertation. Ames, IA: Iowa State University.

Price, K. (2016, May). Eye-tracking for L2 researchers: Guidelines for hardware Selection. Paper presented at the *Computer-Assisted Language Instruction Consortium*, East Lansing, MI.

Rabbany, R., Elatia, S., Takaffoli, M., & Zaiane, O. R. (2013). Collaborative learning of students in online discussion forums: A social network analysis perspective. In A. Peña-Ayala (ed.), *Educational Data Mining: Applications and Trends* (pp. 1–30). Berlin: Springer.

Ranalli, J., Feng, H., & Chukharev-Hudilainen, E. (2017, May). Visualizing engagement in writing processes via integrated keystroke logging and eye-tracking to support EAP writing-skills development. Paper presented at the *Computer-Assisted Language Instruction Consortium*, Flagstaff, Arizona.

Reeves, T. C. (2000). Alternative assessment approaches for online learning environments in higher education. *Journal of Educational Computing Research*, 23(1), 101–111. http://doi.org/10.2190/gymq-78fa-wmtx-j06c

Roscoe, R. D., & McNamara, D. S. (2013). Writing Pal: Feasibility of an intelligent writing strategy tutor in the high school classroom. *Journal of Educational Psychology*, 105(4), 1010–1025. http://doi.org/10.1037/a0032340

Shermis, M., & Burstein, J. (eds.) (2003). *Automated Essay Scoring: A Cross-Disciplinary Perspective.* Mahwah, NJ: Erlbaum.

Shute, V. J., Leighton, J. P., Jang, E. E., & Chu, M.-W. (2016). Advances in the science of assessment. *Educational Assessment*, 21(1), 34–59.

Sockett, G. (2013). Understanding the online informal learning of English as a complex dynamic system: an emic approach. *ReCALL*, 25(01), 48–62. http://doi.org/10.1017/s095834401200033x

Suraj, P., & Roshni, V. S. K. (2015). Social network analysis in student online discussion forums. *Proceedings of the 2015 IEEE Recent Advances in Intelligent Computational Systems (RAICS)*. http://doi.org/10.1109/raics.2015.7488402

Tan, S., O'Halloran, K. L., & Wignell, P. (2016). Multimodal research: Addressing the complexity of multimodal environments and the challenges for CALL. *ReCALL*, 28(3), 253–273. http://doi.org/10.1017/s0958344016000124

Thorne, S. L., Fischer, I., & Lu, X. (2012). The semiotic ecology and linguistic complexity of an online game world. *ReCALL*, 24(3), 279–301. http://doi.org/10.1017/s0958344012000158

Van Geert, P. (2008). The dynamic systems approach in the study of L1 and L2 acquisition: An introduction. *The Modern Language Journal*, 92(2), 179–199. http://doi.org/10.1111/j.1540-4781.2008.00713.x

Vanoni, D., Seracini, M., & Kuester, F. (2013). ARtifact: Tablet-based augmented reality for interactive analysis of cultural artifacts. *Proceedings of the 2013 IEEE International Symposium on Multimedia*. http://doi.org/10.1109/ism.2012.17

Vygotsky, L. S. (1978). *Mind and Society: The Development of Higher Psychological Processes*. Cambridge, MA: Harvard University Press.

Wolf, M. K., Guzman-Orth, D., Lopez, A., Castellano, K., Himelfarb, I., & Tsutagawa, F. S. (2016). Integrating scaffolding strategies into technology-enhanced assessments of English learners: Task types and measurement models. *Educational Assessment*, 21(3), 157–175. http://doi.org/10.1080/10627197.2016.1202107

Yoo, J., & Kim, J. (2014). Can online discussion participation predict group project performance? Investigating the roles of linguistic features and participation patterns. *International Journal of Artificial Intelligence in Education*, 24(1), 8–32. http://doi.org/10.1007/s40593-013-0010-8

12 Argument-Based Approach to Validation in Online Language Education

Erik Voss*

Introduction

The goal of learning-oriented assessment is to provide feedback to support language learning. Language teachers often use scores from assessment procedures to measure learners' language knowledge or progress of content taught in a course, or to make pedagogical decisions. However, in order to be confident that the language assessment scores are appropriate for their intended purpose and correct decisions are being made based on appropriate interpretation of the scores, such assessments need to be evaluated through a validation process. This chapter will first highlight the importance of validation of learner-oriented assessment practices. Next, it will present the framework for the argument-based approach to validation (Chapelle, Enright, & Jamieson, 2008; Kane, 2006). The chapter will conclude with a consideration of how the argument-based framework can provide effective assessment information for evaluation of language learning and pedagogical practices across online language education.

Appropriate Language Assessment

Appropriate language assessments are fundamental for evaluating the quality and effectiveness of language programs, ranging from the evaluation of an entire language program, to an instructor's preparedness to teach online, or appropriate language learning and assessment materials. Language teachers frequently use scores from tests, quizzes, and other assessment

* Northeastern University, Boston, MA, USA; e.voss@neu.edu

procedures to measure language skills, abilities, knowledge, or progress of content taught in a course, or to determine levels of appropriate instruction. Assessment scores can be used to promote learning (assessment *for* learning) and to measure and interpret what has been learned (assessment *of* learning) (Jones & Saville, 2016). However, both assessment for learning and assessment of learning are used to support language learning and, thus, are referred to as learning-oriented assessment. According to Green (2014: 5), "language assessment involves obtaining evidence [about language use] to inform inferences about a person's language-related knowledge, skills or abilities." Such evidence is used to interpret language scores and make pedagogical decisions.

Pedagogical decisions can vary in different contexts and for different purposes toward the common goal of supporting language learning. For example, the primary purpose of a placement test is to group students into level-appropriate language courses. Placement into a level with learning objectives that are too low or too high will not be beneficial for language learning. Teachers need to collect evidence, or language production, to determine how well a student can speak the target language before making a decision about placing the student into an appropriate level of study. Teachers may also administer additional *formative* (assessment for learning) quizzes during the semester to guide further instruction, and *summative* (assessment of learning) tests at the end of a chapter to see how well students mastered the chapter objectives.

When a teacher uses an assessment in a course to determine if students have mastered an irregular past tense form, participated in a group discussion, or demonstrated the ability to identify main ideas and details in an academic lecture, she is relying on the test score to provide information about the student's performance. The interpretation of a test score is based not only on what the test is measuring but also on how the test is delivered. The online delivery of language tests is limited by the available technology and could change the way a student performs on a test. A similar score on a face-to-face and online speaking task might actually reflect different abilities. Take, for example, a speaking test in a traditional classroom. In a face-to-face context, the student is speaking with another classmate or the instructor where the interaction might include an exchange of language or even nonlinguistic cues such as facial expressions or eye contact by the interlocutor. By contrast, an asynchronous speaking task in an online environment might require the student to talk to a computer screen without immediate feedback from a listener. This type of task is considered less authentic and may cause anxiety or poor student performance. Even in a synchronous computer-mediated interview using web cameras, issues such as positioning of the camera, distance to the screen, or maintaining eye contact are different from a face-to-face interaction. Therefore, the effects of test delivery should be taken into consideration when interpreting the meaning of a test score.

As language teachers, we can only infer a student's ability based on our interpretation of the meaning of the assessment score. Traditional multiple-choice tests also need to be evaluated to agree on what the test is actually measuring. For example, if a student obtains a score of 15 out of 20 on a vocabulary test that asks students to match the word with the definition, how could we interpret that score? How many words were matched correctly by guessing? Would a student get the same score on a similar test in a week or a month? Would a student be able to use these words when speaking? What does this score tell us about a student's language ability? In other words, how confident can we be that the language test scores are accurate judgments about student performance? We can be more confident about the meaning of a test score if assessments are planned carefully to include language and tasks that reflect the objectives to be measured. Subsequently, an evaluation of the tests and assessment would give a better idea of how well the tests and assessments are measuring what the teacher believes they are measuring.

The process to evaluate language assessments and tests involves specialized techniques and frameworks to "validate" rather than "evaluate" language test scores. "Validation is the justification of the interpretations and uses of testing outcomes" (Chapelle & Voss, 2013: 1). While teachers might refer to an assessment as valid or not, this is a quick way to say that the interpretation and/or use of a score is valid for its intended purpose. Therefore, in order to be confident that the language assessment scores are appropriate for their intended purpose and correct decisions are being made based on the interpretation of the scores, these assessments need to be evaluated through a validation process.

The argument-based framework is a unique validation method because it guides a teacher as test developer to outline an argument for the interpretation and use of a language assessment score. The rationale, presented as an argument, for the intended score interpretation can be supported or challenged by the amount and quality of evidence for or against the claims in the argument. It is also flexible enough to be applied to a variety of contexts including online language teaching. The characteristics and challenges of teaching online are made more explicit in the argument and thus help language teachers and researchers predict issues they might not think of with a different approach.

In sum, as teachers, we want tests to reflect students' knowledge of language and their ability to use the language. Yet, the available technology might influence the type of test a teacher designs. For example, a multiple-choice test will give us different information from a test that involves matching or writing definitions. Therefore, the teacher must be clear from the beginning about what the test is actually measuring. The process of validating a language test prompts a teacher to reflect on what the test is measuring and what the score actually means, which can be stated as a logical argument. In the next section, I will describe the basic theory behind the concept of a logical argument and how this theory forms the foundation for a complete validity argument.

Argument-Based Validation Framework

The latest framework for validating language assessments is based on a validity argument (Kane, 1992, 2006). This framework has been applied to many pedagogical contexts (e.g., Chapelle et al. 2008; Fulcher & Davidson, 2007) and can support the interpretation of a score on language assessment or the use of an assessment score (Bachman & Palmer, 2010). Based on Toulmin's (2003: 97) informal or practical argument structure, it is used to evaluate the rationale or argument for the score interpretation or use of individual language tests and assessments, language learning materials, pedagogical practices, and language programs.

The argument structure in the original framework (shown in Figure 12.1) guides the collection of evidence to support the plausibility of each of the six types of inferences in a chain from domain definition through utilization (Kane, 2006; Chapelle et al., 2008). Each inference focuses on a different aspect of the assessment and guides the type of research needed. Sufficient research results are needed to strengthen the argument for each claim in the chain in order to move from one inference to the next.

Kane (2011) presents the framework as simple, with only two steps. The first step in the process is to provide a detailed proposal for potential interpretations and uses of the scores as an *interpretive argument.* The interpretive argument specifies the claims, grounds, warrants, assumptions, and inferences that provide the foundation for score interpretation for each inference. A *claim* presents a statement about the interpretation of a score

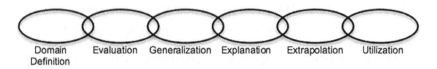

Domain   Evaluation   Generalization   Explanation   Extrapolation   Utilization
Definition

Figure 12.1. Chain of inferences in the interpretive argument

or score use for an inference in an argument chain. Each type of inference guides the type of research needed to support the claim. Backing to support a claim is first presented in statements called *warrants* or *assumptions*. Research is then conducted to collect evidence to support each warrant, which in turn strengthens the claim statement.

Gleason & Schmitt (Chapter 6 in this volume) use two inferences in the argument-based framework to evaluate language teachers with technology-specific literacies. They begin by identifying the online context and technologies used in this context by outlining an argument to support the domain definition inference. The claim presented for the domain definition inference is that types of assessment tasks in the classroom (pedagogical domain) are representative of the academic domains in which teachers will eventually work with their own students (target language use domain). An analysis of both the pedagogical domain and the target language use domain can be used as evidence to support this inference. Similar language in both domains would strengthen the argument. Identification of appropriate language tasks for the target language domain would also provide argument-supporting evidence. Sufficient evidence to support the domain definition inference allows the argument to progress to the next inference in the chain, the evaluation inference. The claim for the domain definition inference then becomes *grounds* for the evaluation inference.

For the evaluation inference the authors developed the claim that "teacher-educators in an MS TESOL program were able to transform their teaching using traditional f2f pedagogies to sophisticated uses of technologies in VC environments" (p. 132). The claim was most likely developed from a guiding question such as "Are teacher-educators in an MS TESOL program able to transform their teaching using traditional f2f pedagogies to sophisticated uses of technologies in VC environments?" The authors present a warrant that equivalent scoring was found in both contexts as backing to support the claim. This warrant was justified through research by examining the scoring rubrics in both teaching contexts to determine their equivalency. The structure for the evaluation inference in this argument is shown in Figure 12.2.

The second step in the framework is to evaluate the overall plausibility of the proposed interpretations and uses through the collected evidence to support and justify the claims in each inference of the interpretive argument. This second step, evaluating the collected evidence, is presented as the *validity argument.*

Theoretical evidence and empirical evidence can be collected to contribute to the confirmation or disconfirmation of a claim. For the evaluation inference, support can take the form of a systematic examination of

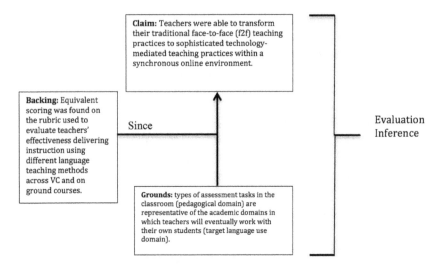

Figure 12.2. Model of evaluation argument structure from Gleason & Schmitt's chapter (this volume)

the scoring procedures and rubrics. Returning to Chapter 6 of this volume, the authors presented evidence from an analysis of assessment scores on a rubric that scores were equivalent in both face-to-face and online contexts. Evidence for the evaluation inference supports the move from one step in the argument to the next. Another way to visualize a validity argument is as a staircase. The information from the example above has been entered for the evaluation step in Figure 12.3. The authors would then move on to evaluate the collected evidence to support the claim for the generalization inference.

A second example is a validation project to evaluate a web-based rating platform called R-PLAT (Yang & Cotos, Chapter 8 of this volume). The authors present part of a validity argument by first identifying a plausible argument for the evaluation inference in an interpretive argument with the claim that R-PLAT captures appropriate diagnostic descriptors of individual speaking ability needed for a strong learner fit quality of online language instruction. To support this claim, the authors collected evidence for the assumption that diagnostic descriptors are indicative of target speaking ability levels used for placement into the respective levels of the course. The authors then analyzed data from diagnostic descriptor markings using descriptive statistics and Chi-Squared tests, and examined descriptive comments about individual students' oral proficiency provided by raters via R-PLAT. They concluded that the evidence was strong enough to support the claim in the evaluation inference. Additional validation research is

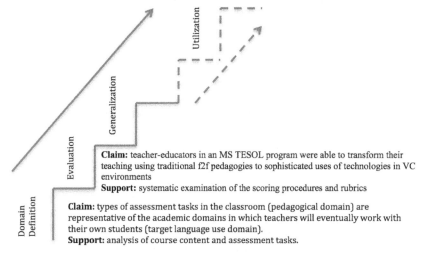

Figure 12.3. Steps in the validity argument from Gleason & Schmitt's chapter (this volume).

necessary to complete the validity argument to support the use of R-PLAT web-based rating platform as a diagnostic tool that may help the development of an online course tailored to learners' individual needs.

The two examples above presented arguments for one or two of several inferences possible, which demonstrates that the argument-based validation framework is flexible and can be applied to high- and low-stakes assessments in face-to-face, hybrid, or online contexts. The number of inferences included in the interpretive argument depends on the context and decisions that will be based on the interpretation of the test scores. Decisions can alter the life of a student or teacher. Therefore, high-stakes decisions should take into account all information possible to support appropriate interpretation of the test results. Stronger conclusions in higher-stakes decisions will require more evidence; whereas, weaker conclusions for lower-stakes decisions can be supported with less evidence (Kane, 2011).

Overall, the argument should seek to collect evidence for claims that are weaker in the argument and test alternative hypotheses to reduce doubts and enhance the robustness of the argument (Fulcher and Davidson, 2007). Focusing only on weak parts of an argument, however, should not be done at the expense of supporting other parts of the argument (Kane, 2013). Stakeholders evaluate the validity argument after the evidence has been presented. Enough evidence has been collected when the stakeholders are convinced either for or against the argument.

In the next section, consideration will be given to the six inferences and how the argument-based framework can provide effective assessment information for evaluation of language learning and pedagogical practices in online language environments.

Argument-Based Validation for Online Environments

Domain Definition Inference

The first step in the validity argument framework is the *domain definition* inference. This inference guides an evaluation of appropriate content and context for the language assessment through an analysis of the appropriate target language. In other words, how authentic is the language on the test? For example, language on an assessment of clinical terminology in a nursing program, such as the one in Chapter 4,would include specific medical vocabulary. Each assessment would need to include an analysis to identify appropriate vocabulary and level-appropriate discourse for both the context and the proficiency level of the test taker. An additional consideration is the authenticity of the language produced by the test taker. For instance, if a student writes a summary of a newspaper article, this cannot be the basis for a claim that the student is able to write in the journalism genre.

Claims can be developed by posing guiding questions that the domain definition inference can help answer, such as:

- Does the language included on the assessment reflect the appropriate register and linguistic mode?
- Has the language on the items been constructed to avoid cultural bias?
- Is the language at the appropriate level for the test taker and construct being measured?
- Is the language authentic for the appropriate context?
- Is the language produced or activity completed by the test taker authentic for the target context and task?

Answers to questions like these can help instructors define the appropriate language for the ability they would like to measure.

In an online program, language is identified through course learning objectives and outcomes. These curricular guides can be used to determine the type and amount of evidence that is necessary to justify the claim that the instruction, lessons, and assessments are appropriate for their intended purpose. An analysis of the content of a textbook or lesson would provide evidence if the language on the assessment is appropriate and representative of the language and skills taught or observed in the lesson or not. For example, a language lesson should include language that is representative of the target language domain and the assessment should include the language and strategies that were introduced in the lesson.

For evaluation of an online course or program, questions prompting the investigation probe if language instructors have the relevant knowledge, skills, processes, and strategies required for teaching and developing an online language course, and if they have the values, beliefs as well as digital literacy skills to teach the course. Gleason & Schmitt (Chapter 6), for example, examined teachers' technological literacies for language instruction in their domain-specific online environment. They began by describing the language teaching methods used by teachers in traditional classrooms and the online environment. Through comparative analysis, the authors could determine the equivalency between both contexts.

Evidence collected to answer the guiding questions related to appropriate content for a particular context would be evaluated to determine if there is enough support to justify the claims created from the guiding questions.

Evaluation Inference

Based on sufficient support to justify that the language assessments are based on language and strategies from the appropriate target language domain, tasks and assessments can be evaluated in the *evaluation inference*. The evaluation inference seeks evidence that scoring rules are reasonable and applied appropriately and consistently. Evidence can include analysis of appropriate scoring rubrics, analysis of task administration conditions, and statistical analyses of item difficulties.

First, appropriate scoring rubrics are developed to reflect appropriate language, skills, and abilities. Consideration should be given to the delivery method in online learning environments to identify if technology has influenced the way the language task is scored. Human scoring is much more complex than machine scoring. Automatic scoring might not capture potentially correct alternative answers. This is often the case with short constructed response items. Decisions about alternative spellings and synonyms, and acceptable answers need to be clarified.

Second, assessments should be presented uniformly to all test takers to support this inference. In an online context, appropriate test delivery is a fundamental consideration. For instance, reading on a 12" screen is different from reading on the screen of a 4" handheld device. Thus, variability in screen size or network speed may weaken a claim for this inference and ultimately the overall argument. Technical issues with weak internet signal or software not loading could prevent successful completion of a test, resulting in a score that is not accurate. Analysis of test administration conditions will reveal the extent to which the assessment is delivered to all test takers in similar circumstances and offer evidence to strengthen or weaken the argument.

Additionally, feedback from students regarding their attitudes toward use of technology can provide evidence to support or weaken the argument for uniform and stable delivery of a lesson or assessment. For instance, Beauvois & Eledge (1996) collected data from student journals and interviews that indicated the students' perceptions and reflections about the benefits and challenges of the new technological methodology for a French as a second language course. They found that students had a positive perception of technology use. Non-uniform test delivery would weaken the support for a claim to use an online format. Goertler, Bollen, & Gaff (2012) report that students selected a hybrid course for the convenience of time and space rather than the delivery format and, as a result, were lacking in some of the skills needed for the online format, which impacted their performance in the course. Such evidence is then used to revise aspects of language testing such as presenting students with training videos on how to use the technology, which was done when the TOEFL shifted from a paper-based to computer-based format (Taylor et al., 1998).

Finally, analyses of scores can also provide information on how individual items on the assessment are performing by showing if items are at appropriate levels of difficulty and if items are able to distinguish those students who have mastered the material from those who are still struggling. An analysis of potential partial credit scoring methods is also appropriate evidence for this inference.

Guiding questions to be answered for the evaluation inference could be:

- Do online tasks appropriately provide evidence of targeted language abilities?
- Does an automated scoring tool enable obtaining accurate and appropriate language performance descriptors to inform the design of online language instruction?
- Do items on a test have different item difficulties?
- Is the delivery of online assessments consistent, uniform, and stable for all test takers?
- Are students familiar with technologies used in online delivery?

Evaluation of the evidence collected to support claims based on these guiding questions would determine the extent to which the argument in the evaluation inference is supported. Sufficient evidence to provide a strong claim would justify moving to the next inference in the chain, the generalization inference.

Generalization Inference

Once the first two inferences have sufficient evidence to support their claims, the argument can move on to the next inference in the argument chain, the *generalization inference.* This inference assumes that the observed score on the performance task is an indication of performance on additional similar tasks. This inference also seeks confirmation of performance across various occasions and contexts. For example, results from an online assessment should be equivalent to those obtained from assessments of performance face-to-face. Evidence is needed to justify the comparison of both assessments if such a comparison is made.

Other questions that can be answered to support this inference could be:

- Does the assessment have enough items or tasks to measure a test taker's knowledge, ability, or skill?
- Is performance on an online assessment consistent with performance on a similar test in a face-to-face context?
- Is the reliability of an online assessment at an acceptable level?

Such questions focus on consistent administration of an assessment. Reliability estimates are used as a measure of consistency of the testing instrument. If an assessment has a high reliability estimate, there is a high probability that a student would get a similar score if they took the assessment a second time. Therefore, higher reliability is an indication that the test is measuring the intended language ability. Tests with many items will statistically have a higher reliability estimate. However, many class assessments are shorter and have a smaller number of items. This could result in lower reliability estimates.

Calculating reliability estimates is the most common form of evidence in both traditional and online assessment. However, calculating reliability coefficients for all course assessments is not feasible for busy online instructors. Fulcher and Davidson (2007) suggest that instead of taking time to calculate reliability statistics, the decisions teachers make about what to teach next or what needs to be repeated could be used as evidence to support this inference. For example, if test results indicate that students have not mastered a particular classroom objective and repeating instruction for that objective was the appropriate decision, this would be evidence for generalizability of test scores. This information would be more beneficial to a practicing teacher than the numerical value from a correlation calculation. However, the search for evidence needed to support decision-making is guided by questions in the utility inference later in the argument chain.

Explanation Inference

Next, the *explanation inference* explores the relationship between task performance and an underlying trait or construct. Implications of theoretical traits can include expected relationships to research variables related to instructional interventions or differences across contexts and groups. An instructor might consider what a multiple-choice grammar quiz is measuring. In many cases the quiz is assessing grammar knowledge rather than the ability to use grammar correctly in spoken or written language production. For example, clicking on a multiple-choice test question would not provide language that could demonstrate a student's writing ability. This distinction is essential when explaining the meaning of the quiz score.

This inference also involves the cognitive processes of taking a test. Inquiry into the following areas is necessary to address this inference. Appropriate questions to ask would be:

- Does the technology impact performance on the assessment such that test takers are not able to express their knowledge?
- Are test takers familiar with the test task or assessment technology?
- Is performance on the assessment attributed to knowledge and skills?

These questions reflect the appropriacy of the assessment for the intended purpose, target population, and target knowledge, ability or skill. Research could take the form of presenting theoretical relationships with other skills based on language learning hypotheses, or a comparison of scores on two tests that claim to measure the same construct (e.g., target knowledge, ability or skill).

Correlations with other measures representing the same construct have been favored as the approach to supporting this inference. Another method asks students, who have been identified at a particular proficiency level, to take the exam to determine if they can perform well on it. Caution must be taken, however, that the external assessment that is used as a corollary instrument has proper validation research to justify its use (Chapelle, 1999).

That is to say, if a test of reading is correlated with another reading test that has not been properly validated, the correlations could be meaningless.

Extrapolation Inference

The score interpretation is extended further through support for the *extrapolation inference*, assuming that performance may be an indication of performance on non-assessment tasks and in non-assessment contexts. The fundamental question for this inference explores the extent to which language proficiency as assessed by online activities/modules/tools accounts for the quality of linguistic performance in the intended context. In other words, is performance in the online learning environment reflective of actual performance in the real world? Other guiding questions can explore the relationship between performance on the assessment in the course and similar performance in the real world.

Observations of performance in the real world are often conducted through similar assessments. In addition to comparing performance on two measures of language ability using traditional tests, course-based test scores can also be compared with alternative assessments such as students' self-assessments or instructors' ratings of the students in the course. Comparisons can be analyzed by calculating correlation coefficients, a statistical analysis to determine the direction and strength of a relationship.

Calculating correlations between two measures of language ability serves as backing for the extrapolation inference. However, collecting data after students have left the program and are out in the "real world" is a difficult task. An alternative source of evidence would be to determine if the assessment instrument is able to distinguish among groups with different proficiency levels.

Utilization Inference

An additional stop, the *utilization inference,* gathers evidence about appropriate decision-making based on assessment scores. The claim to be made is that online assessment practices are useful for gauging language proficiency and supporting learners' needs. That is to say, scores are useful for decision-making. Guiding questions could include:

- Do placement tests group students effectively?
- Are assessments providing appropriate feedback to identify what needs to be taught?

- Are cut scores used appropriately for making decisions?
- Is an assessment appropriate to determine if an instructor is prepared to teach an online course?

Diagnostic decisions can be made to guide the selection of materials, skills to teach, or placement into a course or teaching position. In a course environment, decisions to repeat content or teaching using an additional method could be made based on scores from a language assessment. After graduation, grades from a matriculating degree could be suitable to determine the success of the previous program. Moreover, measurement of the digital literacy of online instructors could determine if they are eligible to teach online. If the decision is made to allow an instructor to teach online, evaluation of the course and teacher performance could be used as evidence to support the strength of the decision. Evaluation of future performance forms the basis for the success of the decisions made and strengthens or weakens the argument for this inference.

Educational decisions are often based on cut scores. Students need to achieve a score above a certain percentage on a test to pass, or achieve a GPA (grade point average) above a certain percentage to complete a program. If a teacher would like to seek utilization evidence for a test, she might begin with a statement that a particular cut score is appropriate for passing a test. She could then look at the performance on the test of those students who achieved the score to determine if they had indeed mastered the material.

Collection of data to support this inference can only occur once the assessment is operational (in use) and decisions have been made. Adequate support for each inference moves the argument to the next inference. Any gap in the chain of inferences weakens the overall conclusion of the argument.

Ramification Inference

Recently researchers have added a seventh inference – the *ramification inference* – to the chain of inferences in the validation argument (Li, 2015; Link, 2015; Gruba et al., 2016) to seek evidence about the impact the test has on all those who use the assessment results – known as stakeholders. Meeting the needs of multiple stakeholders has been a challenge with evaluating online learning (WestEd with Edvance Research, 2008). The claim in this inference should focus on how the assessment has a positive impact on learning, i.e., learning-oriented assessment (Chapelle, Cotos, & Lee, 2015). This inference could also be called the *positive consequences*, *learning reflection*, *objectives reflection*, or *pedagogical reflection* inference. These names reflect the purpose and context of the inference in the validation process.

The design of high-stakes language proficiency tests can have positive and negative consequences. For example, when the TOEFL iBT introduced a speaking section, students became more aware of the need to improve their speaking ability in order to get a higher test score. Speaking instruction was introduced in more language courses to meet this demand. However, because of the large number of test takers, the task was limited to brief one-minute oral responses. This, in turn, was seen as a negative consequence as students prepared short, formulaic answers in an attempt to get higher scores, rather than improve natural oral discourse.

Similarly, application for a lower-stakes language assessment might include inferences relevant to the context (Chapelle & Voss, 2013). For example, an achievement test in an intermediate reading course might include domain definition, evaluation, generalization, objectives reflection, and utilization. The objectives reflection inference specifies a relationship between the ability measured on the test and instructional objectives for the intermediate reading course. In this case, the design of the assessment task should promote language learning that is useful. How many times would someone be asked to complete a multiple-choice task in the real world? How many times is someone asked to match a word with its definition? Unintended consequences should be mitigated to the extent possible.

Whereas the utilization inference posed the question of whether a student was placed into an appropriate level of study based on a placement test score, the ramification inference would ask if the student learned anything in that level. Guiding questions would reflect different perspectives on language learning processes.

- Do students view the assessment positively?
- Does the feedback from the assessment provide learning opportunities?
- Do students become aware of their strengths and weaknesses from the assessment results?

Achievement of the intended consequences of learning language is gauged through assessment feedback. In an online learning environment, issues such as teacher presence and quality of feedback will need to be explored to support claims made for the positive consequences inference. The use of technology can have positive consequences for language learning. For example, records kept in learning management systems report student progress through grades, attendance, and teacher feedback. Students use this feedback to identify where and how they can improve in the course. Teachers use the feedback to identify if learning is occurring.

Conclusion

Assessment practices are part of all online instructional environments. Assessments can take the form of a standardized test or can be an informal observation. The data from these practices informs learning by providing feedback. Scores from any assessment can alter the course of instruction, motivation to learn, and opportunity to enter or proceed with instruction, or apply for a job. The decisions made based on test scores can carry weighted consequences. It is, therefore, necessary to evaluate the assessment procedures and instruments to identify the extent to which the assessment is providing meaningful and useful feedback.

An argument-based approach to validation presents a narrative about the meaning of the assessment information and how the information is used. It begins with an interpretive argument to establish guiding questions and claims to be answered and supported for the intended pedagogical context. Empirical and theoretical evidence is then collected to support or justify the claims. Moreover, the validity argument itself is evaluated to identify its strength. The quality of the evidence for each inference will determine the strength of the overall argument and uncover areas of the assessment which may need attention for improvement.

This approach is the latest interpretation of validation in educational settings and offers a framework that can be applied to various online learning environments. Assessments that use technology pose new benefits and challenges. An approach to validation using this framework has the potential to uncover new areas of research. The particular assessment context guides the purpose of the assessment and the potential interpretation of the score. By developing the argument for a particular interpretation and use for an assessment score, we focus our attention on types of validation research that are specific to the context, which may be overlooked without guiding questions for each inference in the proposed framework. The framework also calls for more evidence to justify weaker links in the argument, thereby drawing our attention to areas that may be challenged by a critical stakeholder.

Finally, because of the strong relationship between assessment and language learning, developing an argument for an assessment using the framework can also lead to reflection on many aspects of language learning. The interpretation of results from an assessment can be used to inform language learning – from the meaning of a score, to decisions based on that score, to opportunities to learn from the assessment feedback. This framework can be applied to research on automated scoring, automated feedback, online delivery methods, assessing learner progress and development, assessing online teachers, and assessing tools for online learning environments.

About the Author

Erik Voss is an Associate Teaching Professor at Northeastern University, Boston. His research focuses on validation research, corpus linguistics, and language assessment and technology. He has presented on technology use in the language classroom and language assessment research, at domestic and international conferences and workshops.

References

Bachman, L. F., & Palmer, A. S. (2010). *Language Assessment in Practice.* Oxford, UK: Oxford University Press.

Beauvois, M. H., & Eledge, J. (1996). Personality types and megabytes: Student attitudes toward computer mediated communication (CMC) in the language classroom. *CALICO Journal*, 13, 27–45.

Chapelle, C. A. (1999). Validity in language assessment. *Annual Review of Applied Linguistics*, 19, 254–257.

Chapelle, C. A., & Voss, E. (2013). Evaluation of language tests through validation research. In A. J. Kunnan (ed.), *The Companion to Language Assessment* (Vol. 3, pp. 1–17). Malden, MA: Wiley-Blackwell.

Chapelle, C. A., Cotos, E., & Lee, J. (2015). Validity arguments for diagnostic assessment using automated writing evaluation. *Language Testing*, 32(3), 385–405.

Chapelle, C. A., Enright, M. K., & Jamieson, J. (eds.) (2008). *Building a Validity Argument for the Test of English as a Foreign Language.* London: Routledge.

Fulcher, G., & Davidson, F. (2007). *Language Testing and Assessment: An Advanced Resource Book.* Oxford, UK: Routledge.

Goertler, S., Bollen, M., & Gaff Jr., J. (2012). Students' readiness for and attitudes toward hybrid FL instruction. *CALICO Journal*, 29(2), 297–320.

Green, A. (2014). *Exploring Language Assessment and Testing: Language in Action.* New York. Routledge.

Gruba, P., Cárdenas-Claros, M. S., Suvorov. R., & Rick, K. (2016). *Blended Language Program Evaluation.* London, UK: Palgrave Macmillan.

Jones, N., & Saville, N. (2016). *Learning Oriented Assessment: A Systemic Approach.* Cambridge: Cambridge University Press.

Kane, M. (2006). Validation. In R. Brennen (ed.), *Educational Measurement* (4th ed.) (pp. 17–64). Westport, CT: Greenwood.

Kane, M. (2011). Validating score interpretations and uses: Messick Lecture, Language Testing Research Colloquium, Cambridge, April 2010. *Language Testing*, 29(1), 3–17.

Kane, M. T. (1992). An argument-based approach to validity. *Psychological Bulletin*, 112, 527–535.

Kane, M. T. (2013). Validating the interpretations and uses of test scores. *Journal of Educational Measurement*, 50, 1–73.

Li, Z. (2015). An argument-based validation study of the English Placement Test (EPT) – Focusing on the inferences of extrapolation and ramification. Doctoral dissertation. Ames, IA: Iowa State University.

Link, S. M., (2015). Development and validation of an automated essay scoring engine to assess students' development across program levels. Doctoral dissertation. Ames, IA: Iowa State University.

Taylor, C., Jamieson, J., Eignor, D., & Kirsch, I. (1998). The relationship between computer familiarity and performance on computer-based TOEFL test tasks. TOEFL Research Report RR-61. Princeton, NJ: Educational Testing Service.

Toulmin, S. E. (2003). *The Uses of Argument* (updated edition). Cambridge, UK: Cambridge University Press.

WestEd with Edvance Research (2008). *Evaluating Online Learning: Challenges and Strategies for Success*. Prepared by WestEd with Edvance Research, Inc. for U.S. Department of Education Office of Innovation and Improvement.

Author Index

Subject Index

9 781781 797013